WHAT EVERY PATIENT WANTS TO KNOW

by
Robert E. Rothenberg,
M.D., F.A.C.S.

A
MEDBOOK
PUBLICATION

A SIGNET BOOK
NEW AMERICAN LIBRARY
TIMES MIRROR

WHAT YOUR DOCTOR MIGHT TELL YOU— IF HE ONLY HAD THE TIME

This book was written to close the information gap. Here you will find the answers to all your questions about heart disease, cancer, arthritis, mental health, and almost every ailment known to modern medical science.

Here are special sections on specific male and female disorders, children's complaints, plus essential guidance in health care and preventive medicine. Here are life-saving first-aid tips, Medicare information, and advice on practically every subject vital to your health needs.

ROBERT E. ROTHENBERG, M.D., is a Fellow of the American College of Surgeons, a Diplomate of the American Board of Surgery, and Attending Surgeon and a member of the Board of Trustees at the French and Polyclinic Medical School and Health Center. From 1950 to 1960, he was Assistant Professor of Environmental Medicine and Community Health at the State University College of Medicine in New York, from 1954 to 1964 he served on the Board of Directors of the Health Insurance Plan of Greater New York, and from 1960 to 1966, he was Civilian Surgical Consultant to the United States Army Hospital, Fort Jay, New York.

Dr. Rothenberg's *The New American Medical Dictionary and Health Manual* and *Health in the Later Years* are also available in Signet editions.

More SIGNET Books of Interest

To Andrew
and Steven

CONTENTS

PART III

PREFACE

Because physicians are extremely busy these days and have so little time to sit down and talk to their sick charges in a leisurely manner, an ever-widening information gap has developed between patient and doctor. Without being aware of it, most doctors tend to hurry through an appointment with a patient, knowing that they have a crowded schedule ahead; the patient senses the rush and often forgets to ask important questions that have been on his mind. Later, when he or a member of his family tries to get the information from the doctor via the telephone, he may have to be content with a hurried or incomplete response from a nurse or secretary. It is to improve, supplement, and expedite the all-important line of communication between the patient and his doctor that this book has been written.

What Every Patient Wants to Know is not a home medical guide through which one must search at length before finding what he wants to know. Its aim is to give specific answers to specific questions about specific medical conditions, answers that can be located almost instantly. Questions are printed in italic type, the answers appearing immediately below. Following virtually every section in this book are a series of questions that can be answered only by the reader's personal physician. The reader is urged to place a marker in the pages on which questions having to do with his particular condition appear, and to get the answers from his own doctor.

Although *What Every Patient Wants to Know* is the title of this book, it covers an even broader area than the title implies. The patient's problems may be more than not knowing the answers to certain questions; he may not even know all the questions he should ask about his condition! In this case, the book will serve as a thorough checklist. Thus, before the patient enters his doctor's office or the hospital, he will already know the answers to most of the questions he could conceivably ask about his condition in general, and will know what questions to ask about his specific case. No longer will it be necessary for him to jot down questions on little pieces of paper that he intends to ask his doctor, only to discover after the visit that there was no time to discuss them.

Another objective of this book is to provide background information that will help patients to use medical personnel and services more effectively. Toward this end, in the front of the book are sections on Choosing a Doctor, Medical Fees and Health Insurance, Medicare, Hospitalization, etc. In addition, in the back of the handbook there is a special section on medical facts, containing information on First-Aid, Immunization and Vaccination, Medicines and Medical Supplies in the Home, Special Diets, and Vitamins.

R.E.R.

HOW TO
USE THIS BOOK

1. Look first for answers to any specific queries you may have regarding the ailment in question.

2. At your convenience, read *all* of the questions and answers pertaining to the topic in which you are interested.

3. In a special section, at the end of each topic discussed, you will find unanswered questions. These are the questions that relate specifically to your problem and they should be answered only by your own doctor. Put a marker in these pages so that you can find them readily.

4. In the space provided at the end of the un-answered question section, jot down any additional questions you may want to ask your doctor.

5. Bring this book to your doctor's office when you visit him, or, if he comes to see you, have it at your bedside. This will make it easy for you to get all your questions answered during the brief time you will spend together.

6. At your leisure, read the information in the opening section of the book to provide yourself with background on such subjects as choosing a specialist, periodic health check-ups, hospitalization, etc.

7. Read Part III, the medical facts section, for information on various medical situations that might confront you or a member of your family, and for guidance on such subjects as immunization, diets, vitamins, etc.

PART I

1. CHOOSING A DOCTOR

A great many people choose a doctor in a haphazard, ill-considered way. They may select him merely because his office is nearby, or because he makes an attractive impression, or because an acquaintance recommends him. These are not the best criteria for choosing someone who will play a vital role when serious illness strikes. The task of obtaining a permanent general practitioner (family doctor) is exceptionally difficult because only 10 percent of physicians practice general medicine today. Thus, American families often find themselves in a situation in which they must engage several doctors, each to treat a different part or system of the body.

CHOOSING A FAMILY DOCTOR

* If you know and like a doctor who lives in your community, check him out by calling your local county medical society. Ask them to tell you what medical school he attended and when he graduated.

* Call the doctor and inquire about his office hours. This will give you a good idea of his ongoing availability.

* When you call the family doctor, ask him what hospital he is associated with. It is always best to select a physician who is on the staff and has admitting privileges at a first-rate, accredited hospital. Then, should you or a member of your family require hospitalization, you can be assured that you will go to an approved institution.

* Ask the doctor whether he will make home calls when necessary. Some family doctors are reluctant to make such calls unless the patient is well known to them.

3

* Find out whether the doctor's practice is covered by an alternate or assistant when he is off duty or on holiday.

* Inquire about what hospital emergency room you should go to if a sudden emergency arises and he is not immediately available.

* If you are concerned about medical expenditures, find out his usual fees for office or home visits.

* Ask if he will accept payments from your medical insurance company in lieu of direct cash payments.

CHOOSING A SPECIALIST

* Ask your family doctor whom you should see in consultation. However, you need not be guided solely by his recommendation.

* If you want further information, call your local medical society and ask:

  What medical school the specialist attended and when he graduated?

  Does he have his American Board qualifications in his specialty?

  Is he a member of the American College of Physicians or of the American College of Surgeons?

  With what hospitals is he affiliated?

  What is his position on the hospital staff?

* Specialists today should be qualified by the American Board in their specialty. The diploma of these boards is more or less a guarantee that the specialists have been well trained and found to be proficient.

* Specialists should be on the staff or have courtesy privileges at an accredited hospital. This will insure you good care if hospitalization is required.

* As with the general physician, if you are concerned about medical expenditures, inquire about your doctor's fees and find out whether he will accept assignment of payments from such agencies as Medicare, Medicaid, or various insurance companies that issue health policies.

FINDING A DOCTOR AWAY FROM HOME

If you are in a strange community when you become sick, call the local medical society or the largest hospital in the area. Ask them to help you select either a general practitioner or a specialist.

CHANGING YOUR DOCTOR

If you have chosen a general practitioner or a specialist whom you do not like, it is a perfectly ethical for you to make a change. Prior to doing this, it is common courtesy to notify the doctor or his nurse that you have decided to make a change. Do not feel embarrassed; you are entitled to be treated by someone with whom you can establish good rapport. And if you do change doctors, it is ethical to request that your medical records be forwarded to your new doctor.

2. HOSPITALIZATION AND HOSPITAL INSURANCE

What is the best way to choose a hospital?

Patients usually have little choice in this matter since they generally go to the hospital where their physician has a staff appointment. This is one good reason for making sure that your doctor, before you choose him, is on the staff of an accredited hospital. In an emergency, if possible, you should always ask to be sent to an accredited hospital.

What is meant by the term "an accredited hospital"?

It is a hospital that has been approved by the Joint Committee of Accreditation of Hospitals. This body, composed of several important national medical societies, periodically inspects hospitals to see if they meet certain high standards. Whenever possible, a patient should discover beforehand whether he is going to an accredited hospital.

Is there some way that I can find out whether my doctor's hospital is accredited without asking him directly?

Yes, you can call the local county medical society. They have a list of all accredited hospitals in your area.

Can my doctor send me to any hospital he chooses?

No. In most areas of this country, hospitals have closed staffs. Only those doctors who are on the staff of that particular hospital can admit patients.

What items shall I take with me when I go to the hospital?

1. Pajamas, slippers, and a bathrobe.
2. Toilet articles.
3. An inexpensive watch or clock.
4. A pen, stationery, and stamps.
5. Your hospital insurance card.
6. A checkbook.
7. Only sufficient cash to make payments for small items such as newspapers, magazines, etc. It is poor practice to bring a large amount of cash to the hospital.
8. A small radio. (TV sets are usually available on a rental basis.)

Do hospitals have provision for the safekeeping of valuables?

They may have, but it is wise not to bring expensive jewelry or valuables to a hospital.

Should a child be told beforehand that he is going to a hospital?

Yes, each child who faces hospitalization must be prepared as much as possible for the experience. Depending on their age, some children may be disturbed by too much preparatory discussion; others may be comforted by specific foreknowledge. A good rule is never to lie to a child about what will take place after he is in the hospital.

At what age can the child understand what it means to go to a hospital?

Usually by the time he reaches four to five years of age.

How long before going to the hospital should a child be told that he is going?

No more than a few days. If he is told too far in advance, this will create unnecessary anxiety.

Do some hospitals have arrangements for the parent to stay overnight with the child?

Yes.

What should a mother take to the hospital with her child?

1. First of all, she should discover the particular hospital rules. Some hospitals will not permit toys or security blankets, etc., to be brought in from the outside. If they can be brought along, the mother should check with the physician to see if he thinks it is a good idea.

2. Toothbrushes, toothpaste, comb and brush, and other items used for personal hygiene should be taken.

3. Pajamas or nightgowns and slippers and bathrobe should be taken.

4. Radios and television sets are best left at home. They are available in most children's wards.

Are there facilities in the hospital for me to be shaved or to get a haircut?

Most hospitals do have barbers.

Do hospitals have hairdressers?

Yes, most of the larger institutions do.

Are children permitted to visit in a hospital?

No, most hospitals only permit young people over fourteen or sixteen years of age to visit.

Do hospitals have recreation facilities during convalescence?

Most larger institutions do.

What bills do I have to pay before I leave the hospital?

It is customary to pay the anesthesia bill as well as bills for such items as delivery of a daily newspaper, TV rental, and telephone.

Can I get an abstract of my medical record from the hospital?

Yes, if the doctor who has taken care of you in the hospital so approves. It must be remembered that the medical record is the property of the physician and the hospital, not the property of the patient.

Are there different types of hospital insurance policies?
Yes. Some are so-called comprehensive policies which cover all the basic hospital charges; others are limited policies which pay so many dollars a day toward the hospital bill.

What is a nonprofit hospital insurance company?
A company such as Blue Cross which issues policies that cover almost all of the regular hospital charges for a semi-private accommodation.
It is estimated that 75,000,000 American are insured under Blue Cross.

What are commercial hospital insurance policies?
These are written by some of the large profit-making insurance companies. Whereas most of these policies pay less than the total cost of hospitalization, some do provide very liberal allowances.

What are "major medical" hospital insurance policies?
They are policies that pay for catastrophic, prolonged hospitalization. One can own both a basic Blue Cross or commercial hospital insurance policy *plus* a policy that pays for extended illnesses.

What are the routine hospital services for which there are no extra charges if one has Blue Cross hospital insurance?
1. Room and board.
2. Floor nursing care.
3. Ordinary drugs and medications.
4. Treatments such as injections and intravenous solutions.
5. The use of the operating room.
6. The use of the X-ray department.
7. The use of laboratory facilities.

What hospital services are usually not included as routine?
1. The payment for rare or expensive drugs or treatments.
2. Special nursing care.
3. Anesthesia, when given by a physician. In most hospitals, anesthesia is now given by medical specialists who may charge their own fees, just as does your surgeon.

4. The cost of blood transfusions.
5. The doctor's fee.

Do hospitals ever charge extra for some of the above services?
Yes. Each hospital has its own individual way of charging. Some have a flat rate for room and board but charge individually for the other items listed above if the patient is not covered by hospital insurance.

If I have Blue Cross, does this mean that I also have coverage for doctor's bills?
No. Blue Cross covers hospitalization only.

How can I distinguish between Blue Cross and Blue Shield insurance?
It is very important to remember that Blue Cross covers hospitalization only. It is not medical or health insurance. Blue Shield is medical or health insurance, but does not cover hospital costs.

How can I tell how much of my hospital bill my hospital insurance will cover?
Some policies will pay all of your hospital bills in a private room, but most of them provide for full care in semi-private accommodations only. This is stated very clearly in your policy and you should read it carefully before you enter a hospital.

Do hospital insurance policies vary in the number of days of payment they will give?
Yes. Some policies are written for 21 days of full coverage and an additional 180 days of half coverage; others are for 120 days of full coverage and an additional number of half coverage days.

Who can help me interpret the provisions of my hospital insurance policy?
Your doctor's nurse or secretary will be willing to go over your insurance policy with you. It is important that she do that if there is any doubt in your mind as to what benefits you are entitled to.

What is the best type of hospital insurance to buy?
One that will give you total payment coverage for the

longest period of time. Most hospitalizations last no longer than ten days, but a catastrophic illness may require hospitalization for a period of several weeks. Therefore, it is wise to purchase a policy with a long period of coverage.

Will all hospitals accept my hospital insurance?
No. Many hospitals insist that you pay the hospital bill and collect back from your hospital insurance company. An exception to this are the large number of hospitals that have contracts with Blue Cross. If you enter a hospital that is affiliated with Blue Cross, in all probability they will not require you to make any down payment but will accept the Blue Cross card as payment in full for a semiprivate accommodation.

Do hospital insurance companies that pay a certain number of dollars a day usually cover the cost in full?
No. These policies which limit the amount of money per day usually fall far short of covering all of your hospital bills. If this is the type of policy you have, make certain how much is covered before you are hospitalized. Otherwise, you may discover that you owe a great deal of money over and above your policy coverage.

Are newborn infants always covered by their parents' hospital insurance policies?
Not in all instances. Read your policy carefully to determine if you are entitled to this benefit.

QUESTIONS TO ASK YOUR DOCTOR

How long will I be in the hospital?

Will I require private nurses?

Will I be in an intensive care unit of the hospital?

How soon after I go to the hospital will I be able to have visitors?

Should I encourage or discourage visitors?

Will I be able to have a room with a bath?

Shall I notify relatives who are out of town that I am going into the hospital?

What tests do you anticipate performing upon me in the hospital?

Will it be necessary to call other doctors in to treat me?

Should I see my attorney and make a will before entering the hospital?

What are my chances of recovering from this illness?

Do I have to pay my entire hospital bill before I leave?

When will I have to pay your bill?

Can I go home from the hospital in my own car?

Do I require convalescent care?

Is it all right for me to travel out of town for convalescence?

Can I take care of myself at home, or will I need help?

When will I be able to:
    shower?
    bathe?
    have my hair done?
    walk up and down stairs?
    go outdoors?
    cook my own meals?
    do housework?
    take a walk?
    take a ride?
    return to work?
    resume marital relations?
    perform all physical exercise?
    drive my car?

Must I eat a special diet and, if so, what?

When will I be able to smoke again?

When will I be able to drink again?

When will I begin to feel completely normal again?

3. MEDICAL FEES
AND MEDICAL INSURANCE

If a patient is concerned about costs, he should feel completely free to discuss fees with his family doctor or specialist. Many doctors leave these matters to their secretaries or nurses to discuss, but if a patient is not satisfied with their explanations, he should ask to talk directly to the doctor. Most physicians will adjust their fees if they are convinced that the patient is unable to pay the full fee.

VARIATION IN FEES

Because the nature of medical services usually varies from case to case, it is common practice for doctors to vary their fees for different patients. Some patients require more time, more attention, and more expert skill than others. In addition, a doctor may charge more for one visit than another because he has performed more tests or has spent more time with his patient. Medical fees also vary greatly in different parts of the country. Here are some of the reasons for these variations:

* Certain areas have much higher rents than others; thus, the cost of maintaining an office is greater. Then, too, in certain areas, doctors are able to cut costs by combining their home and office; in other areas this is not feasible.
* Salaries for nurses, secretaries, and technicians are much higher in some areas than in others.
* Malpractice insurance, auto insurance, fire and theft insurance, and other insurance premiums are considerably more expensive in certain parts of the country than in others.

ARRANGING PAYMENT

People often tender a fee to a physician before he renders a particular service, such as an operation. However, most physicians prefer to be paid after they have rendered the service. If a patient knows that he will be unable to pay an entire fee upon completion of the service, he should so notify his doctor. Most physicians will arrange for larger fees to be paid over a period of time, provided they have confidence in the patient's integrity and intent.

COVERAGE

Medical insurance is owned by a large segment of the population, and, all too often, the owner of the insurance policy thinks that his doctor's fees are fully covered by the policy. Unfortunately, this is infrequently the case. As a result, the patient is disturbed to learn either that a particular medical service is not covered at all, or is covered only partially by his insurance. It is always advisable before embarking upon extensive medical therapy to read your medical insurance policy thoroughly. Be certain of what you are entitled to, and what is not covered by the policy. The doctor's secretary or nurse can be very helpful in explaining the details of most health insurance policies.

ACCEPTANCE OF INSURANCE PAYMENTS

Doctors are not obligated to accept insurance payments as total fees unless they have signed a prior agreement with the insurer. Patients should determine this fact before beginning treatment or undergoing expensive surgery. It should also be mentioned that a great number of physicians do not wish to deal with insurance companies but prefer to make all financial arrangements directly with their patients. They then leave to the patient the task of collecting the fee from the insurance company, after he has paid the doctor out of his own pocket.

Although there is no legal obligation for a doctor to fill out a patient's medical insurance form, it is a courtesy that doctors do extend. However, the filling out of the form does not mean that the doctor has agreed to accept the fee determined by the insurance company for a particular treatment nor that he is willing to wait for his fee until the company has reimbursed the patient.

MEDICARE

The great majority of people over sixty-five years of age have the medical insurance portion of Medicare. Some doctors accept Medicare fees as total payment, others do not. It is the obligation of the patient to discover whether or not his doctor accepts Medicare fees without surcharge. This should be done before beginning treatment.

EVALUATING YOUR POLICY

The best type of medical insurance is one that covers expenses for services rendered in your doctor's office and in your home, as well as expenses incurred while in the hospital. Also, it is better to buy a policy in which the benefits coincide with the going medical charges in your community. It is not very wise to own a policy that pays $100 for an operation when the average fee for that operation is $500, nor is it sound to own a policy that excludes payments for office visits when almost 90 percent of all medical services are rendered in a doctor's office.

4. OFFICE
AND HOME VISITS

Doctors prefer to see patients in their offices rather than going to the patient's home, and they will sometimes request patients to come to their office even when they have an elevated temperature. Formerly, this practice was frowned upon, but since most infections can be controlled by antibiotics, doctors no longer fear complications merely because a patient with fever goes outdoors. The advantages of the more complete examination that is possible in an office where

X-rays and equipment to perform laboratory tests upon the blood and urine are available, far outweigh the danger of complications that might arise from a trip in a car from home to office. Furthermore, the doctor can care for several patients in his office during the time it would take to make one home call. Pediatricians, a particularly overworked group of specialists, frequently advise that a child with fever be bundled up and brought to the office. This practice leads to earlier examination and institution of treatment, since the child does not have to wait until office hours are over and other house calls are made.

AVAILABILITY

As mentioned in another part of this book, it is essential that people clearly understand their doctor's methods of handling office and home calls. No one should engage a new physician until he knows whether his practice includes the making of home calls, whether he is available in his office during hours that are convenient, what days he is unavailable, and whether he is covered by another physician at night and over weekends.

Doctors are often judged by their availability to their patients. In this connection, one should know that the average American physician puts in a ten-hour day, six days a week, for forty-eight to fifty weeks each year. During this year, he renders an average of 5,000 or more services to his patients. Unfortunately, the shortage of doctors in this country will not be overcome for several decades, and, as a consequence, the public will continue to complain about doctor-unavailability. Although it is admitted that easy access to medical care at all times is the right of every citizen, reality dictates that people must call for home medical service only when it is truly necessary. By the same token, until the doctor shortage is relieved, people must be understanding when their overworked doctor is unavailable at night or shows reluctance to make house calls.

SAVING YOUR DOCTOR'S TIME

Here are a few suggestions to aid your doctor in determining the need for a house call:

* If you or a member of your family is suffering from an

infection, take the temperature before calling the doctor.
* Before calling your doctor, jot down the symptoms, unless of course, the illness is emergent in nature. This will enable your doctor to get an idea of how sick you are.
* Do not minimize the symptoms, as this may lead your doctor to conclude erroneously that a house call is unnecessary.
* Do not exaggerate symptoms as this may cause your doctor to visit you unnecessarily.
* Be sure to tell your doctor if you have had similar episodes previously. This will aid him in reaching an accurate diagnosis more quickly.
* If your doctor has decided that a home visit is not needed, but your symptoms persist or increase in intensity, do not hesitate to call him again and urge strenuously that he come to your home.
* In an emergency, if you cannot reach your doctor, call the police for an ambulance. If the patient is up and able to move about, take him to the emergency room of the nearest hospital.

You may be able to save extra visits to your doctor's office if you do the following:
* Whenever possible, call for an appointment beforehand. An impromptu visit may result in your being rushed, or may lead to an incomplete examination.
* Always tell the nurse or secretary as much as you can about the reason for your visit. This will enable her to give you instructions on special preparations prior to your visit.
* If you know in advance that you will want an exceptionally lengthy consultation, tell the nurse or secretary so that she can plan for your doctor to afford you ample time.
* Jot down the questions you will want answered before you see your doctor, or take this book with you and mark the pages containing questions for which you seek answers.
* Be on time for your appointment.

Patients often complain bitterly about having to wait so long in a doctor's office. This situation is unfortunate and is frequently due to the inconsiderate patients who come late for their appointments. However, it may be caused by an emergency situation that has cropped up during office hours. For example, a whole office hour may be knocked out of kilter if the doctor has to suture a laceration, unexpectedly, or a patient at the hospital requires immediate attention.

5. PERIODIC
MEDICAL CHECK-UPS

Ideally, people should seek medical attention not only when ill but when they feel fit. A complete physical examination on a "well" person may reveal a disorder in such an early stage of its development that symptoms have not yet appeared. Naturally, disorders or diseases respond best when treated early.

People under forty-five years of age should undergo a check-up once a year; for those over forty-five, a check-up twice a year is advisable. Infants under a year old should be examined every month; between one and two years of age, every two to three months; and older children two to three times a year.

Periodic medical examinations can be conducted by your general practitioner or pediatrician or, if you wish, by a diagnostic center in your community. These centers, some operated privately, others controlled either by voluntary hospitals or local health departments, are equipped to do thorough medical check-ups, laboratory tests, and X-ray examinations.

During the routine medical check-up, or to use the more technical phrase, a multiphasic screening examination, a complete medical history and physical examination of the entire body will be taken. This will include:

Testing of the eyes for visual acuity, observation of the retina through an ophthalmoscope, testing of intraocular pressure for glaucoma, appearance of the conjunctiva and lens.

A test of hearing and appearance of the eardrum by use of an otoscope.

Inspection of the nose, mouth, and throat.

Examination of the neck for enlarged lymph glands or goiter.

Breast examination, with recommendation for mammographic X-rays if lumps are suspected.

Chest examination with the aid of a stethoscope, noting breath sounds of the lungs and heart action, and the taking of a chest X-ray.

Blood pressure reading and taking of the pulse.

Abdominal examination with observations to note if the liver, spleen, or kidneys are enlarged, and to note if any masses are present.

Examination of the groin for hernia.

Pelvic examination in the female.

Genital examination in the male.

A Pap smear in the female.

Rectal examination digitally, and by use of a sigmoidoscope. In the male, the prostate gland is examined through the rectum.

Examination of the extremities for presence of varicose veins and to note any muscle disorders.

Examination of the skin of the entire body.

Examination of reflexes to note the presence of any nerve disorder.

Weight determination.

Urine analysis.

A complete blood count.

Complete blood chemistries.

The giving of needed booster shots, especially to children.

One of the major benefits of a periodic health examination is that it points the way toward further indicated investigations. Thus, if a patient gives a story of intestinal symptoms, the physician may order a gastrointestinal X-ray series; if a patient has enlargement of the prostate, cystoscopy may be advised, etc.

One of the curious side effects of the periodic health check-up is that many people fail to take them periodically. Having once been assured by the negative findings of a particular examination, there is a tendency for some people to allow several years to elapse before undergoing another check-up. As a result, they live under the false impression that they have remained healthy during the long interval between check-ups. To be of real value, health examinations must be carried out every year.

CANCER DETECTION EXAMINATION

In recent years, examinations to detect cancer have become rather popular. While they are in many instances helpful, they do *not* take the place of a thorough periodic medical check-up. Cancer is not the only disease to be controlled if one is to live a healthy, long life. It's of little benefit to be given a clean bill of health from a cancer detection examination when one may be suffering from untreated diabetes, tuberculosis, coronary artery insufficiency, or a host of other equally disabling conditions. Moreover, a thorough and complete medical check-up usually will uncover the presence of a cancer or allied disease.

6. MEDICARE

Your Medicare Handbook

HEALTH INSURANCE

UNDER

SOCIAL SECURITY

(PART A)   HOSPITAL INSURANCE

(PART B)   MEDICAL INSURANCE

Like Medicare, your handbook has two parts. . .

PART A

● The *first* section describes *hospital insurance*, often called *Part A* of Medicare. This is the part that helps pay for your care when you are in the hospital and for related health services, when you need them, after you leave the hospital.

PART B

● The *second* section describes *medical insurance*, often called *Part B* of Medicare. This is the part that helps pay your doctor bills and bills for other medical services you need.

Your Medicare health insurance card shows the protection you have

The people at the hospital, doctor's office, or wherever you get services, can tell from your health insurance card that you have both hospital and medical insurance and when each started. This is why you should always have your card with you when you receive services.

When a husband and wife both have Medicare, they receive separate cards and claim numbers.

If you ever lose your health insurance card, the people in your social security office will get you a new one.

This is your personal health insurance claim number. It must be shown on all Medicare claims exactly as it is shown on your card—INCLUDING THE LETTER AT THE END.

This shows you have hospital insurance.

This shows you have medical insurance.

The dates your insurance starts are shown here.

Table of Contents

Hospital Insurance

Medical Insurance

This shows that you are entitled to the benefits described in the hospital insurance part of this handbook.

The date your hospital insurance starts is shown here.

HOW HOSPITAL INSURANCE WORKS

Your hospital insurance helps pay for medically necessary covered services provided by health facilities participating in Medicare when you are:

- **A BED PATIENT IN A HOSPITAL,**

And . . . if you need further care *after* a hospital stay, when you are:

- **A BED PATIENT IN A SKILLED NURSING FACILITY,** or
- **A PATIENT AT HOME RECEIVING SERVICES FROM A HOME HEALTH AGENCY.**

The services hospital insurance helps pay for are called *covered services.* When you meet the conditions described on the following pages, your hospital insurance *covers almost all of the services* you would ordinarily receive as a bed patient in a participating hospital or skilled nursing facility or as a patient at home receiving services from a participating home health agency. Your hospital insurance will also, in some cases, help pay for care in certain hospitals that do not participate in Medicare (see page 12).

When you receive covered services from a participating hospital, skilled nursing facility, or home health agency, you do not need to make any claim for your hospital insurance benefits. These institutions or agencies make the claims and receive the Medicare payment. They have agreed to charge you only for services which are not covered by Medicare.

You will always receive a notice from the Social Security Administration when a payment has been made on your behalf.

All outpatient hospital services are covered only by medical insurance. See page 18.

Health Facilities Must Meet Certain Conditions to Take Part in Medicare

To participate in the Medicare program, health facilities must meet standards which help assure that they will be able to provide high quality health care. In addition, they must not charge the Medicare beneficiary for services paid for by the program, and they must abide by title VI of the Civil Rights Act, which prohibits discrimination based on race, color, or national origin.

How Often You Can Use Your Hospital Insurance Benefits—and How Your Benefits Can Be Renewed

Your use of hospital insurance benefits is limited to certain *maximum* amounts for certain periods of time—but there is a way for your hospital insurance benefits to *start over* again (except the "lifetime reserve" described on page 8). You can figure out yourself how this works:

HOW THE USE OF HOSPITAL INSURANCE BENEFITS IS COUNTED

WHEN YOU RECEIVE COVERED SERVICES AS—	YOUR PART A BENEFITS ARE—
• A bed patient in a hospital.	• Up to 90 "hospital days" for *each* "benefit period."
• A bed patient in a skilled nursing facility.	• Up to 100 "extended care days" for *each* "benefit period."
• A patient at home receiving home health services.	• Up to 100 "home health visits" for *each* "benefit period." (Page 11 describes the 1-year time limit on these visits.)

These three kinds of benefits and how you qualify for them are described in more detail on the following pages. But, as you can see, you can get covered services for up to these total numbers of "days" and "visits" for *each* "benefit period." So you need to know what a "benefit period" is to know how often you can use your hospital insurance benefits.

WHAT IS A "BENEFIT PERIOD"?

A "benefit period" is simply a period of time for measuring your use of hospital insurance benefits. (In the first Medicare handbook and in some other Medicare publications, we called this period of time a "spell of illness," which is the term used in the law. But because many people thought this term had something to do with a single illness or a particular "spell" of sickness, we are now calling it a "benefit period.") This is how it works.

The first time you enter a hospital after your hospital insurance starts will be the beginning of your *first* benefit period. Your first benefit period *ends* as soon as you have not been a bed patient in any hospital (or any facility that mainly provides skilled nursing care) for *60 days in a row*. After that, a *new*

benefit period begins the next time you enter a hospital—and *that* benefit period ends as soon as you have *another* 60 days in a row when you are not a bed patient in any hospital (or any facility that mainly provides skilled nursing care). Then *another* benefit period can begin the *next* time you enter a hospital—and so on.

There is no limit to the number of benefit periods you may have. There is an easy way to remember the rule. Just keep in mind that *any time* you are not in any hospital or other facility mainly providing skilled nursing care for *60* days in a row a new benefit period will begin the next time you go into a hospital. And, of course, for each new benefit period, your full hospital insurance benefits are available again to use as you need them.

You Get a Personal Record of Benefits Used

You don't have to bother about trying to keep track of how many "days" or "visits" you use in each benefit period. The notice you receive from the Social Security Administration after you have used any hospital insurance benefits will tell you how many benefit "days" and "visits" you have left in that benefit period. But very few people who enter a hospital or skilled nursing facility, or use home health services, need these services long enough to use all the benefits they have for a benefit period. So most people will never run out of "days" or "visits," because a new benefit period will almost always start with full benefits available again the next time they are needed.

EXAMPLE: Mr. L was in the hospital for 14 days and then went home.

After being at home for 80 days, Mr. L needs to return to the hospital. When Mr. L is admitted this time, he is in a new benefit period. That means he is again eligible for up to 90 hospital days because more than 60 days have gone by since he was last in a hospital (or other facility that mainly provides skilled nursing care). The benefit days Mr. L used the time before do not matter because he is in a new benefit period.

However, because Mr. L had been in the hospital only 14 days, he still had 76 hospital benefit days left in the original benefit period. If he had had to go back to the hospital within 60 days, instead of 80, he could have used any of these remaining days that he needed during this second stay.

How Hospital Insurance Benefits Are Financed

The hospital insurance program is financed by special contributions from employees and self-employed persons, with employers paying an equal amount. These contributions are collected along with regular social security contributions from the wages and self-employment income earned during a person's working years.

The contribution rate for the hospital insurance program is 1 percent of the first $12,600 of earnings in 1974.

These contributions are put into the Hospital Insurance Trust Fund from which the program's benefits and administrative expenses are paid. Funds from general tax revenues are used to finance hospital insurance benefits for people who are insured under a special coverage provision in the initial law even though they are not entitled to monthly social security or railroad retirement benefits. A 1972 change in the law also makes it possible for people 65 and over who are not otherwise entitled to hospital insurance to enroll in the program and pay premiums into the Hospital Insurance Trust Fund.

In addition, the law provides that the various dollar amounts for which the patient is responsible be reviewed annually. These dollar amounts include the first $84 of hospital charges in each benefit period and different per-day amounts after certain periods of benefit use in hospitals and skilled nursing facilities. These are described on the following pages. The law also provides that if this annual review shows that hospital costs have changed significantly, these amounts must be adjusted for the following year.

What Hospital Insurance Can Pay When You Are a Hospital Bed Patient

When you need the kind of special care that *only* a hospital can provide, Medicare can help pay for up to 90 days of bed patient care in *each* benefit period in any participating general care, tuberculosis, or psychiatric hospital.

● For the first 60 days—hospital insurance pays for all covered services, *except for the first $84.*

● For the 61st through the 90th day—hospital insurance pays for all covered services, *except for $21 a day.*

IMPORTANT!

Once you have taken care of the first **$84** of hospital expenses in each benefit period, **you do not have to pay it again,** even if you have to go back in a hospital more than once in that same benefit period.

Also, You Have a "Lifetime Reserve" of 60 Additional Hospital Days

This is like a "bank account" of extra days to draw from if you need them. You can use them if you ever need more than 90 days of hospital care in the same benefit period. For each "lifetime reserve" day used, hospital insurance pays for all covered services, *except for $42 a day.*

Each lifetime reserve day you use permanently reduces the total you have left.

Usually you will want to use your lifetime reserve days if you need hospital care after you have used all your 90 days in a benefit period. *Unless* you decide *not* to use them, the extra days of hospital care that you use are automatically taken from your lifetime reserve.

If for any reason you do not wish to use your reserve days, the hospital will ask you to say so in writing. In making your decision, you should consider any private insurance you have which may pay for some or all of your additional hospital care. And, of course, you may wish to talk to your doctor or the people at the hospital about whether in your particular situation you should draw on your lifetime reserve.

EXAMPLE: Mrs. S had to go to the hospital a number of times in the same benefit period and used up all her 90 days. Before a new benefit period could start, she again needed to go to a hospital. She can draw from her "lifetime reserve" days to help her pay for the hospital care.

Special Rules for Benefits in Psychiatric Hospitals

For care in a psychiatric hospital, there is a lifetime limit of 190 hospital benefit days. Also, for a beneficiary who is a patient in a psychiatric hospital on the day his hospital insurance starts, there is a special limitation which is described in Question 4 on page 13.

Your Benefits When You Are a Bed Patient in a Participating Hospital

The list below describes the kinds of bene- fits that hospital insurance will help pay for when you are a bed patient in a hospital and some of the services that it cannot pay for.

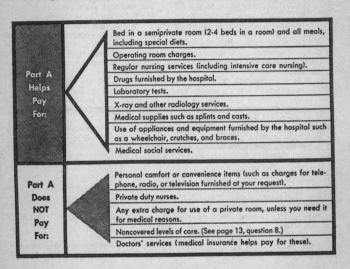

Part A Helps Pay For:	Bed in a semiprivate room (2-4 beds in a room) and all meals, including special diets.
	Operating room charges.
	Regular nursing services (including intensive care nursing).
	Drugs furnished by the hospital.
	Laboratory tests.
	X-ray and other radiology services.
	Medical supplies such as splints and casts.
	Use of appliances and equipment furnished by the hospital such as a wheelchair, crutches, and braces.
	Medical social services.
Part A Does NOT Pay For:	Personal comfort or convenience items (such as charges for telephone, radio, or television furnished at your request).
	Private duty nurses.
	Any extra charge for use of a private room, unless you need it for medical reasons.
	Noncovered levels of care. (See page 13, question 8.)
	Doctors' services (medical insurance helps pay for these).

An Example of How Hospital Insurance Helps Pay for Hospital Care

Mrs. C was in the hospital for 10 days. During her stay in the hospital, Mrs. C had an operation. Her bill included the hospital charges for semiprivate room and all meals, including special diet; use of the operating room; X-rays, laboratory tests; oxygen; and drugs furnished by the hospital. There was also a charge of $15.25 for television and telephone services.

Of the total hospital bill of $967.25, Mrs. C paid $99.25. (This was the first $84 for that benefit period plus the charges for the television and telephone.) Her hospital insurance took care of the remaining $868. (And, of course, Mrs. C's medical insurance helped pay her doctor bills.)

Extended Care Benefits After You Leave the Hospital

Sometimes a patient no longer needs all the care which hospitals provide, but still needs daily skilled nursing care or skilled rehabilitation services.which cannot be furnished in his home. In these cases, the doctor may transfer the patient from the hospital to a skilled nursing facility. This is a specially qualified facility which is staffed and equipped to furnish skilled nursing care or skilled rehabilitation services and many important related health services.

Hospital insurance pays for all covered services in a participating skilled nursing facility for the first 20 days you receive such services in each benefit period and all but $10.50 a day for up to 80 more days in that same benefit period, *but only if all the following are true:*

1. Your medical care needs require daily skilled nursing care or skilled rehabilitation services;

2. A doctor determines that you need skilled nursing or rehabilitation care and orders such care for you;

3. You have been in a participating (or otherwise qualified) hospital for at least 3 days in a row before your admission;

4. You are admitted within a limited period, generally 14 days after you leave the hospital; and

5. You are admitted for further treatment of a condition for which you were treated in the hospital.

If you leave a skilled nursing facility and are readmitted to one within 14 days, you can continue to use your additional extended care benefit days for that benefit period without a new 3-day stay in a hospital.

The following list describes some of the kinds of extended care services hospital insurance will help pay for and some of the services that it cannot pay for.

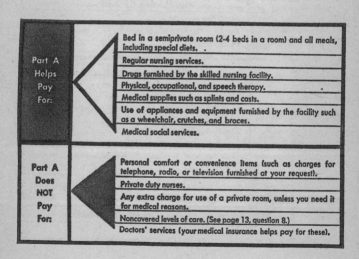

Part A Helps Pay For:	Bed in a semiprivate room (2-4 beds in a room) and all meals, including special diets. .
	Regular nursing services.
	Drugs furnished by the skilled nursing facility.
	Physical, occupational, and speech therapy.
	Medical supplies such as splints and casts.
	Use of appliances and equipment furnished by the facility such as a wheelchair, crutches, and braces.
	Medical social services.
Part A Does NOT Pay For:	Personal comfort or convenience items (such as charges for telephone, radio, or television furnished at your request).
	Private duty nurses.
	Any extra charge for use of a private room, unless you need it for medical reasons.
	Noncovered levels of care. (See page 13, question 8.)
	Doctors' services (your medical insurance helps pay for these).

Home Health Benefits After You Leave the Hospital

After you have been in a hospital (or in a skilled nursing facility *after* a hospital stay), your doctor may decide that the continued care you need can best be given in your own home through a home health agency. If the continuing care you need in your home includes part-time skilled nursing care or physical or speech therapy, Medicare can pay for this care and also for certain additional health care services you may need.

Hospital insurance pays for all covered services—for as many as 100 home health visits after the start of one benefit period and before the start of another.

The visits must be medically necessary and be furnished by a participating home health agency. Benefits can be paid for up to a year after your most recent discharge from a hospital or participating skilled nursing facility, *but only if all the following are true*:

1. You were in a participating (or otherwise qualified) hospital for at least 3 days in a row;

2. The continuing care you need includes part-time skilled nursing care or physical or speech therapy;

3. You are confined to your home;

4. A doctor determines that you need home health care and sets up a home health plan for you within 14 days after your discharge from the hospital or a participating skilled nursing facility; and

5. The home health care is for further treatment of a condition for which you received services as a bed patient in the hospital or skilled nursing facility.

For an explanation of how "visits" are counted, see Question 7 on page 13.

The following list describes the kinds of home health services that hospital insurance will help pay for and some of the services that it cannot pay for.

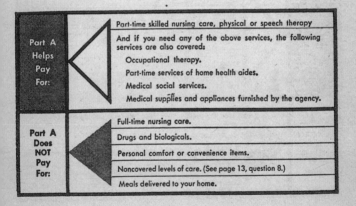

Part A Helps Pay For:	Part-time skilled nursing care, physical or speech therapy
	And if you need any of the above services, the following services are also covered:
	Occupational therapy.
	Part-time services of home health aides.
	Medical social services.
	Medical supplies and appliances furnished by the agency.
Part A Does NOT Pay For:	Full-time nursing care.
	Drugs and biologicals.
	Personal comfort or convenience items.
	Noncovered levels of care. (See page 13, question 8.)
	Meals delivered to your home.

Benefits for Care in Hospitals That Do Not Take Part in Medicare

Nearly all hospitals in the country take part in Medicare. But if you are admitted for emergency care to a hospital that does not take part in Medicare, hospital insurance may still be able to help pay some of the bills.

Your hospital insurance can help pay for emergency care if the hospital: (1) meets certain conditions listed in the law; (2) is the closest or the quickest one to get to that

has a bed available; and (3) is equipped to handle the emergency.

If you receive emergency care in such a hospital, the benefit payment will usually be made to the hospital. If the hospital decides to bill you instead of Medicare, the benefit payment will be made to you. The people at your social security office will help you make your claim.

Utilization Review

Each hospital and skilled nursing facility has a Utilization Review Committee. The purpose of this committee is to help assure the most effective use of hospital or skilled nursing facility services. The committee, which includes at least two physicians, reviews admissions on a sample basis and reviews ALL long-stay cases.

The Utilization Review Committee does not decide whether hospital or extended care services are covered under Medicare. These decisions are made by intermediaries, which are organizations selected by the Federal Government to make Medicare payment determinations.

If a Utilization Review Committee, however, finds in a specific case being reviewed that care in a hospital or skilled nursing facility is not medically necessary, then the law requires that Medicare payments must be stopped. In these cases, the committee always discusses its findings with the patient's doctor before making a decision. But, if the decision still is that further hospital or skilled nursing facility care is not medically necessary, then the patient, his doctor, and the facility are advised in writing, and Medicare payments must stop no later than 3 days after notice has been received by the hospital or skilled nursing facility.

Questions and Answers About Hospital Insurance

1. *Where can I find out if a hospital, skilled nursing facility, or home health agency is participating in Medicare?*
Your doctor, or someone at the institution or agency, can tell you. Or you can ask the people in any social security office.

2. *Does hospital insurance pay for services in a foreign hospital?*

Yes, but only under certain conditions. If you are in the United States when an emergency occurs and a foreign hospital is closer than the nearest hospital in the U.S. which could provide the emergency care you need, then hospital insurance can help pay for the emergency care. If a foreign hospital is closer to your home than the nearest U.S. hospital which can provide the care you need, hospital in-

Questions and Answers About Hospital Insurance (continued)

surance will help pay for the covered services you receive in the foreign hospital whether or not an emergency exists. Hospital insurance can also help pay for inpatient hospital care in a Canadian hospital if you become ill or are injured while you are traveling through Canada between Alaska and another State. Your medical insurance can also help pay for doctors' and ambulance services furnished in connection with covered foreign hospital care.

3. *Can hospital insurance pay anything toward the cost of my care in a Christian Science sanatorium?*

Yes. Your hospital insurance can cover certain hospital and extended care services furnished to inpatients of a sanatorium operated, or listed and certified, by the First Church of Christ, Scientist, in Boston. For more information, ask at any social security office.

4. *Is there a special rule for beneficiaries who are in a psychiatric hospital when their hospital insurance protection starts?*

Yes. When a person is a patient in a psychiatric hospital *at the time* his hospital insurance starts, the days in the mental hospital during the 150-day period just before his hospital insurance starts count against the total number of benefit days he can use in a psychiatric hospital in his first benefit period. These days, however, do not count against his lifetime maximum of 190 days.

5. *What can I do if I think a mistake has been made in the amount of my hospital insurance benefits?*

The first thing to do is to ask someone at the hospital, skilled nursing facility, or home health agency that provided the services. Usually they can answer your questions. Sometimes, however, they may need to refer you to the organization that handles their Medicare payments. If you are still not satisfied, get in touch with your social security office for information about your right to formal appeal.

6. *What if I cannot pay the amounts that hospital insurance does not pay?*

You may want to ask at your local public assistance office about help under a State program such as old-age assistance or medical assistance (sometimes called "medicaid").

7. *What is a home health "visit"?*

One "visit" is counted *each* time you receive a covered health care service from a home health agency. If you receive two *different* services on the same day (for example, both a nurse and a physical therapist call on you), that would be two "visits." It would also be two "visits" if you received the *same* service twice in a day (such as two calls by a nurse).

8. *What is meant by "noncovered level of care"?*

The Medicare law specifies that payment cannot be made for custodial care. This means the level of care that primarily helps people with their personal, daily needs such as eating, getting about, and similar things one ordinarily does for himself, or that can be done for him by people without professional skills or training. When a person's *primary* need is for the skilled health care that a hospital, skilled nursing facility, or a home health agency provides, Medicare payment can be made even though personal care services are also being furnished. But if a person's *primary* need is for personal care services, Medicare cannot pay even if he is in a hospital, skilled nursing facility, or receiving home health care.

This shows that you are entitled to all the benefits described in the medical insurance part of this handbook.

Health **Insurance**
SOCIAL SECURITY 667
NAME OF BENEFICIARY
JOHN Q PUBLIC
CLAIM NUMBER
000-00-0000-A   SEX
                                MALE
IS ENTITLED TO   EFFECTIVE DATE
HOSPITAL INSURANCE   1-1-73
MEDICAL INSURANCE   1-1-73
SIGN
HERE ► John Q. Public

The date your medical insurance starts is shown here.

YOUR MEDICAL INSURANCE PREMIUM

The basic medical insurance premium for each person is $6.30 a month through June 30, 1974. Those who delayed signing up for a long period of time after their first chance or who signed up after canceling this insurance in the past are required by law to pay an additional 10 percent for each full year they were eligible but not enrolled.

The medical insurance program is reviewed each year to make sure that the full costs are being met. The results of the review are announced each December. Any change in your share of the premium would be effective for the 12-month period beginning the following July.

Your premium covers only part of the cost of your medical insurance protection. Up to now, the cost has been shared half and half by the people enrolled in this program and the Federal Government. Because of a recent change in the law, however, there is now a limit on how much your share of the premium can be increased.

In the future, even if the costs of the medical insurance program go up, your share can be increased only if there has been a general increase in social security cash benefits since the last time the premium was increased. The increase in your share of the premium is limited to the percentage increase in cash benefits. As a result, the Government's share may amount to more than half of the total costs in future years.

Medical insurance premiums are automatically deducted from monthly checks for people who receive social security benefits, railroad retirement benefits, or civil service annuities. People who do not receive any of these monthly checks pay their premiums directly to the Social Security Administration (or, in some cases, have premiums paid on their behalf under a State assistance program).

If You Ever Decide to Cancel

You can cancel your medical insurance at any time. Your protection and your premiums will stop at the end of the calendar quarter after the quarter your notice is received. (A calendar quarter is any of the 3-month periods beginning with January 1, April 1, July 1, or October 1.)

If you do cancel your medical insurance, you have only one chance to get it back. You may sign up again in any "general enrollment" period. There is a general enrollment period *every* year—from January 1 through March 31.

If you should ever think of canceling your medical insurance protection, remember that you may not be able to get equal protection from other sources. Many health insurance companies do not offer broad coverage policies for people 65 and over, but only *extra* insurance for those who already have medical insurance under Medicare.

34

HOW MEDICAL INSURANCE WORKS

Your medical insurance helps pay for—

**DOCTORS' SERVICES
OUTPATIENT HOSPITAL SERVICES
MEDICAL SERVICES AND SUPPLIES
HOME HEALTH SERVICES
OUTPATIENT PHYSICAL THERAPY
SPEECH PATHOLOGY SERVICES
—and other health care services.**

To understand the way medical insurance works, it will help to know the following terms.

Covered services: These are the kinds of services medical insurance can help pay for. (The reasonable charges for covered services also count toward the $60 deductible.)

$60 deductible: For each calendar year, medical insurance cannot make any payment until you have had $60 of reasonable charges for covered medical expenses. (Prior to January 1, 1973, the deductible was $50.)

Reasonable charges: Reasonable charges are determined by the Medicare carriers —the organizations selected in each State by the Social Security Administration to handle medical insurance claims—and take into consideration the customary charges of your doctor (or supplier) as well as the charges made by other doctors and suppliers in your locality for similar services.

After Medicare records show that the reasonable charges for covered services you have received are over $60 for a calendar year, medical insurance will pay 80 percent of the reasonable charges for additional covered services for the rest of that year. There are four exceptions to this rule: radiology and pathology services (page 17); home health benefits (page 20); outpatient physical therapy (page 19); and doctors' services for treatment of mental illness (Question 1, page 30). For information on when to send in claims, see page 23. *Important:* There is only *one* $60 medical insurance deductible each year —not a separate $60 deductible for each kind of covered service. Also, medical expenses in the last 3 months of one year can sometimes count toward the $60 deductible for the next year. This carry-over rule is described on page 24.

EXPLANATION OF BENEFITS NOTICE

Whenever a medical insurance claim is sent in, you will receive a statement showing your use of medical insurance benefits. This statement will show you how much of your expenses have been credited to your $60 deductible and the amount of the benefit payment if any. The explanation-of-benefits statements are important because you can use the latest one to show your doctor and others when they want to know how much of the $60 deductible you have met.

35

When a Doctor Treats You

Medical insurance will help pay your doctor bills for all covered services you receive in the United States. Payment can be made no matter where a doctor treats you—in a hospital, his office, skilled nursing facility, your home, or at a group practice or other clinic.

You select your own doctor. He does not have to "sign up" or make any other special arrangements with Medicare.

For covered services you receive from your doctor, the medical insurance payment can be made either to you or to your doctor. See page 22 for the two ways payment can be made.

The following list shows the kinds of doctors' services that medical insurance will help pay for and some of the services it cannot pay for.

Part B Helps Pay For:	Medical and surgical services by a doctor of medicine or osteopathy.
	Certain medical and surgical services by a doctor of dental medicine or a doctor of dental surgery.
	Certain services by podiatrists which they are legally authorized to perform by the State in which they practice.
	Other services which are ordinarily furnished in the doctor's office and included in his bill such as: Diagnostic tests and procedures Medical supplies Services of his office nurse Drugs and biologicals which cannot be self-administered.
	Limited services by chiropractors (beginning July 1, 1973)
Part B Does NOT Pay For:	Routine physical checkups.
	Routine foot care and treatment of flat feet and partial dislocations of the feet.
	Eye refractions and examinations for prescribing, fitting, or changing eyeglasses.
	Hearing examinations for prescribing, fitting, or changing hearing aids.
	Immunizations (unless directly related to an injury or immediate risk of infection such as a tetanus shot given after an injury).
	Services of certain practitioners, for example: Christian Science practitioners Naturopaths

Limited Coverage of Dental Services

Medical insurance covers the services of dentists *only* when the services involve surgery of the jaw or related structures or setting of fractures of the jaw or facial bones.

Medical insurance does *not* pay for dental services such as the care, filling, removal, or replacement of teeth, or treatment of the gum areas nor for surgery or other services related to these kinds of dental care.

Radiology and Pathology Services by Doctors When You Are a Bed Patient in a Hospital

Medical insurance pays *all* (100 percent) of the reasonable charges by doctors for radiology services (such as X-rays) and pathology services (such as blood and urine tests) you receive as an inpatient in a participating or otherwise qualified hospital.

You may not receive any doctor bills for these services because many hospitals and the doctors who perform these services have agreed that the hospital will collect the payments due from your medical insurance. If you do receive doctor bills for these services, send them in as described on page 22 for *full* payment of the reasonable charges, even though you have not met the $60 deductible.

Medical insurance pays 80 percent of the reasonable charges by doctors for all other covered services you receive. Full payment of the reasonable charges can be made only for radiology and pathology services.

SPECIAL RULE: Because the full reasonable charges are taken care of when you receive radiology and pathology services as a hospital inpatient, these charges do not count toward the $60 deductible.

Ambulance Services

Medical insurance will help pay for ambulance transportation by an approved ambulance service to a hospital or skilled nursing facility only when (1) the ambulance, its equipment, and personnel meet Medicare requirements, and (2) transportation by other means could endanger the patient's health. When the patient is taken to a facility other than the *nearest* one that can provide appropriate care, only the reasonable charges for ambulance transportation to the nearest facility can be allowed.

Under similar restrictions, medical insurance can help pay for ambulance services from one hospital to another, from a hospital to a skilled nursing facility, or from a hospital or skilled nursing facility to the patient's home.

Outpatient Hospital Benefits

When people go to the hospital for diagnosis or treatment and are not admitted as bed patients, the services they receive are called *outpatient hospital services.*

Covered outpatient services whether for diagnosis or treatment are paid by medical insurance.

After the $60 deductible has been met, Medicare takes care of 80 percent of the reasonable charges for all covered outpatient hospital services you receive.

The hospital will apply for the Medicare payment and will charge you for any part of the $60 deductible you have not met plus 20 percent of the remaining reasonable charges for the outpatient services.

If the charge is $60 or less and the hospital cannot determine how much of the $60 deductible you have met, then the hospital may ask you to pay the entire bill. If you pay the bill, any Medicare payments that are due will be paid directly to you. Except in unusual circumstances, the hospital will prepare the Medicare claim for you. If you ever need help with your claim, get in touch with your social security office.

When you pay an outpatient bill of $60 or less, here is what happens:

- *If you have already met the $60 deductible*—Medicare will pay you 80 percent of the amount you paid the hospital.
- *If you have not met the $60 deductible* —Medicare will credit the amount you paid toward your $60 deductible. If that amount plus any part of the deductible you have previously met for the year adds up to more than $60, medical insurance will pay you 80 percent of the amount above the $60 deductible.

EXAMPLE: During the year, Mrs. J had met $55 of her deductible *before* she received treatment in the hospital outpatient department. The hospital charged her $10, and she paid the bill at their request. When her claim is received, $5 of the outpatient bill is used to make up her $60 deductible and Mrs. J receives 80 percent of the remaining $5, which would be $4.

IMPORTANT:

When you go to a hospital for outpatient services, be sure to show the people there your most recent explanation-of-benefits statement (see page 15). From this form, they can tell how much of the $60 deductible you have met and how much of the deductible, if any, they may charge you.

Outpatient Hospital Benefits (continued)

The following list describes the kinds of outpatient hospital services that medical insurance will help pay for and some of the services that it cannot pay for:

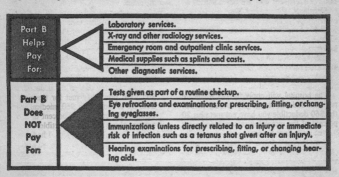

Part B Helps Pay For:	Laboratory services.
	X-ray and other radiology services.
	Emergency room and outpatient clinic services.
	Medical supplies such as splints and casts.
	Other diagnostic services.
Part B Does NOT Pay For:	Tests given as part of a routine checkup.
	Eye refractions and examinations for prescribing, fitting, or changing eyeglasses.
	Immunizations (unless directly related to an injury or immediate risk of infection such as a tetanus shot given after an injury).
	Hearing examinations for prescribing, fitting, or changing hearing aids.

Outpatient Physical Therapy and Speech Pathology Services

Outpatient physical therapy and speech pathology services are covered by medical insurance when they are furnished under the direct and personal supervision of a doctor or when they are furnished as part of covered home health services. Starting July 1, 1973, home and office services furnished by a licensed physical therapist are covered under your medical insurance subject to an annual payment limit of $80.

Also, physical therapy or speech pathology services you receive as an outpatient are covered when they are furnished by a qualified hospital, skilled nursing facility, home health agency, clinic, rehabilitation agency, or public health agency, and they are furnished under a plan established and periodically reviewed by a doctor. This benefit can also help pay for physical therapy you need while you are a bed patient in a hospital or skilled nursing facility, when your care cannot be covered by hospital insurance.

Emergency Outpatient Care from Certain Nonparticipating Hospitals Can also be Covered

If you receive emergency outpatient care from a nonparticipating hospital which meets certain conditions, the hospital will usually bill Medicare for its share of the charges. It will then bill you for any part of the $60 deductible you have not met plus 20 percent of the remaining reasonable charges.

The hospital may choose instead to bill you for the entire amount. In this case, your medical insurance will pay you 80 percent of the reasonable charges (after the $60 deductible has been met).

For help in making your claim, get in touch with your social security office.

Home Health Benefits

Your medical insurance will help pay for up to 100 home health visits each calendar year without the prior hospitalization required under your hospital insurance, *but only if all the following are true:*

1. You need part-time skilled nursing care, or physical or speech therapy services;
2. You are confined to your home;
3. A doctor determines you need home health care;
4. A doctor sets up and periodically reviews the plan for home health care; and
5. The home health agency is participating in Medicare.

For an explanation of how home health "visits" are counted, see Question 7 on page 13.

The home health agency always makes the claim for the benefit payment, so you do not submit a *Request for Medicare Payment* form when you receive home health services. Since medical insurance pays the *full* reasonable charges for home health services, the agency will bill you only for any part of the $60 deductible you have not met.

The following list describes the kinds of home health services that medical insurance will help pay for and some of the services that it cannot pay for.

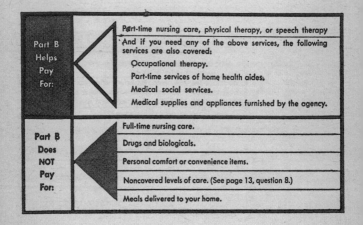

Part B Helps Pay For:

Part-time nursing care, physical therapy, or speech therapy

And if you need any of the above services, the following services are also covered:

Occupational therapy.

Part-time services of home health aides.

Medical social services.

Medical supplies and appliances furnished by the agency.

Part B Does NOT Pay For:

Full-time nursing care.

Drugs and biologicals.

Personal comfort or convenience items.

Noncovered levels of care. (See page 13, question 8.)

Meals delivered to your home.

Other Medical Services and Supplies

This benefit helps you pay for a number of different medical services and supplies which may be necessary in the treatment of an illness or injury. They may be furnished in connection with treatment by your doctor, a medical clinic, or other health facility.

When you get any of these separate services from a participating hospital, skilled nursing facility, or home health agency, it will make the claim for the Medicare payment and will

bill you for any of the $60 deductible you have not met and 20 percent of the remaining reasonable charges. Otherwise, you or the supplier of services will make the claim, as described on page 22.

The following list shows the kinds of medical services and supplies that medical insurance can help pay for when they are medically necessary and ordered by your doctor and some that it cannot pay for.

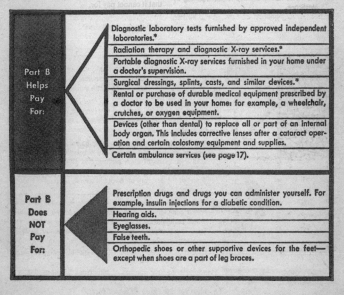

Part B Helps Pay For:	Diagnostic laboratory tests furnished by approved independent laboratories.*
	Radiation therapy and diagnostic X-ray services.*
	Portable diagnostic X-ray services furnished in your home under a doctor's supervision.
	Surgical dressings, splints, casts, and similar devices.*
	Rental or purchase of durable medical equipment prescribed by a doctor to be used in your home: for example, a wheelchair, crutches, or oxygen equipment.
	Devices (other than dental) to replace all or part of an internal body organ. This includes corrective lenses after a cataract operation and certain colostomy equipment and supplies.
	Certain ambulance services (see page 17).
Part B Does NOT Pay For:	Prescription drugs and drugs you can administer yourself. For example, insulin injections for a diabetic condition.
	Hearing aids.
	Eyeglasses.
	False teeth.
	Orthopedic shoes or other supportive devices for the feet—except when shoes are a part of leg braces.

* If you are a patient in a hospital or skilled nursing facility and, for some reason, your hospital insurance cannot pay for these services (for example, because you have used up your benefit days), medical insurance can help pay for them.

How to Claim Medical Insurance Benefits

1. PAYMENT TO YOUR DOCTOR OR SUPPLIER

If you and your doctor (or supplier) agree that he will apply for the medical insurance payment, it will be made directly to him. This is called "assignment" of the benefit.

A. Complete and sign Part I of the *Request for Medicare Payment* (Form SSA-1490). A copy of this form is on page 25. Often your doctor's office or the supplier will complete Part I as a convenience to you.

B. Your doctor or supplier completes Part II of the form.

C. Your doctor or supplier sends in the *Request for Medicare Payment* form.

When your doctor or supplier accepts assignment, he agrees that his total charge will not exceed the reasonable charge (see page 15). This means that you are responsible only for any of the $60 deductible not yet met, plus 20 percent of the balance of the "reasonable charges" and any charges for services that Medicare does not cover.

2. PAYMENT TO YOU

If either you or the doctor (or supplier) do not want to use the assignment method, the medical insurance payment can be made directly to you. *You can make a claim whether or not the bill has been paid.*

A. Complete and sign Part I of the *Request for Medicare Payment* form. Often your doctor's office or the supplier will complete Part I as a convenience to you.

B. Your doctor or supplier will either complete Part II or give you an itemized bill. An itemized bill shows the date, place, and description of each service, and the charge for each service. (Be sure your name and claim number, including the letter at the end, are on each bill exactly as they are shown on your health insurance card.)

C. You send in the *Request for Medicare Payment*, with either Part II completed or with itemized bills, to the organization which handles claims for the *area where you received services*. These organizations are listed on pages 27 to 29.

NOTE:

You may send in a number of bills from the *same* doctor or supplier (or from different doctors or suppliers) with a single *Request for Medicare Payment* form.

Also, if you have health insurance in addition to Medicare or you are covered under a State program which pays all or part of your health care, be sure to fill in Item 5 of your *Request for Medicare Payment* form. (See page 25.)

42

When to Send in Your First Claim Each Year

As soon as your bills come to $60, send them to the office that will be handling your medical insurance claims (see page 27). If the reasonable charges for covered services are $60 or more, an entry will be made in your record to show that you have met the deductible for the year, and any payment due at the time will be made.

In some cases, of course, you may want to send in your bills before you have a total of $60. For example, you may already have $40 in small medical bills when you receive services from a doctor for $25 and he agrees to take your assignment. In that case, you would send in your $40 in prior bills, so that when the assignment is processed for payment the record will show that you have met $40 of the $60 deductible. Also, you need not wait to send in a doctor's bill which meets the special rule for radiology or pathology services described on page 17.

It's a good idea to keep a record of your claim in case you ever want to inquire about it. Before you send it in, write down the date you mailed it, the services you received, the date and charge for each, and the name of the doctor or supplier who performed the services.

Your social security office will always be glad to answer your questions about when to send in your first claim.

If You Belong to a Group Practice Prepayment Plan

Group practice prepayment plans represent a special way of making health services available to their members. Generally, each member pays regular premiums to the plan in advance and this entitles him to receive any of the health services the plan provides, whenever he needs them, without paying a separate fee for each health service he receives. Congress took steps to assure that these plans could participate in the Medicare program while continuing their established method of operation.

Almost all group practice prepayment plans have made special arrangements with the Social Security Administration to receive direct payment for covered services they furnish their members who are medical insurance beneficiaries.

If you are a member of a plan which has made these special arrangements:

You DO NOT need to make a claim for any covered services which are provided through your group practice prepayment plan.

You DO need to make a claim for any covered services you receive which are not provided by your plan. In making your claim, you use one of the two methods described on page 22.

In addition, each plan has developed special methods to credit your membership premium payments or your use of plan services to the $60 deductible. Your plan will, of course, advise you of its method.

If you need more information, get in touch with your group practice prepayment plan.

When the Carry Over Helps You

To help the beneficiary who might otherwise need to meet the annual deductible twice in a short period, there is a special carry-over rule.

If you have expenses in the last 3 months of a year which can be counted toward your deductible for that year, they can also be counted toward the $60 annual deductible for the next year. This is called the carry over. So, even if you have not met the deductible before October, be sure to send in *all* the bills for covered services you receive in October, November, or December. The carry over will be credited to your deductible for both years.

Time Limits for Payment of Claims

Claims *must* be submitted within specific time limits or Medicare payment *cannot* be made. *Medicare can pay your claim only if it is sent in within the time limits shown below:*

If services were received during this period	Claims must be sent in no later than
October 1, 1972 — September 30, 1973	December 31, 1974
October 1, 1973 — September 30, 1974	December 31, 1975
October 1, 1974 — September 30, 1975	December 31, 1976

The Request for Payment Form

Page 25 shows the *Request for Medicare Payment* form. If you do not have a claim form, you can use the form on page 25. Just cut it out along the line. Generally, when you send a claim to the carrier, you will get back a new *Request for Medicare Payment* form to use for your next claim. Also, most doctors' offices usually have a supply of the forms. And you can always get extra copies from your social security office.

REQUEST FOR MEDICARE PAYMENT

Form Approved
OMB No.
72-R0730

MEDICAL INSURANCE BENEFITS—SOCIAL SECURITY ACT (See instructions on Back—Type or Print information)

NOTICE—Anyone who misrepresents or falsifies essential information requested by this form may upon conviction be subject to fine and imprisonment under Federal Law.

PART I—PATIENT TO FILL IN ITEMS 1 THROUGH 6 ONLY

When completed, send this form to:

Copy from
YOUR OWN
HEALTH
INSURANCE
CARD
(See example
on back)

1 Name of patient (First name, Middle initial, Last name)

2 Health insurance claim number (Include all letters)   ☐ Male   ☐ Female

3 Patient's mailing address   City, State, ZIP code   Telephone Number

4 Describe the illness or injury for which you received treatment (Always fill in this item if your doctor does not complete Part II below)   Was your illness or injury connected with your employment? ☐ Yes ☐ No

5 If you have other health insurance or if your State medical assistance agency will pay part of your medical expenses and you want information about this claim released to the insurance company or State agency upon its request, give the following information.

Insuring organization or State agency name and address   Policy or Medical Assistance Number

6 I authorize any holder of medical or other information about me to release to the Social Security Administration or its intermediaries or carriers any information needed for this or a related Medicare claim. I permit a copy of this authorization to be used in place of the original, and request payment of medical insurance benefits either to myself or to the party who accepts assignment below.

Signature of patient (See instructions on reverse where patient is unable to sign)   Date signed

SIGN HERE ▶

PART II—PHYSICIAN OR SUPPLIER TO FILL IN 7 THROUGH 14

7 A. Date of each service	B. Place of service (*See Codes below)	C. Fully describe surgical or medical procedures and other services or supplies furnished for each date given	D. Nature of illness or injury requiring services or supplies	E. Charges (If related to unusual circumstances explain in 7C)	Leave Blank
				$	

8 Name and address of physician or supplier (Number and street, city, State, ZIP code)   Telephone No.   **9** Total charges $

Physician or supplier code   **10** Amount paid $ **11** Any unpaid balance due $

12 Assignment of patient's bill ☐ I accept assignment (See reverse) ☐ I do not accept assignment.   **13** Show name and address of facility where services were performed (if other than home or office visits)

14 Signature of physician or supplier (A physician's signature certifies that physician's services were personally rendered by him or under his personal direction)   Date signed

*O—Doctor's Office
IL—Independent Laboratory   H—Patient's Home (If portable X-ray services, identify the supplier)
IH—Inpatient Hospital   ECF—Extended Care Facility
OH—Outpatient Hospital   OL—Other Locations
NH—Nursing Home

FORM SSA-1490 (8-72)   Department of Health, Education, and Welfare
Social Security Administration

SOME THINGS TO NOTE IN FILLING OUT PART I
(Your doctor will fill out Part II.)

1 & 2 Copy the name and number and indicate your sex exactly as shown on your health insurance card. Include the letters at the end of the number.

3 Enter your mailing address and telephone number, if any.

4 Describe your illness or injury. Be sure to check one of the two boxes.

5 If you have other health insurance or expect a welfare agency to pay part of the expenses, complete item 5.

6 Be sure to sign your name. If you cannot write your name, sign by mark (X), and have a witness sign his name and enter his address on this line.

If the claim is filed for the patient by another person he should enter the patient's name and write "By," sign his own name and address in this space, show his relationship to the patient, and why the patient cannot sign. (If the patient has died, the survivor should contact any social security office for information on what to do.)

HOW TO FILL OUT YOUR MEDICARE FORM

There are two ways that Medicare can help pay your doctor bills

One way is for Medicare to pay your doctor.—If you and your doctor agree, Medicare will pay him directly. This is the assignment method. You do not submit any claim; the doctor does. All you do is fill out Part I of this form and leave it with your doctor. Under this method the doctor agrees to accept the charge determination of the Medicare carrier as the full charge; you are responsible for the deductible and coinsurance. Please read Your Medicare Handbook to help you understand about the deductible and coinsurance. (Because Medicare has special payment arrangements with group practice prepayment plans these plans handle all claims for covered services they furnish to their members.)

The other way is for Medicare to pay you.—Medicare can also pay you directly—before or after you have paid your doctor. If you submit the claim yourself, fill out Part I and ask your doctor to fill out Part II. If you have an itemized bill from him, you may submit it rather than have him complete Part II. (This form, with Part I completed by you, may be used to send in several itemized bills from different doctors and suppliers.) Bills should show who furnished the services, the patient's name and number, dates of services, where the services were furnished, a description of the services, and charges for each separate service. It is helpful if the diagnosis is also shown. Then mail itemized bills and this form to the address shown in the upper left-hand corner. If no address is shown there, use the address listed in Your Medicare Handbook—or get advice from any social security office.

IMPORTANT NOTES FOR PHYSICIANS AND SUPPLIERS

Item 12: In assigned cases the patient is responsible only for the deductible, coinsurance, and non-covered services. Coinsurance and the deductible are based upon the charge determination of the carrier if this is less than the charge submitted.

This form may also be used by a supplier, or by the patient to claim reimbursement for charges by a supplier for services such as the use of an ambulance or medical appliances.

If the physician or supplier does not want Part II information released to the organization named in item 5, he should write "No further release" in item 7C following the description of services.

47

Where to Send Your Claim

The list below gives the names and addresses of the organizations selected by the Social Security Administration to handle medical insurance claims. These organizations are called carriers. In most cases, carriers handle claims for an entire State; a few handle claims for only part of a State. To find out where to send your medical insurance claim, look in the list for the State *where you received the services.* Under the name of the State (or, in some cases, under the list of counties within a State), you will find the name of the organization that will handle your medical insurance claim.

If you are not sure where your first claim should go and happen to send your claim to the wrong office, don't worry. Your claim will be sent on to the right place. Be sure to include the word "Medicare" in the carrier's address on the envelope, and give *your* return address.

NOTE: If you are a railroad annuitant (even if you are also entitled to social security benefits), send your medical insurance claim to The Travelers Insurance Company office which is nearest to your home—no matter where you received services.

ALABAMA
Medicare
Blue Cross-Blue Shield of Alabama
930 South 20th Street
Birmingham, Alabama 35205

ALASKA
Medicare
Aetna Life & Casualty
522 SW. Fifth Street
Portland, Oregon 97204

ARIZONA
Medicare
Aetna Life & Casualty
3010 West Fairmount Avenue
Phoenix, Arizona 85017

ARKANSAS
Medicare
Arkansas Blue Cross and Blue Shield
P.O. Box 2181
Little Rock, Arkansas 72203

CALIFORNIA
Counties of:
Los Angeles   Imperial
Orange   San Luis Obispo
San Diego   Riverside
Ventura   Santa Barbara
San Bernardino
Medicare
Occidental Life Insurance Co.
of California

CALIFORNIA (continued)
Box 54905
Los Angeles, California 90054
Rest of State:
Medicare
California Blue Shield
P.O. Box 7968, Rincon Annex
San Francisco, California 94119

COLORADO
Medicare
Colorado Medical Service, Inc.
P.O. Box 6410
Denver, Colorado 80206

CONNECTICUT
Medicare
Connecticut General Life Insurance Co.
200 Pratt Street
Meriden, Connecticut 06450

DELAWARE
Medicare
Blue Cross and Blue Shield
of Delaware
201 West 14th Street
Wilmington, Delaware 19899

DISTRICT OF COLUMBIA
Medicare
Medical Service of D.C.
550—12th St., S.W.
Washington, D.C. 20024

FLORIDA
Medicare
Blue Shield of Florida, Inc.
P.O. Box 2525
Jacksonville, Florida 32201

GEORGIA
The Prudential Insurance Co.
of America
Medicare Part B
P.O. Box 7340, Station C
1175 Peachtree St., N.E.
Atlanta, Georgia 30309

HAWAII
Medicare
Aetna Life & Casualty
P.O. Box 3947
Honolulu, Hawaii 96812

IDAHO
Medicare
The Equitable Life Assurance Society
P.O. Box 9048
Boise, Idaho 83707

ILLINOIS
County of:
Cook
Medicare
Illinois Medical Service
233 N. Michigan Street
Chicago, Illinois 60601

ILLINOIS (continued)

Rest of State:
Medicare
Continental Casualty Co.
P.O. Box 910
Chicago, Illinois 60690

INDIANA
Medicare
Mutual Medical Insurance, Inc.
120 West Market Street
Indianapolis, Indiana 46204

IOWA
Medicare
Iowa Medical Service
324 Liberty Building
Des Moines, Iowa 50307

KANSAS
Counties of:
Johnson   Wyandotte
Medicare
Blue Shield of Kansas City
P.O. Box 169
Kansas City, Missouri 64141
Rest of State:
Medicare
Kansas Blue Shield
P.O. Box 953
Topeka, Kansas 66601

KENTUCKY
Medicare
Metropolitan Life Insurance Co.
1218 Harrodsburg Road
Lexington, Kentucky 40501

LOUISIANA
Medicare
Pan-American Life Insurance Co.
P.O. Box 60450
New Orleans, Louisiana 70160

MAINE
Medicare
Union Mutual Life Insurance Co.
2211 Congress St.
Portland, Maine 04112

MARYLAND
Counties of:
Montgomery   Prince Georges
Medicare
Medical Service of D.C.
550—12th St., S.W.
Washington, D.C. 20024
Rest of State:
Medicare
Maryland Blue Shield, Inc.
700 East Joppa Rd.
Towson, Maryland 21204

MASSACHUSETTS
Medicare
Massachusetts Blue Shield, Inc.
P.O. Box 2194
Boston, Massachusetts 02110

MICHIGAN
Medicare
Michigan Medical Service
P.O. Box 2201
Detroit, Michigan 48231

MINNESOTA
Counties of:
Anoka   Olmstead
Dakota   Ramsey
Filmore   Wabasha
Goodhue   Washington
Hennepin   Winona
Houston
Medicare
The Travelers Insurance Company
8120 Penn Avenue, South
Bloomington, Minnesota 55431

Rest of State:
Medicare
Blue Shield of Minnesota
P.O. Box 7899
Minneapolis, Minnesota 55404

MISSISSIPPI
Medicare
The Travelers Insurance Co.
P.O. Box 22545
Jackson, Mississippi 39205

MISSOURI
Counties of:
Andrew   Henry
Atchison   Holt
Bates   Jackson
Benton   Johnson
Buchanan   Lafayette
Caldwell   Livingston
Carroll   Mercer
Cass   Nodaway
Clay   Pettis
Clinton   Platte
Daviess   Ray
DeKalb   St. Clair
Gentry   Saline
Grundy   Vernon
Harrison   Worth
Medicare
Blue Shield of Kansas City
P.O. Box 169
Kansas City, Missouri 64141

Rest of State:
Medicare
General American Life Insurance Co.
P.O. Box 505
St. Louis, Missouri 63166

MONTANA
Medicare
Montana Physicians' Service
P.O. Box 2510
Helena, Montana 59601

NEBRASKA
Medicare
Mutual of Omaha Insurance Co.
P.O. Box 456, Downtown Station
Omaha, Nebraska 68101

NEVADA
Medicare
Aetna Life & Casualty
P.O. Box 3077
Reno, Nevada 89505

NEW HAMPSHIRE
Medicare
New Hampshire-Vermont Physician
Service
Two Pillsbury Street
Concord, New Hampshire 03301

NEW JERSEY
Medicare
The Prudential Insurance Co. of
America
P.O. Box 6500
Millville, New Jersey 08332

NEW MEXICO
Medicare
The Equitable Life Assurance Society
P.O. Box 3070, Station D
Albuquerque, New Mexico 87110

NEW YORK
Counties of:
Bronx   Orange
Columbia   Putnam
Delaware   Richmond
Dutchess   Rockland
Greene   Suffolk
Kings   Sullivan
Nassau   Ulster
New York   Westchester
Medicare
United Medical Service, Inc.
Two Park Avenue
New York, New York 10016
County of:
Queens
Medicare
Group Health, Inc.
227 West 40th Street
New York, New York 10018
Counties of:
Livingston   Seneca
Monroe   Wayne
Ontario   Yates
Medicare
Genesee Valley Medical Care, Inc.
41 Chestnut Street
Rochester, New York 14604

NEW YORK (continued)
Counties of:
Allegany   Niagara
Cattaraugus   Orleans
Erie   Wyoming
Genesee
Medicare
Blue Shield of Western New York, Inc.
298 Main Street
Buffalo, New York 14202
Counties of:
Albany   Montgomery
Broome   Oneida
Cayuga   Onondaga
Chautauqua   Oswego
Chemung   Otsego
Chenango   Rensselaer
Clinton   Saratoga
Cortland   Schenectady
Essex   Schoharie
Franklin   Schuyler
Fulton   Steuben
Hamilton   St. Lawrence
Herkimer   Tioga
Jefferson   Tompkins
Lewis   Warren
Madison   Washington
Medicare
Metropolitan Life Insurance Co.
258 Genesee Street
Utica, New York 13502

NORTH CAROLINA
The Prudential Insurance Co.
of America
Medicare B Division
P.O. Box 1482
High Point, North Carolina 27261

NORTH DAKOTA
Medicare
North Dakota Physicians Service
301 Eighth Street, South
Fargo, North Dakota 58102

OHIO
Medicare
Nationwide Mutual Insurance Co.
P.O. Box 57
Columbus, Ohio 43216

OKLAHOMA
Medicare
Aetna Life & Casualty
7 South Harvey
Oklahoma City, Oklahoma 73102

OREGON
Medicare
Aetna Life & Casualty
522 SW. Fifth Street
Portland, Oregon 97204

PENNSYLVANIA
Medicare
Pennsylvania Blue Shield
Box 65
Camp Hill, Pennsylvania 17011

RHODE ISLAND
Medicare
Physicians' Service
444 Westminster Mall
Providence, Rhode Island 02901

SOUTH CAROLINA
Medicare
Blue Shield of South Carolina
Drawer F, Forest Acres Branch
Columbia, South Carolina 29206

SOUTH DAKOTA
Medicare
South Dakota Medical Service, Inc.
711 North Lake Avenue
Sioux Falls, South Dakota 57102

TENNESSEE
Medicare
The Equitable Life Assurance Society
P.O. Box 1465
Nashville, Tennessee 37202

TEXAS
Medicare
Group Medical and Surgical Service
P.O. Box 22147
Dallas, Texas 75222

UTAH
Medicare
Blue Shield of Utah
P.O. Box 270
Salt Lake City, Utah 84110

VERMONT
Medicare
New Hampshire-Vermont Physician
Service
Two Pillsbury Street
Concord, New Hampshire 03301

VIRGINIA
Counties of:
Arlington   Fairfax
City of:
Alexandria
Medicare
Medical Service of D.C.
550—12th St., S.W.
Washington, D.C. 20024
Rest of State:
Medicare
The Travelers Insurance Co.
P.O. Box 26463
Richmond, Virginia 23261

WASHINGTON
Medicare
Washington Physicians' Service
Mail to your local Medical Service
Bureau

WEST VIRGINIA
Medicare
Nationwide Mutual Insurance Co.
P.O. Box 57
Columbus, Ohio 43216

WISCONSIN
County of:
Milwaukee
Medicare
Surgical Care
P.O. Box 2049
Milwaukee, Wisconsin 53201
Rest of State:
Medicare
Wisconsin Physicians Service
Box 1787
Madison, Wisconsin 53701

WYOMING
Medicare
The Equitable Life Assurance Society
P.O. Box 628
Cheyenne, Wyoming 82001

PUERTO RICO
Medicare
Seguros De Servicio De Salud De
Puerto Rico
G.P.O. Box 3628
Hato Rey, Puerto Rico 00936

VIRGIN ISLANDS
Medicare
Seguros De Servicio De Salud De
Puerto Rico
G.P.O. Box 3628
Hato Rey, Puerto Rico 00936

AMERICAN SAMOA
Medicare
Hawaii Medical Service Assn.
P.O. Box 860
Honolulu, Hawaii 96808

GUAM
Medicare
Aetna Life & Casualty
P.O. Box 3947
Honolulu, Hawaii 96812

Questions and Answers about Medical Insurance

1. *Is there a limit on what medical insurance will pay for doctors' services when the services are mainly for the treatment of mental illness?*

Yes. When such services are furnished outside a hospital, the payment is limited to a maximum of $250 a year.

2. *Who makes the decision whether to rent or purchase durable medical equipment my doctor has prescribed for use in my home?*

You do. When considering purchase, particularly of expensive equipment, you should keep in mind that the Medicare payments are made over a period of time, based on the reasonable rental rate for the equipment, and that these payments stop when your need for the equipment ends. So in deciding whether to purchase equipment, you may wish to talk to your doctor about how long you may need it. Your social security office can also help when you have any questions.

3. *What happens if I want to assign the payment to a doctor, but he doesn't want to accept an assignment?*

That is his right. He does not have to take an assignment of your benefits. If your doctor doesn't agree to take your assignment, the payment will be made directly to you, whether or not the bill has been paid.

4. *If I assign the benefit to my doctor or supplier, does this mean all my future benefit claims must also be handled on an assignment basis?*

No. The payment can be made directly to your doctor or supplier one time and the next time it can be made to you.

5. *I understand that the medical insurance benefits are paid on a "reasonable charge" basis. Who decides what the reasonable charge is, and how does this affect payment?*

The carrier determines "reasonable charges" for covered services. If there is an assignment, the doctor or supplier agrees that the reasonable charge will be his total charge and that he will charge *you* only for any of the $60 deductible not yet met and 20 percent of the balance of the "reasonable charge." If there is no assignment, medical insurance can pay *you* only 80 percent of the reasonable charge (after the $60 deductible is met), even if the bill exceeds the "reasonable charge." (See page 15.)

6. *What can I do if I disagree with the amount paid on my claim?*

Write to the carrier which handled the claim and tell why you disagree with the amount allowed. If you are still not satisfied with the reply *and* the amount in question is $100 or more, you can request a hearing from the carrier.

7. *Medicare does not pay all the doctor's bills. What can I do if I can't pay the rest?*

If you do not have any other insurance or other resources with which you can pay the amounts due, you may want to ask at your public assistance office about help. The people there can give you information about a State program such as old-age assistance or medical assistance for the aged (sometimes called "medicaid").

Some Health Services and Items That NEITHER Hospital Insurance Nor Medical Insurance Will Pay For

Under each kind of benefit described in this handbook, there is a list of items and services that hospital insurance and medical insurance cannot pay. There are some other items or services that are not covered under either part of Medicare. These are shown in the following list:

- Services that are not reasonable and necessary for the diagnosis or treatment of an illness or injury.

- Cosmetic surgery—except when furnished in connection with prompt repair of accidental injury or for the improvement of the functioning of a malformed body member.

- Services for which neither the patient nor another party on his behalf has a legal obligation to pay—such as free chest X-ray.

- Certain services payable under other Federal, State, or local government programs.

- Services furnished by immediate relatives or members of the patient's household.

The First 3 Pints of Blood

Medicare cannot pay for the first 3 pints of whole blood (or units of packed red blood cells) that you receive either under hospital or medical insurance.

- Hospital insurance cannot pay for the first 3 pints of blood you receive in a *benefit period.* Usually, when you receive blood under hospital insurance it will be as a bed patient in a hospital.

- Medical insurance cannot pay for the first 3 pints of blood you receive in a *calendar year.* Usually, when you receive blood under medical insurance it will be in a doctor's office, a clinic, or the outpatient or emergency department of a hospital.

These are *separate* rules and they operate independently of each other. For example, if you receive blood under both hospital insurance and medical insurance, Medicare could not pay for the first 3 pints of blood under *either* program. But the blood you get under hospital insurance is fully paid for starting with the fourth pint during a benefit period; medical insurance will help pay for the blood you get starting with the fourth pint during a calendar year.

HOW TO GET HELP TO REPLACE BLOOD

Some people are able to arrange for the replacement of these first 3 pints of blood—that way they don't have to pay for them. There are two ways this can be done. First, you may arrange for replacement from a friend or relative or you may be a member of a blood donor group that will replace these first 3 pints of blood for you. Second—and this is often overlooked—your children (or your son-in-law or daughter-in-law) may belong to a blood replacement plan that includes you as a beneficiary. In that case, you would be eligible for blood on the basis of *their* membership.

You might want to check with your children and children-in-law about this so you'll have the information handy if you ever need it.

In almost all blood donor plans, blood replacement credit can be arranged anywhere in the United States.

PART II

1. THE SKIN

Can I improve my complexion by changing my diet or by taking vitamins?

Only if your usual diet is deficient in essential nutrients and vitamins.

Are cosmetics harmful to my skin?

Not if the face is cleansed thoroughly each day after using cosmetics. People may be allergic to certain cosmetics and this can be harmful. In such cases, cosmetics should be avoided or low-allergenic cosmetics should be used.

Will massage help my skin tone?

Not to any appreciable extent. Exercise is the best aid to improving circulation and, therefore, skin tone.

Are there any medications I can put on my skin to prevent wrinkles?

No. But there are cosmetic substances that can hide wrinkles temporarily.

Is the sun harmful to skin?

Yes. Repeated exposure causes skin to age prematurely. It can also lead in some cases to cancer of the skin.

What can I do to prevent wrinkles?

You cannot prevent them, but you may be able to delay their onset by the following:

1. Avoid overexposure to the sun.
2. Avoid overexposure to wind and cold.
3. Maintain a good diet and satisfactory vitamin intake.
4. Cleanse your face regularly, avoiding harsh soaps.

Is there any way to prevent the formation of brown spots which seem to appear on people's faces and hands as they grow older?

No, except by avoiding overexposure to sunlight.

Will mud packs or other such cosmetic aids help my skin?
No.

How can one lessen the chances of getting acne?
By scrupulous cleanliness, by having blackheads removed before they become infected, and by avoiding chocolate and fried or fatty foods.

Does an acne condition ever improve?
Yes, it tends to clear up as the sufferer grows older and his endocrine system becomes more stabilized.

Are there any permanent effects from acne?
In many cases permanent scars will result, especially if the pimples are repeatedly picked at or squeezed.

What can I do to get rid of the scars left by my acne?
You can have a skin planing performed by a dermatologist.

Is skin planing a painful procedure?
Local anesthesia does away with most of the pain.

How successful is skin planing?
Results range from good to excellent.

Should I squeeze the pimples that occasionally occur on my face?
No. This is bad practice and may lead to a spread of the infection.

Is there any specific treatment for large skin pores?
No.

Who should squeeze the blackheads that form on my face?
It is best done by a physician.

What causes athlete's foot?
It is a fungous infection.

Are soap and water bad for athlete's foot?
Soap often irritates the condition. Water is not harmful, provided one dries thoroughly after washing, especially in between the toes.

Is athlete's foot contagious?
   Yes.

How can I prevent athlete's foot?
   Avoid walking barefoot in places where athlete's foot is most likely to be present, such as in bathrooms, shower rooms of gymnasiums or clubs, or around swimming pools. Also, make sure to dry your feet thoroughly after bathing or showering.

Why do I get repeated attacks of athlete's foot while my wife never gets it at all?
   She takes precautions; you do not.

Is the use of soaps and detergents bad for my hands?
   Some people are extremely sensitive to soaps and detergents; others are not. No one should use strong soaps or detergents any more often than absolutely necessary.

What precautions should I take to avoid getting eczema of my hands from detergents?
   Use a mild soap instead of detergent, or, if you must use a detergent, wear protective gloves.

How often should one bathe?
   Daily.

Should one bathe more often in the summer than in winter?
   Yes, because one perspires more.

What can one do to prevent excessive sweating?
   Dress as lightly as possible and avoid drinking excess liquids.

What can I do to prevent body odor from perspiration?
   Bathe frequently and use a deodorant.

Why do some people get a cold sore whenever they are exposed to the sun?
   Sensitivity to sunlight varies greatly among people; some must avoid the direct rays entirely except for momentary exposure.

What causes ringworm?
   A fungus.

Is there anything one can do to prevent baldness?

Any scalp infection, such as seborrhea, should be treated as soon as it appears. Other than that, very little can be done to prevent baldness.

Is baldness inherited?

The tendency may be.

Are the various treatments so widely adverstised to the public actually helpful in preventing baldness?

No, but if one has a skin disorder of the scalp, medications to clear the condition may stop further loss of hair.

Can anything be done to grow new hair?

No. The various treatments advertised are a waste of money. However, hair transplants are sometimes successful in making one appear less bald.

Will scalp massage prevent me from growing bald?

No.

Does the appearance of premature gray hair mean that my other organs are aging prematurely?

No. It has little or no significance insofar as the aging process is concerned. Premature graying tends to run in families.

Will shaving the hair make it grow in heavier?

Despite the common belief, it will not.

Is electrolysis safe?

Yes.

Is it safe to have the hair removed from my lips and face?

Yes, when the procedure is carried out by an expert electrologist. People should not tweeze their own lips to remove hair.

To whom shall I go for electrolysis?

A licensed electrologist. Have your doctor recommend one to you.

Is it safe to have hair removed from my breasts and other parts of my body?

Yes.

Should a mole be removed if it changes color or enlarges?
Yes, as some of them are potentially malignant.

Should moles be removed with an electric needle or should they be cut out surgically?
Most should be excised surgically. The dermatologist may, on occasion, treat certain harmless moles by electric needle.

Is dandruff contagious?
No.

What is a keloid?
An overgrown scar, usually resulting from a deep scrape, burn, laceration, or surgical incision.

How can they be prevented?
There is no known prevention.

Can keloids be removed?
Yes, but about 50 percent will return, frequently larger than the original keloid.

What is psoriasis?
It is a chronic skin disease characterized by silvery, reddish patches appearing anywhere on the body but having a predilection for the elbows, knees, and scalp. The disease persists throughout life, with periods of subsidence and recurrence. Its cause is unknown.

Is it true that if I have psoriasis, I will always have it?
Yes.

Is psoriasis contagious?
No.

Is psoriasis inherited?
It is thought to be.

Does psoriasis often appear on the face?
No.

Can psoriasis be cured?
No, but it can be suppressed by various medications.

Does psoriasis have an effect on my life span?
   No.

What are these patchy areas of loss of pigment in my skin?
   It is a condition known as vitiligo.

What causes vitiligo?
   The cause is unknown.

Is there any treatment for vitiligo?
   Not a satisfactory one.

What is contact dermatitis?
   An inflammation of the skin caused by contact with a substance to which one is sensitive.

Does an allergic reaction by my skin mean that I will always be allergic to the same substance?
   Yes, usually.

Is it possible for me to be allergic to plants but not allergic to certain chemicals?
   Yes.

What is the treatment for my contact dermatitis?
   The most important thing is to avoid contact with the irritating substance.

How long will contact dermatitis last?
   Anywhere from a few days to a few months.

Should all cysts, warts, moles, and other skin tumors be removed?
   Yes, if they tend to grow, change in color, are irritated repeatedly, bleed repeatedly, or are unsightly.

What are the dangers of leaving some of these skin tumors untreated?
   Occasionally, a harmless skin tumor will become malignant.

Can a biopsy determine whether a lesion of my skin is cancerous?
   Yes.

Is skin cancer curable?
Yes.

Is overexposure to sunlight a cause of some skin cancer?
Yes.

Is frequent contact with petroleum products a cause of some skin cancer?
Yes.

Can you tell whether a particular skin tumor is likely to turn into a malignancy or not?
Yes.

Is it necessary to remain in the hospital for the removal of these tumors?
In some cases it is necessary to stay a day or two; other cases can be treated on an ambulatory basis.

What causes warts?
They are thought to be of viral origin.

Is there any way to prevent warts?
No.

What are the various methods of treatment of warts?
1. By burning with an electric needle.
2. By local application of caustic medications.
3. By X-ray therapy.
4. By surgical excision.

QUESTIONS TO ASK YOUR DOCTOR

Will hormone creams be beneficial to my skin?

What should I do to get rid of acne?

Is exposure to sunlight helpful in the treatment of my acne?

Will a change of diet help my acne?

Are X-ray treatments beneficial for my acne?

Should I use a sunlamp to get rid of my acne?

What treatment should I carry out for my athlete's foot?

Can I protect my hands against eczema by the use of ointments or creams?

Why do I get cold sores whenever I get a cold?

How can I prevent ringworm?

How often should I shampoo my hair?

Are there hormones I can take to prevent excessive growth of hair on my body?

How can I get rid of my dandruff?

What is the treatment for my psoriasis?

Is it safe to tweeze out superfluous hairs at home?

2. ALLERGIES

How is the exact cause of an allergy determined?
If the allergy is due to a pollen or mold, skin tests with injections are often employed to determine the cause of the allergy. Food or drug allergies do not lend themselves to this method of testing. They are diagnosed by noting the allergy after the food is eaten or the drug is taken.

How painful are skin tests?
They cause a minimal amount of discomfort.

Will the skin tests cause an allergy to flare up?
No, because only a tiny amount of the allergen (the irritating substance) is injected.

Is there any way to avoid all of the injections for testing?
Yes, a donor can be obtained to undergo your test for you after he has been deliberately sensitized so as to react to your allergies.

What is a patch test?

A sample of the allergen is applied to the skin and is kept in place for a few days. If the area becomes irritated, it indicates that one is allergic to the substance that has been applied.

How can you tell when a skin test is positive?

The skin becomes red and swollen and itchy.

Are allergies inherited?

The tendency to allergy is. For example, a parent may have hay fever and a child may have asthma. However, children do not necessarily become allergic, even when a parent is.

At what age do children usually show allergic tendencies?

Certain food allergies, such as the one toward milk, may become obvious shortly after birth. Hay fever and asthma may not develop until a child is a few years old.

If both parents are allergic, is there a greater possibility that the children will suffer from allergies?

Yes. Each child will have a 50 to 75 percent chance of becoming allergic.

What are the chances of a child becoming allergic if only one parent has an allergy?

Each child has a 25 percent chance of becoming allergic.

Is it possible for a patient without allergies to develop them during his mature years?

Yes.

Why is it that I am developing an allergy now to a certain drug when I never was allergic to it before?

Sensitivity often develops from repeated use over a span of time.

Will a change of location help to cure an allergy?

If the allergy is due to dust, such a change may help, but dust exists to some degree everywhere. If an allergy is due to a pollen, such as ragweed, it may be overcome by moving to an area where the pollen is nonexistent.

Will it help an allergy to move to another climate?

Climate itself is not the important factor. The presence

or absence of the allergen (pollen or mold or dust) may be
the decisive factor.

What can I do to overcome dust allergy?
    1. Avoid dusty areas.
    2. Get rid of carpets, rugs, and draperies.
    3. Have your home or apartment specially treated to
reduce dust.

*If I am allergic to a certain food, are the chances such that
I will always be allergic to it?*
    In all probability, yes.

*Can an expectant mother do anything to prevent her unborn
child from developing an allergy?*
    No.

*Can anything be done during early childhood to prevent a
child from developing an allergy?*
    If he has a food allergy, avoidance of the substance will
suppress the symptoms but will not cure the allergy. Or, if
he has a contact allergy, the irritating substance should be
kept away from him.

What is a contact allergy?
    One that results from physical contact with an irritant.

Will a run-down condition make an allergy worse?
    It may tend to.

What conditions may aggravate an allergy?
    Emotional strain, as well as an upper respiratory infection,
may make an allergy worse.

Are pills as effective as injections for an allergy?
    No. The antihistamine medications are not as effective
as hyposensitization via injections.

Is there a one-shot injection to control an allergy?
    No. This method of treatment has not proved effective.

Is an allergy truly curable?
    No, but through treatment or avoidance of the allergen,
it is possible to suppress the symptoms.

Does psychiatric treatment ever help to overcome an allergy?
    Yes, in some cases.

Are allergies contagious?
    No.

Is one more susceptible to infections because he is allergic?
    If the allergy is in the respiratory tract, one is more prone to respiratory infections. However, allergic people are not more susceptible to generalized infections.

Does cooking a food reduce allergic reaction to it?
    If may, especially if you are allergic to eggs and milk products.

What can be done about the runny nose caused by an allergy?
    The antihistamine medications may help to cut down on the symptom. Also, certain nose drops containing ephedrine or a similar drug may relieve the condition.

Is there any medication to prevent the eye inflammation caused by allergy?
    Antiallergic eyedrops are sometimes helpful.

What are the dangers of the antihistamines?
    Taken in large doses, they make one drowsy, and thus can be dangerous if one drives a car.

Can I drive my car even when I am taking an antihistamine drug?
    Yes, but one must be careful not to fall asleep when driving. It is, therefore, not advisable to drive alone or to take long drives.

Is there any chance of choking to death from an attack of asthma?
    Some attacks may approach the point of suffocation. It is sometimes necessary to rush a patient with a severe asthmatic attack to the hospital.

What should I do when severe allergic symptoms develop?
    Go to the emergency room of the nearest hospital.

What can be done to overcome a severe asthmatic attack?
    If you get such attacks frequently, you should be taught

how to give yourself an injection, and should keep the appropriate medication on hand at all times. If a member of your family is prone to sudden asthmatic attacks, you should learn how to give them injections, too.

Is hospitalization ever necessary for an attack of asthma?

Yes. It may not be possible to stop an attack with one injection, and emergency measures in a hospital may, therefore, be necessary.

Are there any nonmedical measures that will help to relieve asthma?

Yes, in some cases moistening the air with a vaporizer will relieve it.

Do supplementary vitamins and minerals help an allergic condition?

No. But if one has a vitamin or mineral deficiency, his allergies may be more pronounced. Consult your doctor.

If I am allergic to one substance, does this mean that I necessarily am allergic to other substances?

No.

Will anemia or undernourishment affect my condition?

They may aggravate it.

What is the effect of surgery on an individual with pollen allergies?

It is best to postpone elective surgery until after the allergy season is over.

Is it safe for an allergic child to be vaccinated against the various contagious diseases?

It will depend upon the child's allergies. Children who are allergic to eggs should avoid some vaccinations; children who have allergic dermatitis may have to avoid smallpox vaccination.

Can an allergic child be sent away to camp?

Yes, provided he will be able to stay away from the allergens that cause his allergies.

What emergency measures can I take if I am stung by an insect to which I am allergic?

You should always have an injection ready to give yourself. Your doctor will see that the appropriate medication is available to you.

What can I do to prevent insect bites?
1. Do not wear perfume or hair spray in the vicinity of the insect to which you are allergic.
2. Do not eat out in the open if the insect is in the vicinity.
3. Avoid brightly colored clothing.

What medications should one have available if he is allergic?
Your doctor will prescribe them for you. They may consist of antihistamines, ephedrine, Adrenalin, or cortisone drugs.

Is it safe to take cortisone to control an allergy?
Only when specifically prescribed by your doctor.

Will the taking of antibiotics help an allergy?
No. On the contrary, many people are allergic to some of the antibiotics.

How can I tell if my allergy is due to a certain cosmetic or perfume?
By experiencing one allergic reaction to it and subsequently avoiding its use.

Can one's allergy be affected by a perfume or cosmetic worn by someone else?
Yes.

QUESTIONS TO ASK YOUR DOCTOR

Are patch tests reliable in determining the cause of my allergy?

Are there any blood tests that will indicate the nature of my allergy?

What are the chances of my children having the same allergy that I have?

Will I tend to outgrow my allergy?

Will my child tend to outgrow his allergies?

What can I do to reduce the symptoms of my allergy?

For how many years will I have to take these injections?

How many injections a year will I require?

Will I have to be treated for the rest of my life for my allergy?

Can my allergy be helped through psychotherapy?

Are antihistamine drugs helpful for my condition?

Will my allergy occur all year round?

What times of the year am I most likely to have my allergic symptoms?

Would a change of location help me to avoid my allergies?

Are my allergies affected by animals?

Are my allergies affected by the food I eat?

Are my allergies affected by the air I breathe?

Would air-conditioning help to reduce my allergic symptoms?

Can my child be given all the immunizing substances even though he is allergic to eggs?

Can my allergic child go on picnics or field trips?

Do I have to give up my job because I am allergic to the substances that are used during the performance of my work or can they be controlled through medication?

3. INFECTIONS

What causes infections such as boils and abscesses?
Bacteria are the chief cause, the most common of which are the staphylococcus and streptococcus germs, although other types of bacteria may also produce boils or abscesses.

Do viruses ever cause an infection with pus?
No.

When are people particularly susceptible to infections?
1. When their level of general health is poor.
2. When they are over-fatigued.
3. When they are very old.
4. When they have recently given birth.
5. When they are undernourished.
6. When there is a vitamin deficiency.
7. When they are diabetic.
8. When they have a chronic systemic ailment.
9. When they live in dirty, crowded environments.
10. When they are lax about personal hygiene.

What is the best way to prevent infections?
By avoiding or eliminating the conditions enumerated above.

Is lack of cleanliness a common cause of boils and abscesses?
Yes.

Do boils and abscesses tend to run in groups?
Yes. It is not uncommon for a new boil to develop in a nearby place soon after a previous boil has subsided.

Are recurrent boils an indication that something is wrong with the blood?
Not usually.

What causes acne?
The exact cause is unknown. However, it is most frequently

associated with adolescence and the hormonal changes that take place during this time of life.

Are infections of the skin usually cured by the use of antibiotic drugs?
Not in the majority of instances.

Must all infections be treated?
No. Many will subside spontaneously.

What should be used to bring an infection, such as a pimple, to a head?
A warm, wet poultice will do the job best. Ointments, although widely advertised, are of little value.

Is it wise to squeeze a pimple or a boil?
This should *never* be done.

Are infections around the upper lip and the nose and face especially dangerous?
Yes. They should never be squeezed as it may lead to the spread of the infection to veins within the skull.

Do local infections tend to spread elsewhere in the body?
If they are very virulent, this may happen. Fortunately, generalized spread of a well-treated local infection seldom occurs.

What can be done to prevent an infection from spreading?
1. Keep the area clean.
2. Rest the area; for instance, stay off an infected foot as much as possible.
3. Apply hot, wet dressings.
4. Avoid squeezing the infection.
5. Take those antibiotics prescribed by your doctor.
6. Have the pus let out of the local infection by your doctor.

What is the best way to bring an infection to a head?
By the application of hot, wet dressings.

Is it advisable to work when one has an infection?
Not if one has a fever.

Why do some people get many infections, while others seem always to be free from infection?

Resistance to bacteria varies from person to person. Some may lack resistance to certain bacteria, thus leading to repeated infections, such as boils or abscesses.

Does one tend to develop immunity to the germs that cause most superficial infections?

No.

What is the difference between an ordinary boil and a carbuncle?

A carbuncle has many pockets of pus with several openings; a boil usually is composed of one pocket of pus.

If one has diabetes, is he more likely to develop infections?

Yes, unless the diabetes is under good control.

What is septicemia?

Blood poisoning. In other words, an infection of the bloodstream.

How can you tell whether an infection is in the bloodstream?

By taking a blood culture.

Are generalized virus infections susceptible to treatment by the antibiotic drugs?

Most viruses do *not* respond to antibiotic therapy.

Can I be vaccinated against bacterial infections?

To certain ones, yes; to others, no. Tetanus, typhoid, typhus, and other infections lend themselves to prevention through vaccination.

Can I be vaccinated against viral infections?

Yes, in certain instances, for example, against polio, mumps, measles, etc.

Can I develop immunity to a virus infection?

Yes, to some, such as the contagious diseases of childhood.

QUESTIONS TO ASK YOUR DOCTOR

Is my condition caused by a general infection?

Does this mean that I have bacteria circulating in my blood-stream?

Will this infection in any way affect my heart?

Will this infection affect my kidneys?

Can I work even though I have this infection?

How long must I stay away from work?

What can I do to avoid a recurrence of this infection?

Am I particularly susceptible to infections?

Will taking vitamins help to reduce the possibility of my getting an infection?

4. CONTAGIOUS DISEASES

If I have been exposed to a contagious disease, how can I protect myself against catching it?
Consult your doctor. He will tell you if there is anything to take to prevent it. Antibiotics are beneficial in some cases; an injection of gamma globulin may work in other instances; antitoxins, too, may be prescribed to prevent other types of diseases.

Are contagious diseases spread only by being in the presence of someone who has the condition?
No. Many people can contract a disease from the same source, by drinking infected water or milk, or by eating food contaminated by the causative bacteria.

Are some contagious diseases spread by coughing?
Yes.

Are contagious diseases ever spread by using toilet articles of someone who is ill?

Occasionally, as in trench mouth. Venereal diseases are seldom spread in this manner.

Are contagious diseases ever spread by using the eating utensils and drinking glasses of sick people?
Occasionally, as in certain forms of dysentery.

Are contagious diseases ever spread by using toilets utilized by sick people?
Occasionally, but this is an unusual source of contagion.

Can gonorrhea or syphilis be contracted by using a contaminated toilet seat?
In general, no, since the germs causing these diseases usually die within a minute or two after exposure to the atmosphere. Of course, if an infected vaginal discharge is on a toilet seat and the seat is immediately used by someone else, transmission of disease might conceivably be possible.

Are all people susceptible to all contagious diseases?
No. Some people who have been repeatedly exposed to diseases such as measles, scarlet fever, chickenpox, etc., never contract the disease. Others, who come in daily contact with a person with tuberculosis, may never contract the condition.

Why are some people susceptible to a particular condition and others not?
Variations in susceptibility are thought to be due to the presence or absence of specific protective antibodies which circulate in the blood. An individual who lacks the antibodies to a disease will almost always contract it, if exposed.

Can contagious diseases be contracted from germs that float in the air?
Occasionally, airborne bacteria or viruses can cause disease, but more often the germs are transmitted in droplets of a sneeze or cough, or by direct physical contact with a sick person.

Does a "run-down condition" predispose one to contagious diseases?

Yes, to the extent that one who is fatigued, anemic, or undernourished might not have antibodies that are sufficiently strong to successfully combat a potential infection. However, individual susceptibility is a more important factor in the causation of most contagious diseases.

Will the taking of large quantities of vitamins protect against contagious diseases?

Not if the individual's intake of vitamins is already normal and he is in a normal state of nutrition.

What is the best way to prevent catching a contagious disease?

By staying as far as possible from someone with an upper respiratory infection and from someone with an unexplained rash.

Why is it that some people develop immunity from once having had a condition while others have repeated attacks?

Some diseases naturally confer immunity once one has been afflicted; other diseases produce no immunity because they do not induce the body to produce sufficient antibodies to successfully combat the causative bacteria or virus.

What leads to the recurrence of a disease?

Failure to eradicate the original cause. As an example, if one has bronchitis and continues to smoke heavily, his chances for a recurrent attack are much greater. Other diseases, such as relapsing fever, have a tendency to recur.

Can one receive vaccination so that a condition will not recur?

Having a disease once confers immunity in some illnesses; other illnesses do not produce protective antibodies. In such cases, vaccinations are sometimes helpful, as in certain types of influenza. Revaccination and booster shots are excellent safeguards against the recurrence of disease.

See the section in this book on Immunizations and Vaccinations.

QUESTIONS TO ASK YOUR DOCTOR

How did I get this disease?

Is it necessary to be hospitalized with this condition?

How long after I have been exposed do I have to worry about getting the illness?

Are there any injections that I can take now that will prevent me from catching a contagious disease?

Should I let my other children catch the disease or should I try to protect them against it?

Does my child have to stay in bed with this disease?

When can he get out of bed?

Should my business associates take any special precautions if they were in contact with me during the incubation period?

Must my family also be protected, even though they have had no direct contact with the person with the contagious disease?

Should I isolate myself from members of my family until I am sure I will not get the disease?

For how long a period should I isolate myself?

How soon after I have recovered from the contagious disease may I resume contact with others?

When can I:
    go outdoors?
    go back to work?
    resume physical activity?
    resume marital relations?

How soon after recovery can my children:
    return to school?
    resume full activity?

Can adults contract this contagious disease?

Is this disease more serious when it affects adults?

Is there a chance of my ever getting this disease again?

Do I become a carrier once I have recovered from this contagious disease?

Will this disease influence in any way my ability to have children?

Must I tell someone I intend to marry that I have had this disease?

Will future offspring be influenced by my having had this disease?

Are there any tests to be taken to be sure that I am now permanently immune to this disease?

What are the possible complications of this condition?

Is this disease spread through marital relations?

Will this disease seriously affect any of my vital organs, such as my heart, liver, kidneys, etc.?

Does a run-down condition predispose to a recurrence of an illness?

Is my condition likely to recur?

What can I do to prevent recurrence of my condition?

How will I know if my condition is recurring?

How often should I come to your office for a periodic check-up?

For how long a period must I take precautions to prevent the return of my condition?

If my general health is poor, am I apt to get a recurrence?

Will putting on or losing weight help to prevent recurrence?

Will a special diet prevent recurrence?

Will the avoidance of stress and emotional problems help to prevent recurrence?

Must I reduce my physical activity if I wish to prevent recurrence of my condition?

5. IMMUNIZATIONS AND VACCINATIONS

What childhood diseases can be prevented by immunization and vaccination?
Diphtheria, German measles, measles, mumps, polio, smallpox, and whooping cough.

What is a good immunization schedule for infants and young children?
See Immunization and Vaccination Table (pages 318-319).

Is it possible to alter the immunization schedule or must it be adhered to strictly?
Each pediatrician may have his own preference. For example, some doctors start diphtheria, whooping cough, and tetanus immunizations at two months of age, others at three or four months of age.

Do all immunizations require booster shots?
No. However, whooping cough vaccine should be given again if the child is exposed to another child who has the disease; diphtheria immunization should be carried out again if the child is exposed to a case of diphtheria; a booster shot of tetanus toxoid is frequently given for an injury due to a rusty object or one contaminated by dirt.

Do I have to take special precautions about vaccines if I am an allergic individual?
Yes, especially if you are allergic to eggs. This is because some of the vaccines are grown in chick embryos.

Can allergic children be vaccinated?
Yes, but special precautions must be taken by the pediatrician.

Should I give my child a smallpox vaccination since the disease is so rare in this country?

You must ask your own pediatrician because opinions on this subject vary considerably.

Can I be vaccinated against catching colds?

There are cold vaccines available, but they have not proved to be very effective.

Can I be vaccinated against influenza?

Yes, but the vaccines are not always effective and the length of immunity, when obtained, is only of a few months' duration.

Is it wise to allow my child to catch the ordinary contagious diseases or should I try to prevent him from getting them?

It is better to protect him by vaccination. Even the most minor contagious diseases may have serious complications.

What special immunizations or vaccinations should I get before traveling to a foreign country?

Consult your local health department or the local office of the United States Public Health Service.

In addition to the childhood diseases, for what other contagious diseases are there vaccinations?

Cholera, typhoid fever, typhus fever, yellow fever, the plague, and smallpox.

For how long a period does a vaccination last?

See Immunization and Vaccination Table (pages 318-319).

Do I have to take rabies vaccine even though I have been bitten by my own dog?

Not if the dog is free of the disease. The problem with a bite from a stray dog is that afterward the dog is not always on hand for a determination of whether or not it is rabid.

How can I tell whether my own dog has rabies or not?

He will become sick, if he was not obviously sick at the time of the attack. Your veterinarian will be able to determine whether he is rabid.

6. TRAVEL AND
HEALTH PRECAUTIONS

Should one undergo a thorough physical examination before taking a long trip?

Yes. The entire holiday may be spoiled if one starts out on a trip while incubating an illness or when one is not in good physical condition. Also, your doctor can prescribe certain drugs to be taken along as a precautionary measure.

What can I do to be prepared for medical emergencies if I go on an extended trip?

Take along a medical kit, especially if you are traveling to a rural area where first-aid materials are not readily available.

What items should be in a medical kit?

Band-Aids
packaged alcohol sponges
absorbent cotton
gauze pads
roll of adhesive tape
a cloth sling

a small pair of scissors
tweezers

a bottle of aspirin
a bottle of antihistamine
tablets
a bottle of antibiotic tablets
a bottle of salt tablets
a bottle of bicarbonate of
soda tablets
antidiarrhea medications
sleeping tablets

And, of course, prescriptions for any medicines taken regularly.

Should one take along an extra pair of eyeglasses?

Yes.

Are special vaccinations necessary when traveling to remote places in the United States?

Typhoid and tetanus injections are usually advised.

How can one find out what immunizations and vaccinations are necessary when traveling to a foreign country?

Ask your family doctor. In all probability he will make the same recommendations as your local health department. Smallpox vaccination and tetanus toxoid are standard recommendations, but if one is going to an underdeveloped country, other vaccinations may be indicated. Also, your doctor may recommend an injection of gamma globulin.

What injections are necessary before taking a trip to Asia, the Orient, or Africa?

In addition to the usual smallpox and tetanus vaccinations, some countries in the Orient, Asia, or Africa recommend that inoculations against typhus fever, typhoid fever, yellow fever, the plague, and cholera be taken.

How long before departure on a trip should vaccinations be given?

Several weeks beforehand. It is of no value to be vaccinated a day or two before departure, as most immunizations take a few weeks before they become effective. Moreover, the trip may be spoiled by an exceptionally severe reaction to an inoculation.

What precautions should old people or people with heart conditions take about traveling?

First, they must obtain permission from their physicians to go. Then, they should take along their heart medication, if any, and a portable tank of oxygen. Lastly, they should be sure not to overeat or take too much physical exercise.

What is the highest altitude that a cardiac patient should go?

This varies, but many doctors recommend that these patients not stay in places that are more than 2,500 feet above sea level.

Are high altitude precautions also necessary for air travel?

No. Modern planes are pressurized to about 5,000 feet above sea level, and since plane passengers are inactive during the trip, they tolerate this altitude with little difficulty.

Do children travel well in the air?

Yes. They seem to enjoy it.

What can be done for altitude sickness in a country of high altitudes?

Restrict your food intake; avoid alcohol and smoking; take it easy until the body has adapted to this new level of altitude.

Should a child be allowed to eat everything when visiting a foreign land?

It is best to avoid foods that are uncooked or are very highly seasoned.

Should a child be given ordinary milk to drink when visiting a foreign country?

No. It is best to take along or to purchase canned or dehydrated milk, the latter to be prepared with boiled or bottled water.

What precautions should be taken about drinking the water when traveling to a strange place?

Unless one is specifically told that the water is safe, it is better to buy bottled water. Unless one is certain of its source and purity, avoid drinking water from streams and other outdoor water supplies. Typhoid contamination may be present even though the stream appears to contain pure water.

Should people take special precautions when they travel to very hot climates?

Yes. Dehydration from excessive perspiration is a possibility. For this reason, one should take along salt tablets and should make sure to drink adequate amounts of fluid.

Should special precautions be taken when a child travels from a temperate to a very hot climate?

Yes. Infants and children undergo very rapid dehydration and should be given liberal amounts of liquid.

Should people avoid traveling to cold climates if they are old, or if they have heart trouble?

Yes. Circulatory efficiency is more difficult to maintain in cold climates.

What is meant by the "body clock"?

It is a more-or-less nonmedical term referring to a disturbance in body metabolism affecting some people after they have traveled several thousand miles within a very short time.

Some physicians think the disturbance is primarily psychological rather than physical.

How can I adjust my "body clock" after a long air trip which involves a change in time?

Such an adjustment takes time. Take it easy and don't do too much sight-seeing at first; above all, don't get upset if you feel wide awake when the local inhabitants are asleep, or vice versa.

What special precautions should be taken before going on a boat trip?

Pills to safeguard against seasickness should be taken along.

What medications can be taken to prevent seasickness?

Dramamine, Bonine, and other such medications are the most effective.

Should one take special precautions with infants and small children when going on an extended holiday?

Yes, one must plan for the special care they will require. It is especially important to know whether reliable baby-sitters will be available and, also, whether there will be playmates for the child.

Is it safe to travel with an infant under one year?

Yes. In fact, they often travel better than the two- and three-year-old children, as they tend to sleep more and can subsist quite happily on a readymade formula (available in most countries) and commercially prepared baby food.

What is the limit of automobile travel for young children?

One should try to limit the trip to about 300 miles a day, with frequent stops to break the monotony.

What can parents do to help overcome the strangeness a young child feels in new surroundings?

They should take along whatever special toy or security object the child has come to depend on.

Should special precautions be taken when a child travels from a temperate to a very cold climate?

Yes. Warm clothing is necessary, as the nose, ears, fingers, and toes of infants are easily frostbitten.

Should children be warned to stay away from strange animals when on a trip?

Yes. Rabies is common among squirrels, chipmunks, foxes, and other animals. A child may interpret a sick animal as a tame one, and, as the child approaches, he may be bitten.

Is it necessary to examine a child for ticks when traveling in wooded areas?

Yes. They should be checked each night before going to bed. Rocky Mountain spotted fever, which is passed on by ticks, is rather widespread in many parts of the United States.

QUESTIONS TO ASK YOUR DOCTOR

What vaccinations do I need for my trip?

Should I take an injection of gamma globulin before going on a trip?

How soon before my trip should I be vaccinated?

Is it advisable to take my newborn infant on the trip I have planned?

Is it safe for me to travel to any altitude?

Should I avoid humid places?

Must I continue my diet while on this trip?

Is there a medicine I can take to avoid dysentery?

Will you give me a prescription for an antibiotic in case of an emergency?

Will the abrupt change in climate adversely affect me?

Is it safe for me to stay in a very hot climate?

Is it safe for me to stay in a very cold climate?

What special precautions should I take for my child on this trip?

Can you recommend a doctor or doctors in the areas where we will be traveling?

7. MENTAL HEALTH

If I need help, is it just as satisfactory to go to a psychologist as to a psychiatrist?

No. Psychiatrists have, in addition to their training in psychology, a thorough grounding in the medical aspects of emotional and mental disorders.

How can I tell whether a psychiatrist is well qualified?

Find out whether he is certified by the American Board of Psychiatry. If he is, he is well qualified.

If I am unable to afford private psychiatric care, what can I do?

There are psychiatric clinics attached to many large medical centers that give psychiatric assistance at minimal or no cost to the patient.

What is the difference between a neurosis and psychosis?

A neurosis is an emotional disorder without the loss of insight; a psychosis is a mental disorder usually accompanied by lack of insight. A neurotic is not insane, a psychotic is.

Is there any difference between the terms "insane" and "psychotic"?

No, except that "insane" is more of a legal than a medical term.

If I am very neurotic, does this mean that I might become insane?

No. Neurosis does not often lead to insanity.

What is the difference between psychotherapy and psychoanalysis?

Psychoanalysis is a form of psychotherapy in which mental disorders are treated through analysis of the character, personality, and mind. It is more applicable in the treatment of neuroses than psychoses.

Will a psychiatrist help me to get over my depression?
Yes.

How long do acute depressions usually last?
Anywhere from a few days to several months.

What techniques, in addition to psychotherapy, are used to treat depression?
Electroshock therapy and the administration of drugs.

Is shock treatment very dangerous?
Not when carried out by trained personnel in a hospital equipped for this kind of therapy.

Is shock treatment painful?
No.

Is shock treatment ever used as the sole treatment for depression?
Not often. It is usually followed by psychotherapy.

Are there different forms of depression?
Yes. Depression may be associated with organic disease, with insufferable reality situations, or with emotional problems of unknown origin.

What is melancholia?
It is another term for depression or a depressed state.

What is involutional melancholia?
It is a depression that takes place at or beyond the change of life (menopause) and is frequently associated with feelings of persecution, guilt, and worry.

Does change of life bring on melancholia?
This has not been determined. All we know is that involutional melancholia often occurs during the time of change of life.

What is a manic-depressive reaction?
It is a form of psychosis associated with alternating periods

of great elation and great depression. These reactions sometimes last for several months.

Do people usually recover from a manic-depressive episode?
Yes.

What is the treatment for a manic-depressive reaction?
Treatment varies according to the individual case. It may consist of medication plus psychotherapy, or shock treatment plus psychotherapy. A medication known as lithium frequently helps to bring a patient out of a depressed state.

Does childbirth often cause the mother to be mentally depressed?
Post partum depression is a not uncommon condition. Although it occurs after one has given birth, the actual childbirth is not thought to be the causative factor.

Is it safe to marry someone in whose family there is a history of mental disease?
Yes. However, the matter of having children should be studied closley to make sure that inherited mental disease does not exist in both partners' families.

What are the chances of inheriting mental disease or mental defects?
Slight, unless one is the product of a marriage in which inherited mental illness exists on both sides of the family. Genetic counseling is very helpful in these cases.

Does overindulgence in sex cause mental disturbance?
No.

Does lack of sex cause mental disturbance?
It may cause neurotic reactions but it does not lead to psychosis.

Should I receive psychotherapy because I am afraid of being in enclosed spaces?
Yes.

Is psychotherapy advisable when marital difficulties of a major nature arise?
Yes.

Is lack of sleep (insomnia) indicative of an emotional upset?
Yes, usually.

Should someone who has chronic insomnia consult a psychiatrist?
Yes.

How successful are medicines in treating mental illnesses?
There are many new drugs that can help depressed or mentally ill people.

What is hysteria?
An extremely emotional state, out of all proportion to the stimulus. It is seen most often among people with neurosis.

Can high blood pressure be caused by emotional upset?
Yes, in some cases.

Can an ulcer be mainly emotional in origin?
Emotion is a major factor in some cases although other factors, such as excess acidity, poor dietary habits, overwork, etc., also play important roles.

Can the colitis from which I suffer be due to emotional upset?
Yes, but other factors, such as infection, may also play an important role.

Should I be sympathetic toward a member of my family who imagines he is ill when he is really physically fit?
Yes, but more important, see that he seeks psychiatric care.

How seriously should I take threats of suicide on the part of a member of my family?
All threats of suicide should be taken seriously. Notify your doctor immediately.

How can someone be safeguarded against suicide?
By being placed in a hospital or a mental institution especially equipped to handle this type of patient.

Are patients ever made worse by consulting a psychiatrist?
This doesn't happen frequently but, as in every branch of medicine, there are those doctors who fail to help their patients.

Does a patient usually suffer more when he is placed in a mental institution?

Some may; others suffer a great deal less because they are under constant treatment and supervision.

What chances of recovery are there for people who go to mental institutions?

This will depend upon the diagnosis and the response to treatment. However, considerably more than half those who enter mental hospitasl are discharged as cured or greatly improved.

Do mental hospitals ever hold patients longer than they should?

Virtually never. If they make any mistake, it is in not holding some patients long enough.

What is schizophrenia?

It is a form of mental illness formerly known as dementia preacox in which there is a withdrawal from reality. It tends to occur in young adults.

Is there any satisfactory treatment for schizophrenia?

Various forms of psychotherapy are helpful in treating patients with schizophrenia. This therapy, in conjunction with drugs, can sustain many schizophrenics for long periods of time so that they can lead useful, productive lives.

What is a paranoid reaction?

One in which a person is affected by delusions of persecution.

What is the outlook for a patient who is paranoid?

This is a very difficult aberration to overcome. The patient, because of his lack of insight, often cannot be persuaded that he is free from persecution. Logic fails to reach him.

Is there any treatment for paranoia?

With repeated reassurances and psychotherapy, many of these people can be helped, and can be maintained as useful citizens. However, paranoia among aging people seldom responds well to psychotherapy.

At what age can I tell whether my child is mentally retarded?
Within the first few months of life.

Are IQ tests reliable?
Yes, in denoting comparative levels of intelligence.

Is an IQ test a satisfactory indication of mental health?
No. It merely tests intelligence.

Is mental deficiency inherited?
Some cases are; others are not.

Can mental deficiency be prevented during pregnancy?
No.

Is there any treatment for mental deficiency?
Yes. Modern methods aim toward adjusting the child to his level of ability and to training him to use whatever mental capacities he has to their fullest extent. In this way, a large number of mentally deficient people can lead useful lives.

Are aptitude tests reliable?
Only to a limited extent. People make a great mistake if they depend solely upon an aptitude test in choosing a career or making an important life decision.

QUESTIONS TO ASK YOUR DOCTOR

Is my condition one that will lend itself to psychoanalysis or do I just need psychotherapy?

How many times a week will it be necessary for me to visit?

For how long a period will the treatment last?

With my limited means, how can I obtain psychiatric help?

Is my condition a psychotic or a neurotic one?

Am I having a nervous breakdown?

Does a nervous breakdown mean that I am becoming psychotic?

Can this condition lead to my being placed in a hospital?

How can I tell if my symptoms are due to organic mental disease or to emotional difficulties?

Are sedatives helpful in treating my emotional condition?

Is it wise for me to take sleeping pills to overcome insomia?

Will group therapy benefit my condition?

What are the advantages or disadvantages of group therapy over individual therapy for my condition?

Should I tell my family that I am considering psychiatric treatment?

8. NERVE DISORDERS

FAINTING

What should be done for someone who has fainted?
1. Stretch him out flat, face up.
2. Loosen any tight collars, belts, or other constricting clothing.
3. Elevate the chin to improve the air passageway.
4. Elevate the feet about one foot above body level.
5. Encourage deep breathing.

Is there a tendency for women to faint during early pregnancy?
Occasionally.

Why is it that some people faint and others don't?
Those who are emotionally unstable are more prone to fainting.

Does too little blood sugar ever cause fainting?
Yes. This can occur in normal people who have gone for long periods of time without eating.

Will an overdose of insulin in a diabetic patient ever cause fainting?
Yes, and occasionally a convulsion.

Is fainting a sign that I have heart disease?
Not necessarily, although heart attacks may occasionally have their onset with a fainting spell.

How long does the usual faint last?
One to five minutes.

Do patients ever die in a faint?
Not unless the faint is accompanied by a fatal fall.

HEADACHES AND DIZZINESS

Are most headaches caused by physical or emotional conditions?
Either can cause them but emotional conditions probably constitute the more frequent cause.

Are frequent headaches usually symptomatic of physical disease?
Yes; see your doctor.

How can a doctor tell whether symptoms such as headache and dizziness are caused by emotional factors or by physical disease such as a brain tumor or a blood vessel problem within the skull?
By a thorough physical examination, plus the taking of various tests, including X-rays, arteriograms, brain scans, and electroencephalograms, which enable the physician to distinguish and diagnose the disorder.

What is an electroencephalogram?
It is a procedure to determine the brain waves. Electrodes are attached to the scalp, and the electrical impulses that pass through the brain are recorded. Deviations from normal brain waves may indicate the presence of brain disease, such as epilepsy or a tumor.

Is an electroencephalogram painful?
No.

How accurate are electroencephalograms in diagnosing epilepsy or brain tumors?
They are extremely helpful, although other confirmatory tests are usually done too. (See the section on Cancer.)

Will an electroencephalogram show whether I have a tendency toward a stroke?
Usually not.

Are there medications that will control my dizziness?
Most episodes of dizziness can be controlled by appropriate medication and diet.

Are headaches ever caused by excessive fatigue?
Yes.

What is the difference between an ordinary headache and migraine?
Migraine usually affects only one side of the head and is accompanied by nausea and vomiting.

Is migraine inherited?
It may be, especially if it is allergic in origin.

Does migraine ever disappear?
Yes. In many people, this does happen as they grow older.

Are headaches frequently associated with menstruation?
Yes, especially among emotionally unstable women.

Are headache medicines, such as aspirin, habit-forming?
No.

What should I do if my headache is not relieved by ordinary medication?
Consult your doctor.

Are dizzy spells related to blood pressure?
In some patients, dizzy spells are caused by high blood pressure. Low blood pressure in a healthy person seldom causes any symptoms.

PARKINSONISM

What is Parkinsonism?

It is a disease associated with degenerative changes in certain brain cells known as basal ganglia. Parkinsonism is associated with a shaking palsy and a mask-like facial expression. As the disease progresses over a period of years, it tends to become markedly disabling.

Is Parkinsonism inherited?

No.

How can Parkinsonism be controlled?

Through a drug called L-dopa. Its use must be carefully controlled and continuously supervised by your doctor.

Can surgery relieve the symptoms of Parkinsonism?

Yes, in certain selected cases.

What surgery is performed for Parkinsonism?

An intricate brain procedure is carried out whereby electrodes are inserted into the brain to destroy the cells that cause the palsy. In expert hands, good results are obtained in more than 80 percent of cases.

Is Parkinsonism fatal?

No, but in severe cases it tends to shorten the life span.

Can I drive a car even though I have Parkinsonism?

Yes, if the palsy is under control.

NEURITIS

What is neuritis?

It is an inflammation of a nerve.

What causes neuritis?

In most cases the cause is not known. Some are thought to be due to vitamin deficiencies, while others may be caused by viral inflammations or by pressure upon the nerve from surrounding tissues.

What is sciatica?

A form of neuritis. Another term for it is sciatic neuritis.

What is the relationship between a slipped disk and sciatica?
The herniated (slipped) portion of the intervertebral disk presses upon portions of the sciatic nerve. In such cases, surgery may be indicated to remove the pressure.

Do most cases of sciatica clear up spontaneously?
Yes, but it may take several weeks or months to subside completely.

What is a myelogram?
It is an X-ray of the spine taken after injecting an opaque substance into the spinal canal. A myelogram may reveal the presence of a slipped disk or a tumor of the spinal cord. There is no danger in having a myelogram.

What is tic douloureux?
It is an inflammation of the trigeminal (fifth cranial) nerve which supplies the face.

What is shingles?
A form of neuritis thought to be caused by a viral infection of the nerve endings.

What is the treatment for shingles?
There is no truly effective treatment that will shorten the course of the condition. However, analgesics are prescribed to relieve pain.

Is facial paralysis a form of stroke?
No. The typical Bell's palsy (facial paralysis) is a condition affecting the facial nerves. It is *not* a stroke.

What is the prognosis for facial paralysis?
In time, most cases clear, but some leave a certain amount of partial paralysis. There is no truly effective treatment to speed recovery although stimulation of the facial nerves with electric current is frequently employed.

BRAIN TUMORS

Is it possible to make an accurate diagnosis of a brain tumor?
Yes.

How can the presence of a brain tumor be diagnosed?

1. By noting the patient's symptoms.

2. By physical examination of the patient, noting changes in various nerve reactions.

3. By X-ray examination of the brain.

4. By performing a brain scan after first giving the patient a radioactive isotope.

5. By taking an angiogram, an X-ray to outline the blood vessels of the brain.

6. By performing an electroencephalogram.

Are these methods accurate in arriving at a diagnosis of brain tumor?

Yes, by utilizing some, or all, of these tests, a diagnosis of brain tumor can be made with great accuracy.

Are brain tumors curable?

Most benign tumors are curable, whereas most malignant tumors cannot be cured.

EPILEPSY

What is epilepsy?

A brain disorder accompanied by periodic convulsions and loss of consciousness.

If a member of my family has epilepsy, does this mean that I or my children are more likely to develop the condition?

There is an inherited aspect to epilepsy, but unless several members have the condition or unless it exists on both your father's *and* mother's side of the family, your chances of inheriting epilepsy are slight.

Can people of any age develop epilepsy?

Yes. However, it rarely has its onset within the first years of life or after fifty to sixty years of age.

Should epilepsy be a bar to marriage?

No. However, genetic counseling is advisable before deciding to have children.

What precautions must one take if he has epilepsy?

1. He should make sure to take his medications regularly.

2. He should avoid excitement and emotional stress whenever possible.

3. He should carry with him instructions on how he should be treated should he develop a seizure.

4. He should not drive a car if he has forgotten to take his medicine.

5. He should lie down and remain quiet if he feels a seizure coming on.

Are there medications that will prevent the convulsion seen in epilepsy?

Yes. Many patients with epilepsy can be maintained for indefinite periods of time without seizures, provided they take their medication regularly.

If my child has convulsions associated with acute illness, does this mean that he is likely to develop epilepsy?

The convulsions seen in infants and young children are associated with high fevers or vitamin deficiency and have nothing to do with epilepsy.

ENCEPHALITIS

What is encephalitis?

An inflammation of the brain.

How is encephalitis likely to occur?

It is sometimes caused by vaccinations against diseases such as smallpox or mumps, or as a complication of one of the contagious diseases of childhood.

Is the encephalitis following a childhood contagious disease usually very dangerous?

It can be, but the great majority of children so afflicted recover with few, if any, permanent aftereffects.

What is sleeping sickness?

It is an epidemic form of encephalitis usually caused by a virus.

Is encephalitis associated with a childhood disease likely to develop into sleeping sickness?

No. This unfortunate complication occurs with epidemic viral encephalitis, seldom with that seen after a contagious disease such as chickenpox or mumps.

MENINGITIS

What is meningitis?
It is an inflammation of the covering membranes of the brain. Sometimes it is caused by bacteria, at other times by viruses.

Is meningitis contagious?
To a certain extent. Actually, it is infectious rather than contagious. In other words, it can be transmitted by intimate contact with the afflicted individual. When two people in a family contract the condition at the same time, the infection has probably originated from the same source.

Is meningitis curable?
Yes, in the great majority of cases.

Does meningitis usually leave permanent aftereffects?
Most patients will make a complete recovery; a small number may suffer permanent aftereffects such as impairment of sight or hearing, or a weakness in one of the limbs.

CEREBRAL CONCUSSION

What is a cerebral concussion?
A cerebral concussion is a sudden head injury associated with loss of consciousness. It is not accompanied by a skull fracture.

What is a common complaint following concussion?
Headaches ranging from mild to severe that last for weeks or even months.

How can one tell definitely whether a concussion has given rise to brain damage?
By careful neurologic examination, including X-rays, electroencephalography, angiograms, brain scans, etc.

FRACTURED SKULL

What is a fractured skull?
Any break of a bone of the skull constitutes a skull fracture.

Is a fractured skull always associated with brain damage?
    No.

Do most people recover from a fractured skull?
    Yes, provided the brain damage is not too extensive.

Is it common to have headaches for a long period of time after a fractured skull?
    Yes.

Is surgery always necessary for a fractured skull?
    No. It is done when a piece of the skull is pressing upon the brain. It is also done to relieve excess pressure within the skull cavity and, occasionally, to stop intracranial bleeding.

HIGH BLOOD PRESSURE

Is high blood pressure likely to lead to a stroke?
    Yes, in some people, especially if it is accompanied by hardening of the arteries that supply the brain.

Are operations to relieve hardening of the arteries in the neck helpful in preventing a stroke?
    Yes. It has been found that endarterectomy, an operation to widen the passageway within the carotid arteries of the neck, may prevent stroke or relieve the symptoms if stroke has occurred. It accomplishes this by allowing for a greater blood supply to the brain.

Are such operations helpful after a stroke has already taken place?
    Yes, in some cases, the paralysis caused by the stroke will improve or disappear entirely.

Will the paralysis that results from a stroke tend to clear up as one recovers?
    Yes. Full recovery, however, is not the general rule.

Do all people lose their power of speech as a result of a stroke?
    No. A right-handed person who has a stroke on the right side of his brain will not lose his speech. A stroke on his left

side may cause him to lose it. The opposite happens in left-handed people. But in neither case is the power of speech invariably affected by a stroke.

MULTIPLE SCLEROSIS

What is multiple sclerosis?
This condition, also known as disseminated sclerosis, is a disease of the central nervous system associated with the loss of the myelin sheaths covering the nerve fibers.

What are the symptoms of multiple sclerosis?
Any one, or more, of the following symptoms may occur at various times during the course of this disease: double vision, temporary loss of vision in one or both eyes, weakness of one or more limbs, spasticity of the limbs, difficulty in voiding, slurring of speech, etc.

Who is most likely to contract multiple sclerosis?
People between twenty and forty years of age.

Is multiple sclerosis either inherited or contagious?
No.

What is the outlook for patients with multiple sclerosis?
This is a progressive degenerative disease ultimately leading to bed confinement and invalidism. In some people this takes place within a few years; other can go for ten to twenty years or more before the disease eventually overcomes them.

Is there a cure for multiple sclerosis?
No, but there are methods of treatment that may bring about a prolonged remission of symptoms.

MUSCULAR DYSTROPHY

What is muscular dystrophy?
It is a progressive disease of the muscles leading eventually to degeneration of skeletal muscle fibers. Unfortunately, there is no regeneration of destroyed muscle fibers.

Does muscular dystrophy occur more often in males?
Yes, the incidence is three times greater than among females.

What causes muscular dystrophy?

The cause is unknown but there are thought to be strong hereditary factors.

When does muscular dystrophy have its onset?

In childhood, at some time between the ages of four and fifteen years.

What symptoms are characteristic of muscular dystrophy?

A disinclination to run and play, clumsiness with frequent falls and unsteadiness of gait. Later, the child may waddle as he walks and appears swaybacked. All body muscles tend to become weak and inefficient.

Does mental retardation accompany muscular dystrophy?

No.

What is the outlook for one who has muscular dystrophy?

The disease is always progressive, but its course can frequently be slowed by administration of ACTH, cortisone, and other steroid medications. Some children may live for many years with this condition, occasionally attaining adulthood.

QUESTIONS TO ASK YOUR DOCTOR

Are my headaches caused by an allergy?

What can I do to control my migraine?

Is my dizziness associated with a physical condition or is it emotional in origin?

Can you tell whether I will need surgery for my Parkinsonism?

Is it safe for me to drive a car even though I have epilepsy?

What restrictions should I place upon my choice of job and physical activity because of my epilepsy?

Is there any surgery that can cure my epilepsy?

Is my epilepsy psychological in origin?

How can I protect myself against a stroke?

How long will my symptoms last from the concussion I have received?

Will my recovery from skull fracture be complete?

Will the fact that I have had a concussion predispose me to headaches indefinitely?

Am I more subject to headaches because I have had a skull fracture?

Can I return to full physical activity even though I have had a concussion and/or skull fracture?

9. SEX

Where can I obtain reliable information on sex?
Your family doctor is undoubtedly well informed on most sexual matters and should be consulted if you have a problem. Also, the American Medical Association has a list of excellent books on the subject which they will forward on request. The Sex Information and Education Council of the U.S. is another good source of materials on sex.

Is sex necessary for mental health?
For most people, yes. Without it, they can become apathetic and depressed. However, many people lead happy, productive lives without sexual contacts.

Can a doctor tell by physical examination whether a young couple will be physically suited to one another?
Almost all people are physically suited to each other in the sense that no penis is too large for the normal vagina.

Can physical or mental harm result from excessive indulgence in sex?
If the excessive indulgence is associated with too much drinking and inadequate sleep, physical harm can result.

Excessive indulgence, as in satyrs and nymphomaniacs, is usually compulsive and, therefore, a neurotic way of life.

Is masturbation natural?

Yes. According to the Kinsey Report, most males and females reported masturbation during at least some period of their lives.

Does harm result from frequent masturbation?

Not from the masturbation itself but it can from the sense of guilt that often accompanies the practice.

Are sexual desires controlled by hormones?

Yes, to a certain extent. However, the psyche (mind) plays an equally important role.

Is it harmful if a couple has incomplete sexual relations?

Yes, it is natural to want to reach a climax. If incomplete sexual relations, or "coitus interruptus," is used repeatedly as a form of birth control, the woman may become so conditioned that she is unable to achieve a climax.

What are the dangers of intercourse during menstruation?

None. Some couples avoid it on aesthetic grounds, but others find that the woman is particularly eager for intercourse at that time. Certainly, no harm can result.

If I presently lack interest in sex, does this mean that I will always be indifferent to it?

No. People's attitudes vary frequently throughout life, depending on the circumstances. An overworked mother or a man with pressing demands at the office may be less interested in sex than at other periods of their lives.

Is the first sex act usually very painful for a woman?

Usually not. However, a premarital examination will readily determine whether the maidenhead requires stretching prior to marriage.

Do all women bleed on first intercourse?

No. Many women do not bleed at all even though they are virginal.

What is the most common cause of sexual incompatibility?

Psychological incompatibility.

If I am having marital troubles with my spouse, whom shall I consult?

First, your family doctor. He may refer you to a specialist if he thinks it necessary.

Is simultaneous orgasm necessary for a well-adjusted relationship?

No. However, it may be attained eventually in the great majority of cases.

If I fail to reach a climax, does that mean I do not love my mate?

Not at all. Inability to reach climax may be indicative of the need for sexual counseling. Often, such guidance will eliminate the problem.

Can I become pregnant even though I don't reach a climax during intercourse?

Yes, climax has nothing to do with conception.

Is it natural for men to reach a climax more rapidly than women?

Yes, especially among young men.

Is it natural for men to have a greater sexual desire than women?

No. This idea is a hangover from the previous century when women were supposed to conceal their sexuality along with their legs. Some recent studies suggest that women may have an even stronger sex desire than men.

What is the normal number of times a week that a person should have sexual relations?

This depends upon the sexual needs of the partners, their attitude toward each other, their age, and other facts. There is no such thing as a "normal number of times."

Are contacts between the genitals and the anus abnormal?

Most physicians consider this act abnormal, or at least undesirable.

Are mouth–genital contacts abnormal?

They are considered abnormal when they repeatedly serve

as a substitute for genital–genital contacts; otherwise, they are not considered abnormal.

Is it natural for me to want sexual intercourse even though I am over sixty years of age?

Yes. There is no age limit on either male or female sexual desire.

Is loss of interest in sex common after change of life?

No. Many women find that their sexual interest increases at this time.

If I have my uterus and tubes and ovaries removed, will I lose sexual desire?

No. The operation should not in any way influence sexual desire or the enjoyment of sex.

What is frigidity?

It is lack of sexual desire and an inability to reach a climax in a female. Some psychiatrists believe it has its roots in early childhood experiences and is treatable through psychotherapy. Others, such as Masters and Johnson, believe it can be treated through reeducation and the practice of certain physical techniques that emphasize foreplay in the sexual act.

Will frigidity interfere with my ability to have children?

No. Frigidity has nothing to do with conception.

What is a nymphomaniac?

A female who craves sex constantly, indulges in sex indiscriminately, and cannot ever obtain complete satisfaction. It constitutes neurotic behavior.

Is impotence caused by a physical or a mental disturbance?

Except in aged men, impotence is usually of psychological rather than physical origin.

At what age in life do men become impotent as the result of physical causes?

It varies greatly, from sixty to seventy-five years of age. Some men become psychologically impotent at much earlier ages; others retain potency well into their seventies and eighties.

Is there a difference between impotence and sterility in men?

Yes. A man may be potent but have no sperm capable of impregnating an egg, or he may be impotent yet have an adequate supply of active sperm.

Are there any diseases other than syphilis and gonorrhea that can be transmitted through sexual intercourse?

Yes, a condition known as chancroid. Also, certain fungal infections of the vagina, such as monilia or trichomonas, and of the urethra of the penis can be transmitted through intercourse.

Is syphilis transmissible through intercourse even though a thorough course of treatment has been given for the syphilis?

No.

What causes homosexuality?

It is thought by most physicians to be of neurotic origin although a few investigators now think that it is linked to changes in hormonal secretions.

Are homosexual tendencies inherited?

No, although a small group of investigators believe that genetic factors may play a role in its development.

If a person shows homosexual tendencies in early adulthood, will they usually continue for the rest of his or her life?

They usually do unless the individual undergoes intensive, prolonged psychotherapy.

What can one do to overcome homosexual tendencies?

Consult a psychiatrist.

Is psychotherapy valuable in overcoming homosexual tendencies?

Yes, because even if it does not result in heterosexuality, it often makes the homosexual a better-adjusted individual.

Is it possible for a heterosexual person to be seduced into homosexuality?

As an occasional experience, yes. However, one must have very strong homosexual tendencies to live a homosexual life for any length of time.

QUESTIONS TO ASK YOUR DOCTOR

What can I do to overcome painful intercourse?

How can I tell if I am oversexed?

How can I know if I am undersexed?

How do I know if I am truly frigid?

What causes me to be frigid?

How do I overcome frigidity?

Is it natural for me to have erotic dreams?

How can I know whether my impotence is physical or emotional in origin?

Is there a hormone treatment for my impotence?

Would psychotherapy be helpful in overcoming my impotence?

At what age should I begin to lose interest in sexual activities?

Since my heart attack, should I limit my sexual activity?

Is it harmful to my heart if I indulge in sexual intercourse even though I am beyond sixty years of age?

10. THE EYES

How often should the eyes be checked?
Once a year for most people; twice a year for those over sixty.

Should I go to an eye specialist to have my eyes examined or is it sufficient to go to an optometrist?

For a thorough examination, one should see an eye specialist. He will refer you to an optometrist if you need glasses. ·

How can I prevent eyestrain?
1. Read only in good light.
2. Wear your glasses, if you need them.
3. Avoid reading when a strong light is in your eyes.
4. Do not expose your eyes for long periods to the direct rays of the sun.
5. Read legible type.

Can I permanently damage my eyes by reading too much or working too long?
Not if you observe sensible reading habits, as mentioned above.

Are headaches often caused by eyestrain?
Occasionally, but headaches are more likely to come from other sources. (See Headache under Nerve Disorders.)

What causes eyes to tear excessively?
A blockage of the tear duct leading from the inner corner of the lower lid to the nose. Of course, a cold wind or irritating vapor or gas can stimulate the lacrimal gland to produce more tears than even a normal tear duct can carry. Tears then spill over the eyelids.

Is it safe to wear contact lenses?
Yes, for most people.

Are the soft contact lenses better than the conventional type?
Yes, for most patients.

For how long a period each day is it safe to wear contact lenses?
Many people put them in when they get up in the morning and take them out upon retiring in the evening, without any untoward effect. However, not all people have that much tolerance. Contact lenses take practice. Try using them for a trial period at first, then extend it until you are able to wear them comfortably for the greater part of the day and evening.

Can contact lenses be prescribed for people who need bifocal glasses?
Yes, but they are not easy to become accustomed to.

What is the effect of television viewing on a child's eyesight?
As far as has been determined, none.

Is nearsightedness or farsightedness inherited?
Yes.

Do children tend to outgrow nearsightedness?
No.

Can anything be done to prevent nearsightedness?
No.

Will the wearing of proper glasses lead to the improvement of nearsightedness?
The condition will not disappear but sight will be improved.

Can wearing eyeglasses make nearsightedness worse?
No.

Can I use my eyes just as much as normal-sighted people even though I am nearsighted?
Yes.

How can one tell if a child is nearsighted?
He can be tested by three years of age.

Is there an operation that will help nearsightedness?
Yes, but it is limited to selected cases in which the nearsightedness is extremely severe.

Is farsightedness inherited?
Yes.

Does farsightedness tend to get better by itself?
No.

If I wear proper eyeglasses, will this improve my farsightedness?

The vision will be improved even though the farsightedness will persist.

When can you tell whether a child is farsighted?
All newborn infants are farsighted. At about three years of age it can be determined by an oculist whether the child's vision is normal, or whether he is far- or nearsighted.

Will farsightedness improve as I grow older?
No.

Is it safe to use my eyes as much as I wish even though I am farsighted?
Yes.

Can contact lenses aid farsighted people?
Yes.

Are there any medicines that will help to cure farsightedness?
No.

Are farsighted people prone to develop glaucoma in their later years?
Some may, but nearsighted people also can develop this disease.

Do all people experience a change in vision in middle age?
Yes, some may become more farsighted; others more nearsighted.

ASTIGMATISM

What is astigmatism?
An irregularity in the curved shape of the eyeball, leading to an uneven projection of the image to the retina in the back of the eye. It is frequently inherited, nothing can be done to prevent it, and only the wearing of corrective glasses will help it.

Does astigmatism ever get better by itself?
No.

Does astigmatism lead to blindness?
No.

CONJUNCTIVITIS

What is conjunctivitis?
An inflammation of the membrane covering the eye.

What are its causes?
An allergy is one frequent cause; pollutants in the air are another; but most often, it is caused by a bacterial or viral infection.

What is the danger of conjunctivitis?
It can occasionally lead to an ulcer of the cornea (the membrane covering the colored portion of the eye). Such ulcers may lead to scarring of the cornea, with impaired vision.

What is pinkeye?
Pinkeye is one form of conjunctivitis. It is highly contagious and may take several days to clear up.

What is the treatment for conjunctivitis?
1. Appropriate eyedrops or eye ointments, many of which contain an antibiotic and a steroid medication.
2. Protecting the eyes from bright light.
3. Eye rest.
4. Eye lotions to wash out the eye.
5. Avoidance of contamination from rubbing the eyes.
6. Antiallergic medications if the conjunctivitis is allergic in origin.

FOREIGN BODIES AND SCRATCHES

What should be done about a speck of dust in the eye?
The important thing is to remove it as soon as possible, preferably immediately, before any damage is done. Tearing will often take care of it; if not, use an eye cup with warm water. If your own efforts are not immediately successful, see your doctor at once.

To whom should I go to have a foreign body removed from my eye?
To a doctor, not to a layman. If it occurs at night, go to

the emergency room of the nearest hospital. Left for even a few hours without treatment, a foreign body can cause serious damage in the form of a corneal ulcer in the eye.

What should I do when my eyeball has been scratched?
See your doctor at once.

Is there any danger to my eye from a scratch?
Yes, a corneal ulcer may result.

Do most scratches of the surface of the eye heal without causing permanent damage?
Yes, but not without proper treatment.

Is vision ever impaired by a scratch of the eye or by having a cinder in it?
Yes, if the scratch or ulcer heals and leaves a scar, especially if the scar is located over the pupil of the eye.

Is it possible to replace a cornea that has been damaged irreparably?
Yes. In many cases, corneal transplants are successful in improving vision.

What can be done if a corneal transplant fails?
It is possible to reoperate and implant a fresh one.

STIES AND CHALAZIONS

What is a sty?
An infection of one of the small glands of the eyelid.

Can vision be damaged by recurrent sties?
No.

Must all sties be opened surgically?
No. Most of them will open of their own accord or subside without surgery.

What is the usual treatment for a sty?
1. Warm applications to the eye.
2. Antibiotic ointment applied to the eyelid.
3. Surgical lancing of the sty if it gets large and comes to a head.

What is a chalazion?
A cyst due to blockage of a duct of one of the small glands in the eyelid.

Are chalazions very common?
Yes.

Is there any danger to the eyesight from a chalazion?
No.

What is the treatment for a chalazion?
Some will absorb by themselves; others must be excised surgically.

ENTROPION AND ECTROPION

What do the terms "entropion" and "ectropion" mean?
Entropion is the turning-in of the lower eyelid; ectropion is the turning-out of the lower eyelid.

Are there problems associated with entropion?
Yes, there is the danger of scratching the cornea, plus the tendency to excessive tearing.

Can entropion or ectropion be corrected?
Yes, by relatively simple surgical operations.

DACRYOCYSTITIS

What is dacryocystitis?
Blockage of the tear duct leading from the lower eyelid to the nose.

How common is it?
It is often found in infants and elderly people.

Will dacryocystitis interfere with my child's eyesight?
No.

What is the treatment for dacryocystitis?
The duct must be reopened either by probing or with a surgical incision.

GLAUCOMA

What is glaucoma?
A disease of the eye characterized by increased pressure in the eyeball with decreasing vision.

How can an eye specialist tell if I have glaucoma?
By noting your symptoms and by testing the pressure within your eyeball.

What are the symptoms of acute glaucoma?
1. Pain in the eye.
2. Impaired vision.
3. Redness of the eye.
4. Markedly increased pressure within the eyeball.

Is there any way to prevent an attack of acute glaucoma?
Yes. People with a tendency toward glaucoma, as evidenced by increased intraocular pressure, should be on continuing eye medication. The use of eyedrops that keep the pupil constricted will help to prevent acute glaucoma. Also, one must avoid drugs containing belladonna as this will tend to dilate the pupil.

How long must I continue to take eyedrops to prevent glaucoma?
Indefinitely.

Does glaucoma tend to run in families?
Yes.

What harm comes from glaucoma?
Sight can be lost unless surgery is performed promptly upon a patient suffering from severe acute glaucoma.

Are the diagnostic tests carried out in the oculist's office accurate in determining glaucoma?
Yes.

How often should I have the pressure within my eyeballs tested?
At your annual eye check-ups or at any time that you have eye symptoms.

Is it painful to have my eye pressure taken?
No. The drops put into your eyes may sting a bit, but on the whole, the procedure is painless.

Does glaucoma usually affect both eyes at the same time?
No, not at first, but eventually it does tend to affect both eyes.

What is the treatment for glaucoma?
Chronic glaucoma is frequently treated by giving eyedrops to keep the pupil constricted. Acute glaucoma may require an operation to permit drainage from the eyeball of excess fluid.

Does glaucoma eventually clear up by itself without treatment?
No. Early diagnosis and treatment are essential in keeping the disease under control.

What are the chances for recovery following surgery for acute glaucoma?
Results are excellent if the surgery is performed early; results are poor if surgery is performed late.

What anesthetic is used when operating for glaucoma?
Often local anesthesia is used; occasionally, a general anesthesia is given.

Can you tell when a person has had such an operation?
No, there is no visible scar or eye deformity resulting from glaucoma surgery.

Does glaucoma recur after it has been operated upon successfully?
No, but preventive medication is often continued indefinitely.

CATARACT

What is a cataract?
A clouding or opacity of the lens of the eye.

How do you determine the presence of a cataract?
By a simple eye examination.

Do all cataracts require surgery?
No. Some never mature and, therefore, interfere with vision only slightly.

Can you tell accurately when a cataract is ready for surgery?
Yes, again through a simple eye examination to determine the cataract's "ripeness," that is, readiness for removal.

Do cataracts usually affect both eyes?
Yes, but there may be an interval of many years between the first and second cataract.

What happens if a cataract is not operated upon?
Eventually, vision will be greatly impaired.

Is there any way to prevent a cataract?
Only to a limited extent. If there is an associated generalized disease, such as diabetes, the patient should be under continued medical regulation. Cataracts frequently grow more quickly when the general health is poor.

Do cataracts ever disappear by themselves?
No.

What type of surgery is carried out for cataracts?
The lens is removed.

What are the chances of a good result after operation for cataracts?
In most cases, surgical results are excellent and vision is improved markedly. Of course, to obtain better vision, the patient must wear glasses.

What kind of anesthetic is used during a cataract operation?
Local, and in some cases general anesthesia.

Is there a visible scar after removal of a cataract?
No, as the incision in the eye is made beneath the upper eyelid.

Can contact lenses be worn after cataract removal?
Yes.

Do cataracts recur once they have been removed?
No.

CROSSED EYES

What causes crossed eyes?
Weakness of one or more of the muscles that control eye movements.

What are the medical terms for crossed eyes?
Strabismus, or squint.

Are crossed eyes inherited?
No.

Can I tell immediately upon birth if my child is cross-eyed?
Not always, because eye coordination is not well developed at birth, thus giving a false impression of crossed eyes.

What is the condition known as a cast in the eye?
It is similar to being cross-eyed.

What is the medical treatment for crossed eyes?
1. Eye exercises.
2. Wearing corrective glasses.
3. Patching (covering the normal eye) in order to strengthen the muscles of the weak eye.

How effective is the medical treatment for crossed eyes?
If the crossing is marked, in all probability medical treatment will not be sufficient to cure the condition, in which case surgery is indicated.

Is surgery for crossed eyes dangerous?
No.

How successful is surgery for crossed eyes?
It is very successful in the great majority of cases. If results are not totally satisfactory with the first operation, re-operation may be indicated.

What operation is performed for crossed eyes?
The involved muscles are either shortened or lengthened, as indicated by the type of crossing that exists in the eyes.

Is an operation for crossed eyes painful?
   No.

Are there any visible scars from an operation for crossed eyes?
   No.

Is there any further treatment after surgery for crossed eyes?
   Yes, some children have to wear glasses.

Will the crossed eyes recur once they have been operated upon successfully?
   No.

Is vision ever lost because of crossed eyes?
   If the condition is not corrected, it is possible to lose the sight in the eye that is crossed. However, this takes place only if the condition is neglected for years.

DETACHED RETINA

What is a detached retina?
   It is the separation of a portion of the retina from its underlying tissues in the back of the eyeball.

How can I tell whether I have a detached retina?
   Sight is lost from a portion of the visual field of one eye.

Is there a predisposition to the development of detached retina?
   Yes, in people who suffer from marked nearsightedness.

Are there any other conditions that might cause detached retina?
   Yes, an eye tumor can cause it. The presence of an eye tumor can be determined by examination.

Can you tell whether a detached retina is or is not caused by a tumor?
   Yes, by ophthalmoscopic examination.

Can detachment of the retina result from a source outside the body?
   Yes, if there is a predisposition toward the condition, such

as in extreme nearsightedness, then a severe blow to the head, or directly on the eye, can cause it.

What treatment is necessary for detached retina?

Various types of surgery are performed to induce the retina to reattach itself to its underlying structures. This is accomplished by using the laser beam (extreme heat), cryosurgery (using extreme cold), or by electrocoagulation.

Will detached retina heal itself without treatment?

No.

What are the chances of full recovery following surgery for detached retina?

This depends upon the degree of detachment, whether or not the retina is torn as well as detached, and on technical factors such as the location of the detachment. Recovery, however, occurs in a great number of cases.

Can people see again immediately after an operation for detached retina?

Usually, although they are not permitted to use their eyes fully until several days or weeks after the operation.

Is the operation for detached retina painful?

There is discomfort, but no severe pain.

Does detached retina ever recur once it has been successfully treated?

Yes, in some cases.

EYE TUMORS

Can a diagnosis of an eye tumor be made by routine eye examination by an ophthalmologist?

Yes, usually.

Are all eye tumors malignant?

No, but many are.

What is the treatment for eye tumor?

If it is malignant, the eye must be removed.

What will happen if the eye is not removed?
The malignancy will spread to other parts of the body.

SYMPATHETIC OPHTHALMIA

What is meant by the term "sympathetic ophthalmia"?
A severe inflammation of an eye, often leading to blindness, caused by a severe injury or disease of the other eye.

How can one prevent the loss of the other eye through sympathetic ophthalmia?
By having the injured or diseased eye treated promptly, even if it involves its removal.

How can one tell if he is developing sympathetic ophthalmia?
The normal eye will become inflamed.

Is it possible to overcome sympathetic ophthalmia?
Not always. Use of the cortisone drugs can sometimes reverse the process, but once it has started, it usually is progressive.

QUESTIONS TO ASK YOUR DOCTOR

What can I do to prevent redness and irritation of my eyelids?

What is the meaning of the spots that I see floating in front of my eyes?

Can I get rid of the spots before my eyes?

Why do I get frequent attacks of conjunctivitis?

Is my conjunctivitis contagious?

What can I do to avoid conjunctivitis?

What can I do to prevent sties?

How can I prevent the development of a chalazion?

Will my nearsightedness tend to get better as I grow older?

What kind of operation will you perform for my glaucoma?

How soon after my glaucoma surgery will I:
   be released from the hospital?
   have the patch removed from my eye?
   be able to see again?
   bathe or shower?
   go outdoors?
   resume household duties?
   drive a car?
   return to work?
   resume all physical activities?

What caused my cataract?

How long will it take for my cataract to mature?

Is it necessary to have a cataract removed from my eye if the other eye is normal?

Has diet anything to do with the formation of my cataract?

Will my vision return to normal immediately after my cataract operation?

How soon after my cataract surgery will I:
   be released from the hospital?
   have the patch removed from my eye?
   be able to see again?
   wear glasses?
   bathe or shower?
   go outdoors?
   resume household duties?
   drive a car?
   return to work?
   resume all physical activities?

How frequently after my cataract operation should I return for periodic check-ups?

Is surgery required to cure my child's crossed eyes?

How long will it take for the eyes to straighten with the help of glasses?

How soon will you know whether the wearing of glasses will help the crossed eyes?

What is the earliest age at which my child will be able to wear glasses?

Will my child's crossed eyes correct themselves without treatment?

Will my child's eyes be absolutely straight following the surgery?

Will my child see double after a crossed-eye operation?

How soon after surgery will my child be able to move his eyes normally?

How soon after surgery for crossed eyes can my child:
    have the bandages removed from his eyes?
    see again?
    get out of bed?
    leave the hospital?
    go outdoors?
    bathe or shower?
    resume physical activities?
    return to school?

How soon after an operation for detached retina can I:
    get out of bed?
    use my eyes again?
    leave the hospital?
    bathe or shower?
    go out of doors?
    walk up and down stairs?
    resume hosuehold duties?
    return to work?
    resume all physical activities?

How frequently must I return for a check-up after an operation for detached retina?

Will removal of my eye for the tumor result in cure?

11. EAR, NOSE,
AND THROAT CONDITIONS

THE EARS

How often should I have the wax cleaned out of my ears?
Once a year, if it is necessary.

Why shouldn't I do the job myself?
Injury to the eardrum or ear canal may result.

Should I protect my ears when swimming?
Yes. Wear earplugs if you do a great deal of underwater swimming.

What is the best way to get water out of an ear?
Lie down on your back and turn your head to the side. Eventually, the water will run out by itself.

What is the first-aid treatment for a foreign body in the ear?
It should be floated out by pouring mineral oil (or any available vegetable oil) into the external ear canal. One should not try to pick it out.

How can I tell whether I am losing my hearing?
By an audiometric test administered by an ear specialist.

What is otitis media?
Is is an infection of the middle ear, usually secondary to an upper respiratory infection, and accompanied by severe earache.

What is the treatment for otitis media?
Antibiotics are given, as prescribed by your physician. In cases where pus has collected behind the eardrums, it may be necessary to incise the drum.

Do most cases of otitis media clear up without impairment of hearing?
Yes.

Does a mastoid infection often follow a middle ear infection?
Not if the infection has been treated adequately with antibiotics.

What should I do about a pain in an ear?
Consult your physician at once. This will prevent many serious infections.

Other than infection, what can cause permanent damage to the hearing?
A blow in the ear, or persistent exposure to loud noises.

THE NOSE, THROAT, AND SINUSES

What causes colds?
Many different types of viruses cause colds. However, exposure to drafts and cold temperatures, as well as walking around in wet clothing, all predispose one to catching a cold.

Does smoking of cigarettes predispose one to more sore throats and colds?
Yes.

What effect do so-called cold-prevention drugs have in warding off the onset of a cold?
In all probability, they are totally ineffective.

Will large doses of vitamin C prevent me from getting colds?
Only if you have a vitamin C deficiency and are otherwise run down in health.

What effect do cold vaccines have on reducing the incidence of colds?
Some people are benefited by these vaccines, the majority are not.

Are certain people more susceptible to colds than others?
Yes.

Are all colds contagious?
Yes.

How does one avoid catching a cold if a colleague or member of the family has such an infection?

Avoid getting within twelve feet of him; avoid being sneezed on; sleep in a separate room; avoid drafts and wet feet.

Is it safe to take nose drops or use a nasal spray to relieve a congested nose?

They should be used only on the advice of your doctor.

When should I go to bed with a cold?

Whenever you have a temperature elevation.

How often should I take my temperature when I have a cold?

Three times a day.

Do cold remedies cure a cold?

No. Regardless of how they are treated, colds have to run their course and will go away by themselves. However, aspirin or similar medications, while unable to shorten the length of a cold, may relieve some of the discomfort.

Are antibiotics helpful in curing a cold?

No. Antibiotics have little or no effect on viruses.

Can a cold develop into pneumonia?

Colds do not usually turn into pneumonia. A neglected cold, however, may so lower body resistance that pneumonia ensues.

Is whiskey helpful in curing a cold?

No.

Is there any validity in the saying "Stuff a cold and starve a fever"?

No. A light, normal diet should be taken during a cold.

What is the most effective thing you can do for a cold?

Keep warm, get plenty of rest, and drink large quantities of liquid. Moist rather than dry air will help a cold, and a vaporizer will often relieve congestion.

How can I distinguish between an ordinary cold and grippe or influenza?

Influenza and grippe have many general symptoms that most colds do not have, such as high fever, aches and pains in the muscles, bronchitis, etc.

What is meant by the term "allergic rhinitis"?
It is an inflammation of the mucous membranes of the nose, with discharge, due to sensitivity to an allergen.

Is allergic rhinitis the same thing as hay fever?
Not exactly. Hay fever is due to pollen sensitivity; allergic rhinitis may be due to sensitivity to substances other than pollens.

Can air pollution cause stuffy nose and runny eyes?
Yes.

Are X-rays accurate in diagnosing sinus infections?
Yes.

How can you tell whether I have a streptococcus sore throat?
By taking a swab and culturing the germs from the inflamed throat.

Is it safe for me to treat a sore throat by myself?
Yes, if you do not have an elevated temperature.

Are commercial gargles advertised for sore throat helpful?
No. Gargling with plain salt water is just as beneficial.

Are lozenges effective in treating a sore throat?
No, but they may relieve some of the soreness temporarily.

Should antibiotics be taken whenever I have a sore throat?
No. They should be taken under the direction of a physician only.

What is the significance of chronic sore throat?
It may be due to a chronic infection that requires intensive treatment. It may also be due to poor living conditions, to throat-abuse due to smoking, or to breathing irritating vapors.

What is the significance of a chronic hoarseness?
It may mean tuberculosis of the larynx, a tumor of the

larynx, or it may be due to throat-abuse from smoking or the continued inhalation of irritating substances.

THE TONSILS AND ADENOIDS

Is it safe to remove my child's tonsils at any time of the year?

Yes. It is assumed that he has been completely protected against polio. However, they should not be removed when the child has an acute respiratory infection.

Does one attack of tonsillitis predispose toward another attack?

Yes.

Should one have his tonsils removed if he has frequent attacks of tonsillitis?

Yes.

How soon after an attack of acute tonsillitis is it safe to have the tonsils removed?

Within one month.

What harm can result from neglect of tonsils that become infected frequently?

One may develop rheumatic fever, heart disease, or kidney disease.

Should tonsils be removed in a doctor's office or in a hospital?

Preferably in a hospital.

Is tonsillectomy a dangerous operation?

No.

Will I receive general or local anesthesia for tonsillectomy?

Children are always operated upon under general anesthesia, whereas in adults, one or the other may be employed.

Should I follow a special diet after my tonsils have been removed?

Yes, avoid spicy foods.

Must I have a special diet for my child following his tonsillectomy?

No.

Do stitches have to be removed after taking out the tonsils and adenoids?
   No.

Do tonsils and adenoids ever grow back once they have been removed?
   Yes, if they were incompletely excised.

How long will my throat be sore after my tonsils are removed?
   For one to two weeks.

Do tonsils ever bleed after they have been removed?
   Yes, in some cases this happens about the fifth to seventh day postoperatively.

What should I do if there is bleeding after tonsillectomy?
   Call your doctor.

Are there permanent voice changes after tonsillectomy?
   No.

What is the effect of enlarged adenoids in children?
   They cause mouth-breathing and interfere with hearing.

Are the adenoids always removed when the tonsils are removed?
   In children, yes, but not in adults.

Will a child's hearing be improved by removing chronically infected adenoids?
   Yes, if the impairment was due to the adenoids.

THE LARYNX

What are the usual symptoms of acute laryngitis?
   1. Pain in the region of the Adam's apple.
   2. Hoarseness or loss of voice.
   3. A hacking cough.
   4. Fever, in some cases.

What is the treatment for laryngitis?
   1. Plenty of liquids.
   2. A cool compress to the throat.

3. Pain-relieving medications such as aspirin.
4. Silence (no talking).
5. Bed rest, if there is fever.
6. Antibiotics when prescribed by your doctor.

Does laryngitis often appear as the complication of a cold?
    Yes.

How long does an attack of acute laryngitis usually last?
    Four to seven days.

Does the voice return after an attack of acute laryngitis?
    Yes.

Can you tell the difference between an ordinary inflammation of the larynx and one that is due to a tumor?
    Yes, by inspecting the larynx with a laryngoscope.

Is ordinary laryngitis a serious condition?
    No.

Is there any chance of my choking to death when I have laryngitis?
    No, unless the laryngitis has been caused by diphtheria.

Is prolonged hoarseness something to worry about?
    Yes, it is often a sign of disease of the vocal cords.

How is a tumor of the larynx diagnosed?
    A small piece of tissue is snipped away from the larynx (the procedure is called a biopsy) and examined under the microscope to determine the presence of a tumor.

What is the most common tumor of the larynx?
    A benign polyp on a vocal cord.

What is the treatment of a polyp of the vocal cords?
    Removal through a laryngoscope.

Will the voice return to normal after removal of a polyp?
    Yes, but it may take several weeks, during which the patient is urged to speak as little as possible.

What is the treatment for tuberculosis of the larynx?
    The same drugs are given as for tuberculosis of the lungs,

and the same isolation of the patient is required during the active stages of the disease.

Is tuberculosis of the larynx curable?
Yes. The patient may require isolation for a month. Thereafter, the antituberculosis drugs must be continued for about one year.

Is a cancer of the larynx curable?
Yes, if apprehended in the early stages of its development.

What is the treatment for cancer of the larynx?
Removal of the larynx.

Is cancer of the larynx ever treated without surgery?
Yes, in some cases radiation therapy is used instead.

How effective is the X-ray treatment of a cancer of the larynx?
If gotten early, it has resulted in control of the tumor for indefinite periods of time.

Can one be taught to talk after the larynx has been removed?
Yes.

CROUP

What is croup?
It is a catarrhal infection of the larynx, occurring in infants and children.

How can one prevent it?
Since many attacks follow an upper respiratory infection such as a cold, it is important to safeguard a child who displays a tendency toward croup against children who have colds.

Is croup a serious infection?
Yes. Your doctor should be notified whenever your child has a croupy cough or shows any evidence of difficulty in breathing.

If my child has difficulty in breathing with croup, what shall I do?

Unless you can reach your doctor immediately, take the child to the nearest hospital.

What is the treatment for croup?
1. A croup tent to improve breathing.
2. Antibiotic medications as prescribed by your doctor.
3. Medications to make the child vomit seem to alleviate the croup attack.
4. Intake of warm fluids.
5. In severe cases, a tracheotomy is performed to relieve obstruction of breathing.

Do most cases of croup get well without hospitalization?
Yes.

Is croup recurrent?
Yes, it tends to be.

QUESTIONS TO ASK YOUR DOCTOR

Is my stuffy nose the result of an allergy?

What can I do to get rid of my allergy?

Can air-conditioning help my nasal condition?

Can a humidifier help my nasal condition?

What causes my postnasal drip?

How can I stop the coughing during the night from my postnasal drip?

Is my postnasal drip curable?

How can I tell whether my headaches are due to sinus infection?

Is my sinus condition due to an allergy?

What is the treatment for my sinus condition?

Is my sinus condition curable?

Do I need an operation for my sinus condition?

Should I move to another climate to help my sinus condition?

How can you tell the difference between a viral and a bacterial infection of the nose and throat?

Should I have my child's tonsils removed?

How soon after tonsillectomy can I:
    leave the hospital?
    go outdoors?
    bathe or shower?
    resume household duties?
    smoke?
    drive a car?
    return to work?
    resume all physical activities?

How soon after tonsillectomy can my child:
    leave the hospital?
    bathe or shower?
    go outdoors?
    return to school?
    resume all physical activities?

Is my loss of hearing to be permanent?

12. THE HEART

What are some of the common types of heart disease?
    * Congenital heart disease with defects in the partitions between the heart chambers or deformities of the blood vessels of the heart.
    * Rheumatic heart disease with impaired valve function.
    * Heart failure, a condition in which the heart pumps inadequate supplies of blood throughout the body.
    * Irregularities in heart rhythm, including fibrillation, a frequent symptom in heart failure.

* Angina pectoris.
* Coronary artery disease.
* Arteriosclerotic heart disease.
* Hypertensive (high blood pressure) heart disease.
* Myocarditis, an inflammation of the heart muscle.
* Endocarditis, inflammation of the heart valves, often due to infection.
* Pericarditis, an inflammation of the membrane surrounding the heart.

How can I tell if I have heart trouble?

Your doctor will readily make a decisive diagnosis after taking your history, listening to your heart with a stethoscope, X-raying it to note any enlargement, and taking an electrocardiogram. In cases of obscure heart disease, an angiogram (X-ray of the heart and its blood vessels after injecting an opaque substance into the bloodstream) will reveal the presence or absence of any heart deformities.

Does swelling of the ankles mean that there is something wrong with the heart?

It may or may not. However, ankle swelling is an indication for studying heart function.

Does shortness of breath mean that there is something wrong with the heart?

It may or may not. However, it is an indication for investigation of both heart and lung function.

Is heart pain felt in the chest located on the left side or more in the center?

More in the center of the chest.

Is a tendency to heart disease inherited?

Some types are, such as coronary artery disease and hypertensive heart disease. Also, a family in which there is a high incidence of birth deformities is more likely to have an offspring with a congenital heart defect than one in which no such history is present.

What is the significance of pain beneath the breastbone that spreads down the left arm?

It may indicate angina pectoris, a symptom of coronary artery disease. The pain is thought to be caused by decreased blood supply to the heart muscle resulting from a spasm of the coronary artery.

Can an episode of angina be brought on by stress?
Yes.

How long does the usual attack of angina pectoris last?
For a few minutes up to a half hour.

Will physical rest tend to make an attack of angina subside spontaneously?
Yes.

What can one do to shorten an attack of angina?
A nitroglycerin tablet under the tongue will usually overcome the angina within a matter of a minute or two.

Is it dangerous to take nitroglycerin to relieve heart pain?
No.

Is nitroglycerin habit-forming?
No.

What is a heart murmur?
An abnormal sound produced by the beating heart.

Do heart murmurs cause symptoms?
No. Usually the patient is unaware of their existence.

Are all heart murmurs serious?
No, some are harmless and do not indicate a diseased heart; others may be due to valvular disease of the heart.

Must one limit exercise because he has a murmur of the heart?
Not if the murmur is functional. If the murmur is due to defective valves, it may be necessary in some cases to limit physical activity.

Does heart trouble tend to be inherited?
No, but congenital defects of the heart are.

Do stout people tend to get heart trouble more frequently than thin people?
Yes.

Do young people tend to outgrow heart trouble?

No, not if it is due to a defective heart valve or to a birth deformity of the heart.

What can be done for congenital heart condition?

Surgical correction of most defects is possible.

What is the effect of smoking on the heart?

Prolonged use of nicotine is not good for the heart as it causes blood vessel constriction, a situation that may decrease the amount of blood supplying the heart muscle. The incidence of coronary thrombosis is greater among smokers than nonsmokers.

Are heart symptoms sometimes of little importance?

Yes. An occasional skipped heartbeat or occasional elevation of the heart rate usually has little significance. Also, some people have pain in the left chest which is unassociated with true heart disease. Such people are thought to have a cardiac neurosis. A physician can distinguish between actual heart diseases and heart symptoms of neurotic origin.

Is alcohol bad for the heart?

Excess alcohol may be damaging to the heart. Alcohol in moderate amounts is not thought to be harmful.

Is aspirin bad for the heart?

No.

Is excess emotional strain bad for the heart?

Yes, especially for those who already have heart disease or who show a tendency, such as high blood pressure, toward developing heart disease.

How can you tell whether the pain in my heart region is due to a heart condition or due to trouble in some other organ?

By listening to your heart, noting your symptoms, recording your blood pressure, X-raying your heart, and interpreting your electrocardiogram.

What is the significance of a skipped heartbeat?

It is not usually a sign of real heart disease. Excess fatigue, emotional strain, excess smoking, excess alcohol, or coffee, and many other things may cause skipped heartbeat. They usually subside without treatment.

How often should the heart be examined?

People over forty years of age should be examined twice a year. Those with known heart conditions or a family history of heart disease should be examined more often.

What is an electrocardiogram?

The heart muscle generates a characteristic electrical current as it contracts and relaxes. This current can be picked up and recorded on paper by a sensitive instrument known as an electrocardiogram. Variations in amplitude and direction of the current may give important information concerning the heart's function and state of health.

Will an electrocardiogram always show the state of health of the heart?

No. It is only of supplementary value in determining heart disease. Some serious heart conditions may exist with a normal electrocardiogram.

Should adults have a periodic electrocardiogram?

A yearly electrocardiogram is indicated for people over thirty-five years of age even if they are in perfect health.

Are changes from one electrocardiogram to another significant?

Yes.

What is heart failure?

A condition in which the heart fails to pump sufficient blood to adequately supply all the organs of the body.

Can heart failure be controlled?

Yes, usually by appropriate doses of digitalis plus drugs to rid the body of excess fluid accumulation.

Is it dangerous to take digitalis over a long period of time?

Not if you are under ongoing medical supervision.

Is digitalis habit-forming?

No.

Is it possible for one to return to normal physical activity after recovery from an episode of heart failure?
Yes, but certain precautions must be taken to avoid strain. Also, if overweight, the patient must slim down.

Does high blood pressure damage the heart?
Yes, because it requires the heart to pump blood with greater force, thus straining the heart muscle.

Can this condition be improved?
Yes, if the blood pressure is lowered, in many instances the heart condition is improved.

How can the blood pressure be lowered?
By the use of so-called hypotensive medications, and the control of certain other factors such as weight, low salt diet, elimination of tobacco, etc.

Does excess weight tend to heighten the blood pressure?
Yes.

Does nicotine tend to heighten the blood pressure?
Yes.

What diet must I follow to keep my high blood pressure down?
A low salt, low cholesterol, low calorie diet.

Should I discontinue high cholesterol foods if I have a heart condition?
Yes.

Should I limit my salt intake because I have a heart condition?
Yes.

Do emotional upsets tend to raise blood pressure?
Yes.

What is the effect of high blood pressure on life expectancy?
It tends to shorten the life span.

Is low blood pressure bad for the heart?
No.

How many hours of sleep should I get with my type of heart condition?

Eight hours of sleep is sufficient for most adults, whether or not they have a heart disorder.

With my heart condition, is it safe for me to fly in a plane?

Because the cabins of planes are pressurized and passengers rest most of the time in their seats, for most people with a heart disorder, a plane flight is safe. However, you should consult your physician before planning a plane trip.

What should I do if my heart gives me trouble when I am in a foreign country?

Call the American Embassy wherever you are. They will refer you to a good doctor or hospital.

What can I do to ward off heart disease?

1. Keep your weight within normal limits.
2. Eat a low cholesterol, low salt diet.
3. Avoid excess physical strain, but exercise regularly.
4. Avoid excess emotional strain.
5. If you have high blood pressure, take hypotensive drugs as prescribed by your physician.
6. If you have a chronic urinary infection, see that it is treated vigorously.
7. Stop smoking.
8. Seek care for any chronic respiratory disorder.

QUESTIONS TO ASK YOUR DOCTOR

Can you tell by examining me whether I am likely to develop heart trouble?

Is strenuous physical exertion bad for my heart?

Is regular physical exercise good for my heart?

Is it safe for me to go up and down stairs with my heart condition?

Can you predict whether or not my heart condition will shorten my life span?

Should I limit my sexual activities because of my heart condition?

Do I have to stop playing golf because of my heart condition?

Is it all right for me to drive a car even though I have a heart condition?

Is heart surgery indicated for my heart condition?

How dangerous is heart surgery for the relief of my heart condition?

Is walking good exercise for my heart condition?

Is swimming good exercise for my heart?

Are calisthenics good for my heart?

Should I limit the altitude to which I travel?

Is it safe for me to visit a foreign country?

How long must I stay on a restricted diet?

Should I take tranquilizers to lessen the chances of emotional strain?

How much sleep should I try to get each night?

Can I put in a full day's work with my heart condition?

CORONARY ARTERY DISEASE

Exactly what happens when one has a coronary thrombosis?
A clot closes down the passageway in one of the coronary arteries, the vessels which supply blood to the heart muscle.

What causes coronary artery disease?
The exact cause is not known, but certain factors have been singled out as important in the etiology of this condition. They are:
1. Hardening of the arteries.
2. Continuous, excessive emotional stress.
3. A high cholesterol blood level.
4. A family history of coronary thrombosis.

5. Obesity.
6. Excessive use of tobacco.
7. Diabetes mellitus.

Is coronary artery disease always associated with hardening of the arteries throughout the body?
No.

Must I go to the hospital or can I be treated at home?
Most episodes of coronary thrombosis should be treated in the hospital.

Will I be placed in a special intensive coronary care unit?
If your hospital has such a facility, it is the best place to go.

How can my rate of recovery be determined?
Periodic electrocardiographs will be taken, but other signs, obtained on chemical and physical examination, are also important indicators of recovery.

Must I stay in bed when I go home from the hospital?
Not usually, although periodic bed rest is advisable.

What shall I do if my bowels do not move regularly?
Your doctor will prescribe a laxative, a bulk-forming substance, or a rectal suppository.

What special diet should be followed after a coronary?
Dairy products and meat fats should be avoided and a low cholesterol diet should be followed.

How many hours of sleep should I try to get each night?
Eight hours.

Is it all right to fly after a coronary?
If one has made good recovery, he can fly in a pressurized plane.

Will surgery help to prevent another coronary attack?
In certain selected cases, this is possible.

When is surgery advised in coronoray artery disease?
When there is narrowing or blockage of only a segment of

the coronary artery with an open passageway beyond the point of blockage. This can be ascertained by taking angio-cardiographic X-rays.

What surgery is recommended for those with coronary artery disease?

A so-called coronary bypass operation is often performed. This involves suturing a graft from the saphenous vein from the thigh in such a way that it sends blood from the aorta directly to that part of the coronary artery that is beyond the thrombosis. In this way, the clogged portion of the coronary artery is bypassed, allowing ample quantities of blood to reach the heart muscle.

What are the dangers of surgery for coronary disease?

Mortality rates for the coronary artery bypass procedure have been reduced to less than 5 percent when performed by surgeons adept at this type of surgery.

Does the coronary bypass operation often relieve the angina pectoris associated with coronary artery disease?

Yes.

QUESTIONS TO ASK YOUR DOCTOR

How long must I stay in the hospital with my coronary?

What are the chances of my making a full recovery from this coronary attack?

What surgical procedure should be taken if I don't recover fully?

In the hospital, how much of my time should I spend in bed and how much will I be able to be out of bed each day?

How soon after I come home can I:
  go up and down stairs?
  go outdoors?
  ride in a car?
  drive my own car?
  go back to work?
  resume physical activity?
  resume marital relations?

Can I shower or bathe, or must I continue to have sponge baths?

What weight should I maintain?

Should I take medications to help to keep my weight down?

How often shall I take my temperature?

How often will I require electrocardiograms?

Should I take medication to help me sleep better?

Are there any heart medications that I will have to take?

How often should I check with you on the telephone?

What precautions must I take in having marital relations?

How frequently will I be able to have marital relations?

Should I go away for a holiday before returning to work?

What restrictions are there on the altitudes of places to which I may travel?

Should I return to partial work, or can I start right in doing a full day's work?

Is it necessary for me to change my job because I've had a coronary?

Is it safe to resume smoking?

Can I resume drinking alcohol? If so, what limit should I place on the amount I drink?

What types of emotional stress are most important for me to avoid?

How will I know if another coronary attack is imminent?

13. THE LUNGS
AND BRONCHIAL TUBES

What is the function of the lungs?
To extract oxygen from the air breathed in and to expel carbon monoxide in the exhaled air.

What is meant by someone having "weak lungs"?
It usually means he is suffering from a pulmonary disease.

What are the most common conditions affecting the lungs?
Bronchitis, asthmatic bronchitis, influenza, pneumonia, emphysema, tumors, pulmonary embolism, tuberculosis, and other infections.

Is there a tendency for some people to inherit lung disease?
No.

What are the symptoms of lung disease?
Coughing, production of sputum containing pus or blood, shortness of breath, pain in the chest.

How often should the lungs be checked?
At least once a year, or at any time lung symptoms appear. A chest X-ray should also be taken yearly.

How does the condition of the air affect people with lung disorders?
Those with normal lungs are seldom affected by air that is too moist or dry, or too cold or hot. However, people with lung disorders may find extremes difficult to tolerate.

How important to the health of the lungs are the air pollutants that normally exist in urban and heavily industrialized areas?
It has been found that some pollutants cause great lung irritation and, if breathed over a period of years, may result in serious lung disease, including cancer.

Will constant exposure to irritating dust and fumes always lead to impairment of lung function?

Yes, but in varying degrees, depending upon an individual's sensitivity or lack of sensitivity to the irritants.

How long must one be exposed to dust and other air pollutants for it to permanently damage the lungs?

For several years.

How can I know whether air pollutants have damaged my lungs?

By a thorough chest examination by a qualified physician, including a chest X-ray.

What can be the significance of coughing up blood?

It may indicate pneumonia, bronchitis, tuberculosis, lung cancer, etc., or it may be just due to a severe episode of coughing, as in spasms of whooping cough.

How can one distinguish between blood that has come from the lungs and blood that has come from the nose or throat.

Blood from the lungs is coughed up by deep coughing and the blood is found to be mixed with air. Blood from the nose or back of the throat is not mixed with air.

What is a pulmonary function test?

A test of the adequacy of the exchange of inhaled and exhaled air. Good pulmonary function means that the lungs are extracting an adequate amount of oxygen from the inhaled air, and are ridding themselves of adequate amounts of carbon dioxide.

How do I know that my shortness of breath is due to a lung condition and not to a heart condition?

A complete examination of the heart and lungs, including chest X-rays and electrocardiograms, will tell the difference.

Is it dangerous to take long walks or to indulge in physical exercise when one gets short of breath?

No, but moderation is advisable so that one does not suffer too severely from oxygen starvation.

Is it dangerous to have the chest X-rayed?

No.

Is it safe to take chest X-rays of my child?
Yes, when advised by your pediatrician.

Can I have my chest X-rayed if I am pregnant?
Yes. The radiologist will shield the abdominal area against the X-rays.

What is the meaning of pulmonary therapy?
These are exercises to improve breathing and to increase lung capacity.

Where can I go to get pulmonary therapy?
Most large hospitals have pulmonary therapists.

How helpful is pulmonary therapy for lung conditions?
It helps some, but not others, depending upon the particular lung condition. Exercises alone cannot be expected to effect a cure if there is an underlying chronic lung disease.

Should normal people do breathing exercises?
Yes. It is good practice to inhale as deeply as one can, and to exhale as deeply as one can, for ten minutes each day. It should not be done so quickly as to cause dizziness.

Are operations upon the lungs dangerous?
No more so than an operation upon one of the major organs within the abdominal cavity.

BRONCHITIS

What is bronchitis?
It is an inflammation of the bronchial tubes. It may be bacterial or viral in origin; it may be acute or chronic.

How can one make a diagnosis of bronchitis?
By the symptoms of coughing, wheezing, the production of yellow or green sputum, fever, and by listening to the chest with a stethoscope and hearing abnormal breath sounds (rales and rhonchi).

Will bronchitis show on X-ray examination?
No.

Is chronic bronchitis dangerous?

Yes, as it leads to destruction of lung tissue and eventual impairment of respiratory function. Bronchiectasis and emphysema are both more likely to occur if one has chronic bronchitis.

Is bronchitis contagious?

Yes, if one is exposed to droplets from coughing.

Are there accurate tests to show whether my bronchitis is allergic?

No, but a history of repeated episodes following exposure to an allergen usually indicates that the bronchitis is allergic in origin.

Does climate affect bronchitis?

The condition is more prevalent in cooler, damper climates where upper respiratory infections flourish.

Does the condition of the atmosphere affect bronchitis?

Yes, keep your bedroom air moist. It will lessen coughing.

How helpful are inhalations and vapors to relieve the symptoms of bronchitis?

They help considerably.

Are cough medicines helpful in treating bronchitis?

Yes, but they should not contain sedatives that suppress the ability to expel infected sputum.

Are some cough medicines habit-forming?

They may be, depending upon their content.

Should I go to bed when I have an attack of bronchitis?

Only if you have a fever.

What are the symptoms of an ordinary bronchitis that may have developed into pneumonia?

The appearance of a rusty-colored sputum.

Is pneumonia a frequent complication of bronchitis?

Yes, especially when the bronchitis is neglected.

Will antibiotics help to prevent pneumonia?

Yes, but they should be taken only when prescribed by your doctor.

Is bronchitis more frequent among heavy smokers?
Yes.

Should I stop smoking if I get frequent attacks of bronchitis?
Yes.

INFLUENZA AND PNEUMONIA

How can you diagnose influenza?
By the symptoms, the physical findings, and a characteristic low white blood cell count. In addition to an upper respiratory infection, people with influenza usually have a rasping cough, roughened breath sounds, moderate temperature, and severe malaise and aches and pains throughout their muscles and joints. Chest X-ray findings are usually normal in influenza.

Do antibiotics help influenza?
No, but they may act prophylactically so that pneumonia does not ensue.

What is the nature of influenza?
There are many different kinds of influenza, each caused by a particular germ distinguished one from the other by very complicated blood tests. Since most cases occur during epidemics, bacteriologic studies are conducted by various health agencies in Washington and elsewhere to determine what type is prevalent. Vaccines have been developed for a number of types of influenza.

Should I take influenza vaccine?
Yes.

How effective are the various influenza vaccines?
It is estimated that most are effective in only about two out of three cases. At best, the immunity lasts only a few months.

Is influenza contagious?
Yes, exceptionally so.

Is there any way for me to avoid influenza?

Stay away from crowds; take particular care to stay clear of anyone with an upper respiratory infection; avoid exposure to cold, wet and damp, avoid fatigue; take the vaccine.

How long must one stay in bed with influenza?

Until the temperature is normal for forty-eight hours.

What are the aftereffects of influenza?

One may feel washed out and weak for several weeks after an attack. Also, a hacking cough may persist for weeks.

Is pneumonia, in general, as dangerous today as it was years ago?

Not the pneumococcus type, but staphylococcal pneumonia and those caused by viruses or other rare organisms can be just as dangerous as the old-fashioned lobar pneumonia of yesterday.

What is the difference between a virus pneumonia and the usual type of bacterial pneumonia?

The viral pneumonias come on insidiously and seem to last longer than the bacterial types. Diagnosis of virus pneumonia is more difficult because X-rays of the lungs may not be diagnostic, and cultures of sputum often do not show the causative organism.

Should one go to the hospital if he has pneumonia?

Yes, if the temperature is high and symptoms are severe. Old people and those with chronic lung conditions should certainly be hospitalized with pneumonia.

How effective are antibiotics in curing bacterial pneumonia?

They are extremely effective in this type of pneumonia, often causing symptoms to subside within two to three days. An exception is staphylococcal pneumonia.

How effective are antibiotics in treating viral pneumonia?

Their only effectiveness is in preventing a bacterial infection from complicating viral pneumonia.

What are the aftereffects of viral pneumonia?

Much the same as a severe case of influenza.

How long does bacterial pneumonia usually last?
About one to two weeks.

How long does viral pneumonia usually last?
Several weeks.

How long must I stay in bed with pneumonia?
Until the temperature is normal for at least two to three days.

Does permanent lung damage usually follow influenza or pneumonia?
No, but a chronically diseased lung may be further damaged by such an infection.

TUBERCULOSIS

Is tuberculosis as common today as it was years ago?
Not in affluent and middle-class homes. It is just as prevalent among the poor where nutrition and living conditions are bad.

Is tuberculosis contagious?
Yes.

Is there any effective vaccination against tuberculosis?
The BCG vaccine, when given in childhood, is thought by most investigators to be a definite deterrent to tuberculosis.

How can one tell if he has tuberculosis?
A routine chest X-ray is usually sufficient to rule out active tuberculosis.

Is there such a thing as latent tuberculosis?
Yes, it is thought that many people have harbored the tuberculosis germ in their bodies since childhood, even though they have never had active tuberculosis.

How can one tell if he has ever harbored the tuberculosis germ?
By having a tuberculin test. A positive test denotes the presence of the germ within the body.

Does one require treatment if he has a positive tuberculin test?

Only if there is evidence of a possible active infection, or only if one has been exposed to someone with active tuberculosis.

What can a family do to protect itself against the tubercular infection of one of its members?

They should stay completely isolated from that individual until his disease has been controlled to a point where it is no longer contagious.

How accurate is sputum examination in determining pulmonary tuberculosis?

Repeated sputum examinations sooner or later will show the tubercle bacillus if there is an active lung infection.

Do I have to go to bed for a long period of time if I have tuberculosis?

No, only until your temperature remains steadily normal. This, of course, assumes that you will be receiving adequate treatment with one or more of the antituberculosis medications and that the diseased area in the lung is subsiding, not spreading.

How effective are the various antituberculosis drugs?

They are extremely effective. Tuberculosis specialists use them in various combinations, depending upon the site and extent of the tuberculous lesion.

Is most tuberculosis curable?

One uses the word "controllable" rather than curable. Most tuberculosis can be controlled and arrested.

Is there a tendency for tuberculosis to recur?

Yes.

What can one do to prevent a recurrence of tuberculosis?

Maintain a high level of general health and see your doctor frequently for check-ups.

EMPHYSEMA

What is emphysema?

A condition in which the air spaces in the lungs are enlarged, thus reducing lung capacity. It makes breathing more difficult and is conducive to recurrent lung infections.

What causes emphysema?

Repeated bronchial infections and repeated lung irritations are thought to be prime causes. Emphysema is extremely common among heavy cigarette smokers and among those who suffer from chronic bronchitis.

What can I do to prevent emphysema?
1. Don't smoke.
2. Avoid air pollutants.
3. Avoid respiratory infections.
4. Receive prompt and vigorous treatment for the respiratory infections you do contract.

Does chronic bronchitis predispose toward emphysema?
Yes.

Is emphysema contagious?
No.

Will chest X-rays tell whether or not I have emphysema?
Yes. The extent of involvement can be ascertained by pulmonary function tests.

If I stop smoking, will my emphysema improve?
Yes.

What is the treatment for emphysema?

There is no specific drug for the condition. However, someone with emphysema should be placed on antibiotics whenever he develops the most minor respiratory infection. Pulmonary exercises are sometimes helpful in treating this disease.

BRONCHIECTASIS

What is bronchiectasis?

Abnormal dilatation and destruction of the small bronchial tubes, often associated with chronic inflammation and infection within the lungs. Bronchiectasis is often patchy and limited to one lobe of the lung.

What causes bronchiectasis?

Repeated attacks of bronchitis and repeated irritation, as from cigarette smoking. However, some people have bronchiectasis the origin of which is unknown.

How is bronchiectasis determined?

By examining the bronchial tubes with a bronchoscope and by taking special X-rays after instilling a radiopaque substance into the bronchial tubes. This is known as a bronchogram.

How painful is bronchoscopy?

It is uncomfortable but not truly painful.

Is bronchiectasis often complicated by attacks of pneumonia?

Yes, because secretions stagnate in the small bronchial tubes, thus blocking air spaces.

What is the treatment for bronchiectasis?
1. Avoidance of respiratory infections.
2. Stop smoking.
3. Postural drainage exercises to get rid of stagnant mucus.
4. Surgery in certain cases.

Is the diseased portion of the lung ever removed in bronchiectasis?

Yes, in advanced cases.

How successful is surgery for bronchiectasis?

It is very successful in advanced cases if the disease is limited to one or two lobes of the lung and those lobes are removed.

PULMONARY EMBOLUS

What is pulmonary embolus?

It is the blockage of an artery to the lung by a piece of clotted blood that has traveled to the lung through the circulatory system from some other part of the body.

From what source does a pulmonary embolus usually come?

1. From a vein involved in phlebitis with clotted blood within its passageway. These veins are most often located in the leg or pelvic region.

2. An embolus can also arise from a piece of clotted blood lodged on a heart valve on the right side of the heart.

Is a pulmonary embolus dangerous?
Yes, if it obstructs one of the major arteries to the lungs.

Will an X-ray usually show the presence of a pulmonary embolus?
Yes.

What are the symptoms of pulmonary embolus?
1. Sudden chest pain.
2. Coughing up of blood.
3. Signs of shock.
4. In extreme cases, sudden death.

What is the treatment for pulmonary embolus?
1. If the patient is in shock, he must be treated promptly and vigorously.
2. Anticoagulant medications are given to keep the blood fluid and prevent extension of the embolus.
3. If the embolus has arisen from the pelvis or lower extremities, a filter is placed across the inferior vena cava to prevent further embolization.
4. In rare instances, chest surgery is done to remove the clot from the pulmonary artery.

How long must the anticoagulant medications be continued in treating pulmonary embolus?
For two to three weeks after the original embolization.

What are the chances of a second pulmonary embolism?
If the source of the embolus is still present, a second embolus may occur. This is the reason for blocking the vena cava so that another embolus is prevented from reaching the lungs.

How long does it usually take to recover from a pulmonary embolus?
Several weeks.

How can one ward against a pulmonary embolus after surgery?

By getting out of bed and walking as soon as possible after surgery. This activity lessens the possibility of stagnation of blood in the legs and pelvis, which is one of the prime causes of pulmonary embolus.

LUNG CANCER

Is lung cancer a common condition?
Yes, and it has been on the increase during the past twenty-five years.

Does cigarette smoking increase the chances of developing lung cancer?
Cancer of the lung is at least ten times more common among cigarette smokers than among nonsmokers.

How is it that cigarette smoking predisposes to lung cancer but pipe and cigar smoking do not?
One does not inhale the smoke from a cigar or pipe.

Can I develop cancer of the lungs from polluted air?
Not from polluted air alone, but curiously, the incidence of lung cancer is substantially greater among city dwellers than among those who live in rural areas where the air is less polluted.

If I stop smoking will I lessen my chances of developing lung cancer even though I have been smoking for many years?
Yes!

Is a negative chest X-ray sufficient to rule out the presence of cancer?
No. A tiny cancer may not show on X-ray.

How accurate are sputum tests in telling whether or not I have cancer of the lung?
A negative sputum cytology doesn't rule out lung cancer, but the presence of suspicious cells may indicate the presence of lung cancer some time before it can be seen on X-ray.

Can a diagnosis of lung cancer be made by bronchoscopy?
Yes, in most cases.

How is bronchoscopy performed?

By passing a metal tube through the mouth and throat into the trachea.

Is a biopsy usually taken through the bronchoscope?

Yes. A positive result is a positive indication of the presence of cancer.

Can cancer of the lung be cured by surgery?

Yes, in many cases, if it is caught early enough.

Is the entire lung always removed for cancer, or is only a portion of the lung removed?

Usually, the involved lobe of the lung is removed. If more than one lobe is involved, then the entire lung is taken out.

How serious an operation is lung removal?

It is very serious, but recovery from the surgery takes place in well over 90 percent of cases.

QUESTIONS TO ASK YOUR DOCTOR

Why is it that I am subject to repeated lung infections?

How often should my lungs be X-rayed?

Would I be helped if I moved to another climate?

Is it safe for me to travel to high altitudes even though I have impaired lung functions?

How high an altitude is safe for me?

Is it safe for me to travel in a plane?

Why do I get frequent attacks of bronchitis?

Should I go away to a sanitorium for my tuberculosis?

Is my tuberculosis controllable?

Will emphysema shorten my span of life?

How soon after a lung, or portion of a lung, is removed can

I:
   get out of bed?
   leave the hospital?
   walk up and down stairs?
   go outdoors?
   bathe or shower?
   resume household duties?
   drive my car?
   resume marital relations?
   return to work?
   resume physical activities?

14. THE BREASTS

Is it natural for one breast to be slightly larger than another?
   Yes.

Is it harmful to go without a brassiere?
   No.

Are brassieres with metal supports harmful to the breasts?
   No.

Is there a tendency for breasts to get smaller as one advances in age?
   Not necessarily. Much will depend on overall body weight.

Can small breasts be made larger?
   No, but plastic inserts can be placed beneath the breasts, giving them the appearance of being larger.

How successful are operations to make the breasts appear larger?
   Results are usually excellent.

Can breasts be made smaller?
   Yes, through plastic surgery.

How successful are plastic operations that make the breasts smaller?
   Results are usually excellent.

If a first operation for plastic repair of the breasts is not successful, can it be done over again?
  Yes.

Will the scars following a breast plastic operation be visible?
  Unclothed, scars can be noted.

Will I be able to wear an evening gown or a bathing suit following a plastic operation upon my breasts without the scars showing?
  Yes.

Will I have to wear a special support after a plastic operation upon my breasts?
  No.

Are most plastic operations carried out upon both breasts simultaneously?
  Yes, except when operating for dissimilar-sized breasts.

How long a stay in the hospital will be necessary after a plastic operation on the breasts?
  Four to six days.

Is it possible for me to nurse a child after a plastic operation upon my breasts?
  It is inadvisable to do so if the milk ducts have been cut across during the performance of the operation.

Are there any exercises I can do to prevent my breasts from sagging?
  No.

What can I do to retain the youthful contour of my breasts?
  1. Maintain a normal weight.
  2. Wear a good supporting brassiere.

Will pregnancy alter the shape of my breasts?
  It will tend to make them larger during the pregnancy. After childbirth, they will return to their normal size, but they may sag a bit.

Will nursing permanently alter the shape of my breasts?
  In some women it does; in others nursing has no effect

upon breast shape. The more children a woman nurses, the more the breasts will tend to sag and become flatter.

Does nursing predispose one to the development of breast tumor or cancer?

No. On the contrary, many investigators think that nursing decreases the chances of developing breast cancer.

Can I stop nursing my child whenever I want to?

Yes. Without the stimulation of nursing, the secretion of milk will cease in a few days. Medication prescribed by your doctor will hasten the process.

Can a blow or injury to my breast cause cancer?

No.

Is it natural to have tender, enlarged breasts prior to a menstrual period?

Yes, this occurs in many women.

What can be done to stop the pain and enlargement of my breasts prior to a menstrual period?

Hormones and dehydrating medications are sometimes helpful, but most physicians do not advise their use. One should make an effort to withstand the premenstrual discomfort without resorting to hormones or other medications.

Is it safe for me to have the hair removed from around my nipples?

Yes.

Will any harm come to my breasts from manipulation or suckling during intercourse?

No.

How often should I have my breasts examined?

At least once a year if you are under thirty-five years of age; twice a year if you are older.

Is breast self-examination sufficient to rule out the presence of a tumor or cancer?

No, but it is very important in detecting the possibility of such growths, which should be reported at once to your doctor.

Are most lumps in the breast cancerous?
No. Most are benign.

Can you tell whether a lump is cancerous before you operate upon it?
In many cases, yes. However, a microscopic examination of the tissue removed at surgery is much more accurate.

Should all lumps within the breast be operated upon or removed?
Yes, except when the breasts are involved in a process associated with hundreds of small lumps, as in some cases of cystic disease of the breasts.

Can the scars ever be hidden by making an incision around the nipple rather than on the breast when you remove a simple breast tumor or cyst?
Yes, in many, but not all, cases.

How unsightly are the scars from the removal of a simple, benign breast tumor or cyst?
Usually they fade into a barely discernible thin line.

What is the significance of a discharge from the nipple?
If it is bloody, green, or brownish, it often indicates the presence of a small warty growth (papilloma) within one of the breast's ducts. This is an indication for surgical removal of the growth.

Is a bloody discharge from the nipple a very serious thing?
No, but it is an indication for surgery.

How soon after a minor breast operation will I be able to get out of bed?
The day of, or the day after surgery.

Can a cancer of the breast be detected before a lump appears?
In a very small percentage of cases, a mammogram X-ray will reveal a tumor when it is so small that the examining physician is unable to detect it.

If a breast X-ray is negative, does this mean that cancer is not present?
Not necessarily. The ultimate proof is the examination

of the removed tissue under the microscope. In about 15 percent of cases, cancer can be present despite a negative mammogram.

Is it possible to tell while removing the tissue whether the lump in my breast is cancerous?

Yes, in most instances the diagnosis will be apparent, but the final diagnosis will rest upon the microscopic examination of the lump that has been removed.

How accurate is a frozen-section examination carried out during surgery?

Almost 100 percent.

What are the chances for a complete cure if I have cancer of the breast?

Over 80 percent, if the cancer is limited to the breast only, and about half as much if the cancer has spread beyond the breast.

How soon after a breast removal will I be able to get out of bed?

The day following surgery.

Will I be able to return to normal living even though I have had a breast removed?

Yes.

Will the removal of a breast interfere with my future sex life?

No.

Should I become pregnant if I have had my breast removed for a malignant condition?

No.

Is breast cancer inherited?

No. However, the tendency toward the development of malignancy frequently runs in families.

Are the chances of a cure lessened by doing a simple mastectomy rather than a radical mastectomy?

The overall statistics, including tens of thousands of cases, indicate that the chances for cure are greater when a radical mastectomy is done for breast cancer.

If my breast is removed, will I develop swelling in my arm?

Some patients do, others don't. There is no way to predict beforehand whether swelling will occur.

Will the swelling of my arm interfere with its function?

No.

Is there any way to reduce the swelling in the arm following breast removal?

Exercises, arm elevation, and elastic bandages may be helpful in reducing swelling, but no treatment can guarantee good results. Some patients will have permanent swelling of the arm.

Will the fact that I have had my breast removed show when I wear a bathing suit or evening gown?

Not in most instances. Of course, if one wears a very skimpy outfit, a small portion of the scar may be visible.

How good are the prosthetic brassieres in hiding the fact that my breast has been removed?

Excellent.

How soon after breast removal can I get a special brassiere?

Within a few weeks.

Is X-ray or cobalt treatment given following breast removal for cancer?

Not if the tumor was limited to the breast; if the malignancy has spread to the glands in the armpit, cobalt or X-ray therapy is given.

When is chemotherapy or hormone therapy given to a patient who has had breast cancer?

When the tumor shows evidence of having spread beyond the breast.

QUESTIONS TO ASK YOUR DOCTOR

How soon after the removal of a localized lump will I be able to:

take a bath or shower?
go out of doors?
return to household duties?

resume marital relations?
return to work?
drive a car?
resume all physical activities?

How soon after breast removal will I be able to:
take a bath or shower?
go out of doors?
return to household duties?
resume marital relations?
return to work?
drive a car?
resume all physical activities?

Will I be permitted to become pregnant after the removal of the lump in my breast?

How often will you want to see me following removal of my breast?

Will you give me X-ray or cobalt treatments after removal of the breast?

Will the operation disfigure my breast?

If a cancer is found, will you tell me?

If a cancer is found, will you remove the breast?

Do you believe in a radical removal of the breast for cancer or do you do just a simple mastectomy?

What are my chances of a permanent cure if a radical breast removal is carried out?

What are the chances of cure if only a simple breast removal is done for my cancer?

15. THE STOMACH AND INTESTINES

Do certain combinations of foods, each one harmless on its own, form poisons when eaten at the same time?
No.

What is meant by "nervous stomach"?
One that is hyperactive, with exceptionally strong contractions and spasms of the muscles at its outlet. It may also produce excess acid.

Is there any way for me to minimize indigestion?
Yes. Eat slowly, avoid greasy and highly seasoned foods, do not drink too much alcohol, and consult your doctor to make sure you do not have a stomach or gallbladder disorder.

Is gas due to swallowing of air while eating?
A major portion of it does come from air-swallowing.

How can I avoid swallowing air while eating?
Eat slowly, chew thoroughly, and refrain from talking while you eat.

What are the causes of belching and heartburn?
Eating too fast, overeating, or eating certain foods that tend to create gas. Greasy or spicy foods can also cause indigestion.

If one eats an improper diet, can it cause an ulcer?
It may, but there are other important factors, too.

Is it all right to eat a large meal before going to bed at night?
It is best not to eat large quantities of food before retiring as it is more difficult to digest food when one has a full stomach and is lying down.

Can indigestion be caused by an allergy?

Yes, but it is an infrequent cause.

Is it true that certain people have "stronger stomachs" than others?

Yes, if by that, one means that certain people tolerate dietary indiscretions better than others.

Should I make myself vomit when I feel uncomfortable and my stomach feels upset?

Yes, if it can be accomplished without undue strain.

How can I distinguish between an upset stomach and a more serious condition such as appendicitis?

The symptoms of an upset stomach tend to subside spontaneously, whereas the symptoms of appendicitis tend to be continuous and progressive.

Is it safe for me to take a laxative when I have a stomachache?

Absolutely not. In the case of appendicitis or some other serious intestinal condition, it may make the condition worse.

When should I call a doctor for a stomachache?

Whenever it continues for more than an hour.

Is it bad to drink fluids at the same time that one eats solids?

No. On the contrary, one should drink fluids when eating solids.

Does hot weather have any effect on digestion?

Yes, it tends to make digestion more difficult. Moreover one should eat more lightly when it is hot.

Is it dangerous to eat a heavy meal before I go swimming?

No, but it is wiser to wait a half hour or so before going in the water.

Do tranquillizing drugs tend to improve digestion?

Only in the case of a hyperactive stomach which is affected inordinately by emotional stress.

Are there certain foods one should avoid when drinking alcohol?

No, but one should avoid drinking alcohol to excess, as it may lead to marked stomach malfunction and upset.

If I have an ulcer, is it safe for me to drink alcohol?

No, as it will cause greater acid secretion and aggravation of ulcer symptoms.

Is it harmful for me to take iced drinks when I am overheated?

No.

Does excess stomach acid ever cause symptoms?

Yes. Heartburn, belching, nausea, and upper abdominal pain may accompany hypersecretion of acid.

Does too little stomach acid ever produce symptoms?

In the occasional case, indigestion results from too little acid.

Does excess stomach acid mean that I will develop an ulcer?

Not necessarily. Many people secrete excess acid but never develop ulcers or other stomach disorders.

How can I overcome excess acid by diet?

Avoid spicy or very sour foods; avoid greasy, rich foods; avoid excess alcohol. Eat slowly; avoid unnecessary excitement and stress.

Is it safe to take the antacid medications that are commercially advertised?

Yes.

Is ptomaine poisoning another name for "upset stomach"?

Yes, but both are lay rather than medical terms. Most ptomaine poisoning is caused by bacterial infection of ingested foods.

What are the symptoms of an ulcer?
* Gnawing pain, or sharp pain, in the upper abdomen.
* Relief of pain on eating.
* Heartburn, with occasional nausea and vomiting.
* Aggravation of pain on eating sharp, spicy foods.
* Occasional vomiting of blood or black stools due to bleeding from the ulcer.

Are X-rays accurate in diagnosing in the presence of an ulcer?
Yes.

Where are most ulcers located?
About 90 percent are in the duodenum, the portion of small intestine immediately beyond the outlet of the stomach; the rest are in the stomach itself.

Does emotional upset affect an ulcer?
Yes, it seems to worsen the symptoms.

Do most ulcers get well by themselves?
Yes, if proper diet and medications are taken.

When is it necessary to operate for an ulcer?
1. When the ulcer ruptures.
2. When uncontrollable bleeding from the ulcer takes place.
3. When symptoms continue to be severe even though one has followed a strict medical regime.
4. When the ulcer obstructs the free passage of food.
5. When there is a threat that malignant changes may be taking place within the ulcer.

How can I tell if my ulcer is bleeding?
Vomiting of blood may occur, or there may be passage of jet-black stool.

Do ulcers ever lead to cancer of the stomach?
Occasionally. A stomach ulcer should be X-rayed periodically to note any suspicious changes.

How can one distinguish between an ulcer of the stomach and a cancer?
By X-rays; by direct view of the inside of the stomach through a gastroscope; by examination of the stomach at surgery.

Is gastroscopy a dangerous procedure?
No.

Is gastroscopy painful?
It causes discomfort but little pain.

If my ulcer heals through medical management, is there a tendency for it to recur?

Yes, if one abandons good eating habits, works too hard, or is subject to prolonged stress.

Are operations for ulcer dangerous?

No, but they are serious. Mortality rates are extremely low from this type of surgery.

How effective are operations for ulcer?

They are curative in well over 90 percent of patients.

Will I eventually be able to eat a full diet even though I have part of my stomach removed?

Yes.

Will the removal of a portion of my stomach for ulcer affect my span of life?

No.

Is there a tendency to become anemic after an ulcer operation?

Yes, if a large portion of the stomach has been removed.

What can I do to overcome the anemia following an ulcer operation?

It may be necessary to take supplementary iron and vitamins.

Do ulcers tend to recur after an operation?

This happens in less than 3 percent of cases.

How often should I return for a check-up after an ulcer operation?

Every three to four months.

Where is my food digested after a portion of my stomach has been removed?

Where it always is, in the small intestine. (Relatively little food is ever digested in the stomach.)

What operation is carried out for removal of a tumor of the stomach?

Partial or total removal of the stomach (gastrectomy).

Food then passes from the remnant of the stomach, or from the esophagus, directly into the small intestine.

How often should I undergo X-rays of my stomach and intestinal tract?

If you have no symptoms and are over forty-five years of age, you should undergo such X-rays every other year. Of course, whenever you have symptoms, you should be X-rayed.

QUESTIONS TO ASK YOUR DOCTOR

Why do I have heartburn?

Why do I belch so much?

Are there any medicines that can reduce the amount of gas I have?

Does having heartburn mean that I have excess acid in my stomach?

Does having heartburn indicate that I have a hiatus hernia?

What causes my indigestion?

What is the treatment for my indigestion?

What causes my excess stomach acidity?

Will my ulcer get well if I follow a bland diet and take antacid medications?

What operation do I need to cure my ulcer?

Will I need special nurses after an operation for ulcer?

How long will I be in the hospital for my ulcer operation?

How soon after an ulcer operation will I:
    get out of bed?
    go outdoors?
    eat solid foods?
    resume my household duties?
    resume marital relations?

drive my car?
return to work?
resume all physical activities?

Do I have a stomach ulcer?

Is my stomach tumor curable?

THE SMALL AND LARGE INTESTINES

Should I consult a doctor if there is a change in my normal bowel habits?
Yes, if the change persists.

How often should I have a rectal examination?
At least once a year as part of your annual physical examination or whenever you have symptoms referrable to your bowels.

What is a sigmoidoscopy?
Sigmoidoscopy is direct examination of the rectum and sigmoid through passage of a hollow, lighted metal tube which permits inspection of the terminal ten inches of the bowel.

Is a sigmoidoscope painful?
No, but it may be uncomfortable.

How often should I have a routine sigmoidoscopy?
Once a year.

What is the significance of rumbling in the abdomen?
It is caused by gas being propelled through the small and large intestines. It is a normal phenomenon.

Why do I pass so much gas from my rectum?
Excess gas is caused by eating large quantities of raw vegetables and fruits, overeating, eating very spicy foods, and drinking to excess.

Is it natural to have a bowel evacuation every day?
Most people do; however, some evacuate more than once daily, and other move their bowels only two to three times a week.

Can it do me harm to skip a day or two in moving my bowels?
No.

Can I safely take laxatives?
Only when prescribed by your doctor.

Are laxatives habit-forming?
Most of them are.

Are commercially advertised laxatives safe and effective?
Some are, others are not.

How is it that a laxative that has once been effective no longer works?
A laxative taken over a prolonged period of time tends to lose its effectiveness.

Is it harmful to take a lubricant such as mineral oil for my constipation?
No, but it should be taken on an empty stomach before retiring at night.

Will the taking of mineral oil regularly cause me to develop a vitamin deficiency?
Not if taken at night, several hours after the evening meal.

Is it harmful to take an enema for constipation?
Not if recommended by your doctor.

Will I develop headache or other symptoms from constipation?
Some people do have headaches when they are constipated.

How important is diet in causing constipation?
It may be very important. Lack of fresh fruits and vegetables and too little roughage may be instrumental in causing constipation.

Can an allergy to certain foods or medicines cause diarrhea?
Yes.

How can I tell if my diarrhea is due to nervousness or to an inflammation of my intestines?
By X-raying the intestinal tract and by having a thorough

rectal examination, including sigmoidoscopy (see page 168), and a study of the stool for the presence of ova, parasites, or dysentery bacteria.

Is it bad practice to drink water and eat raw fruits and vegetables in foreign countries?
Yes.

How important is the food one eats in causing diarrhea?
It may cause diarrhea because of a food allergy, because the food is tainted or infected, or because the food contains parasites.

How can you distinguish between functional diarrhea and that caused by serious disease?
Through sigmoidoscopic examination, stool examination, and X-rays.

Does bloody diarrhea indicate that I have an inflammation in my intestines?
In some cases, it may; in others it may be due to a bowel tumor. In all cases, you should consult your physician.

Do antibiotics ever cause diarrhea?
Yes.

Will examination of the stools show the cause for my diarrhea?
Yes, in many instances.

What is the treatment for diarrhea caused by antibiotics?
Special medications and diet will overcome most cases without difficulty.

Does mucus in the stool mean that one has actual colitis?
Not necessarily. It may be of minor importance due only to an irritable large bowel.

What are hemorrhoids?
They are varicosities of veins draining the anus and rectum.

How are they treated?
If hemorrhoids bleed, become painful, cause constipation,

or protrude markedly from the anus, they should be removed surgically.

How can you distinguish between blood due to hemorrhoids and that due to a tumor of the bowel?
Usually by rectal examination, sigmoidoscopic examination, and X-rays of the large intestines.

Can all tumors of the bowel be seen through a sigmoidoscope?
No, only those that are within the last ten inches of the large intestine.

How can you diagnose a tumor high up in the bowel?
By use of a colonoscope and by special X-ray examinations following a barium enema.

Is a barium enema X-ray painful?
No.

How accurate is a barium enema X-ray in diagnosing a bowel tumor?
It is very accurate.

Are all tumors of the bowel malignant?
No. The great majority are benign polyps.

Can you tell before surgery whether my bowel tumor is malignant?
Yes, in most instances.

Should all polyps of the rectum and bowel be removed?
Not if they are small, do not bleed, are high up in the bowel, and show no tendency to grow or to cause obstruction of the bowel passages.

What is the significance of inability to pass stool or gas from the rectum?
It indicates an obstruction of the bowel.

Does intestinal obstruction require immediate hospitalization?
Yes.

What is a colostomy?
It is an operation in which a portion of large bowel is

brought out onto the abdominal wall. The patient then passes stool through the colostomy opening rather than through the rectum.

Will I be able to live a normal, productive life even though I have a colostomy?
    Yes.

QUESTIONS TO ASK YOUR DOCTOR

How can I reduce the amount of gas I pass?

How can I overcome my constipation?

How often can I safely take an enema?

What causes my diarrhea?

Do I have spastic colitis?

Is it normal for me to have mucus in my stool?

Do I have functional colitis or one that is due to disease?

What is the treatment for my colitis?

Is my colitis curable?

Is there any way for me to prevent onsets of attacks of colitis?

What is the significance of the blood I am passing from my rectum?

Is it necessary to perform a colostomy to cure my bowel tumor?

16. THE GALLBLADDER

What is the function of the gallbladder?
It concentrates and stores bile from the liver. The bile is discharged by the gallbladder into the ducts and into the small intestines where it aids in digesting fats.

What are the symptoms of gallbladder disease?
   * Pain in the right upper part of the abdomen, often radiating to the back.
   * Indigestion after eating fried, fatty, or greasy foods.
   * Indigestion after eating turnips, cabbage, radishes, sprouts, etc.
   * Indigestion after eating certain raw fruits and salads.
   * Nausea, heartburn, flatulence, and constipation.

How can you tell for sure that I have gallbladder disease?
X-rays may show the stones, or the gallbladder may not show up (visualize) at all on X-ray examination. The latter situation indicates that the duct of the gallbladder is blocked, a sure sign of a diseased organ.

Do gallstones always show up on X-rays?
Not if the duct is blocked and the dye (taken the night before) fails to enter the gallbladder.

Is gallbladder disease inherited?
No.

What causes acute gallbladder disease?
The duct of the gallbladder may be obstructed by a stone, thus pressing upon the blood supply of the bladder and resulting in gangrene. In other instances, the bile in the gallbladder stagnates because of the blocked duct, and infection sets in.

Must an inflamed gallbladder be removed even if there are no stones?

Not in most cases. However, some people do suffer severe gallbladder attacks even though they do not have stones.

Is there any medication that will dissolve gallstones?
No, but experiments are proceeding to find such a medication.

Why does jaundice complicate gallbladder disease?
Because it usually indicates that a stone has passed into the common bile duct and is obstructing the passage of bile into the intestinal tract. When operating upon a patient with gallstones and jaundice, the common bile duct must be opened and the stones removed. This is a more serious operation than simple gallbladder removal.

What takes the place of the gallbladder after it has been removed?
Since the gallbladder acts only as a storage area for bile, it is not actually necessary. Thus, its function does not have to be taken over by any other organ.

Do people with untreated gallbladder disease ever develop cancer of the gallbladder?
Yes, in about 1 percent of cases.

Is a gallbladder operation dangerous?
No. It is a major operation, but not dangerous.

Where will the incision be for my gallbladder operation?
In the upper right quadrant of the abdomen.

Is the entire gallbladder removed or just the stones?
In almost all cases, the entire gallbladder is removed. This will prevent new stones from forming.

What kind of anesthesia will I get?
General anesthesia, induced by an intravenous injection.

How long will it take for my wound to heal?
Approximately eleven to fourteen days.

Is it natural for me to have pains in my wound area for several weeks or months after gallbladder removal?
Yes.

Will removal of my gallbladder shorten my life expectancy?

No. One does not need a gallbladder. When it is removed, biliary function returns to normal within a few weeks' time.

Can I become pregnant even though my gallbladder has been removed?

Yes.

Do stones ever form again once the gallbladder has been taken out?

Not in the gallbladder, but in a small percentage of cases, stones may form in the common bile duct. Such an eventuality may require re-operation.

Can one return to an unrestricted diet after the gallbladder has been removed?

Not immediately afterward. One should stay on a low fat diet for several weeks or months after the operation until biliary function returns to normal.

Do people ever have gallbladder symptoms after undergoing gallbladder removal?

Yes, in a small number of patients. Eventually, the symptoms disappear unless gallstones were inadvertently left behind at operation.

Can I live a completely normal life without a gallbladder?

Yes.

Is there a tendency to put on weight after gallbladder removal?

Yes, once one has returned to a normal diet. The absence of indigestion and pain after eating often creates an excessively lusty appetite.

QUESTIONS TO ASK YOUR DOCTOR

Why must my gallbladder be operated upon?

What can happen if I do not have my gallbladder and gallstones removed?

Will my scar show if I have a bare midriff?

How soon after removal of my gallbladder can I:
    get out of bed?
    leave the hospital?
    walk up and down stairs?
    bathe or shower?
    go outdoors?
    resume marital relations?
    perform household duties?
    drive a car?
    resume all physical activities?
    eat anything I want?
    have a drink?

17. THE LIVER

What are the main functions of the liver?
    1. The storage of sugar and regulation of the amount of sugar circulating in the blood.
    2. The production and storage of protein, and control of the by-products of protein metabolism.
    3. The storage and utilization of fats.
    4. The production of bile and bile salts which are excreted into the intestinal tract and aid in digestion.
    5. The manufacture of substances important to blood coagulation.
    6. The production and storage of substances important to the making of red blood cells and other components of blood.
    7. The neutralization of toxic and harmful substances in the body.

What causes impaired function of the liver?
    1. Liver infection, either by viruses or bacteria.
    2. Infestation of the liver with parasites.
    3. Poisoning of the liver by toxic substances, including harmful drugs.
    4. Invasion of the liver by cancer.
    5. Obstruction to the outflow of bile.
    6. Damage to the liver secondary to alcoholism.
    7. Prolonged, severe malnutrition.
    8. Impairment of the blood supply to the liver.

9. Cirrhosis (see page 178).
10. Severe upset in liver chemistry.

Can most livers continue to function sufficiently to maintain life even though they are badly damaged?

Yes, one requires only a portion of the normal liver to survive.

How is liver disease diagnosed?

1. Through tests of liver function, performed through chemical tests upon the blood.

2. By carefully noting the patient's symptoms.

3. By examination of the liver to see if it is enlarged.

4. By taking a liver scan after ingestion of a radioactive isotope.

5. By performing a liver biopsy (inserting a needle through the side of the lower chest into the liver and withdrawing a small sample of liver cells through the needle).

6. By various tests upon the urine and stool.

What is a liver scan?

It is a photographic recording of radiation from an isotope tracer. The record, on paper, will reveal either the normal outline of the liver or some abnormality.

Are liver scans very accurate?

Yes, if the disease is localized to one or more sizable portions of the liver.

Is jaundice always associated with liver disease?

No. It may be due to a blood disease with excessive destruction of red blood cells.

Can a diseased gallbladder lead to liver disease?

Yes, inflammation of the gallbladder sometimes spreads through lymph channels to the liver.

Can heart disease affect the liver?

Yes. If the heart functions inadequately, the liver may become congested and enlarged.

Does infectious mononucleosis ever cause liver damage?

Yes, almost always. Fortunately, the liver usually recovers fully from such involvement.

Do parasites cause liver damage?

Yes. Amebic dysentry, schistosomiasis, and other infestations can cause considerable liver damage, as can invasion by an echinococcus parasite.

How is a parasitic infection of the liver diagnosed?

Blood tests, X-rays, liver scans, and liver biopsies can usually pinpoint the diagnosis.

What is a fatty liver?

One in which liver tissues are replaced by fat cells. Such livers often function poorly.

What is the treatment for fatty liver?

Remove the cause. Thus, if the fatty liver is secondary to alcoholism, one must stop drinking; if it is due to taking harmful, toxic drugs, these must be discontinued.

Can a liver recover from fatty infiltrations?

Yes, unless the damage is great and has been going on for many years.

Does injury to the liver occur frequently?

Yes. The liver is the largest organ in the body and is often injured during an accident. Its capsule is thin and a tear of liver substance may be followed by severe hemorrhage into the abdominal cavity. In many such cases it is necessary to operate and to suture the torn portion of liver.

Can people recover from severe liver injury?

Yes, but they are usually very sick. Extensive liver injury may be fatal.

CIRRHOSIS

What is cirrhosis of the liver?

Cirrhosis is a general term meant to signify chronic generalized destruction and scarring of liver tissue, with impairment of liver function to a slight or greater degree.

What are the symptoms of cirrhosis of the liver?

* Enlargement of the liver eventually associated with liver destruction and a collection of fluid (ascites) in the abdominal cavity.

* Loss of appetite, weight loss, anemia, and weakness.
* Jaundice as the disease progresses, with eventual collapse of liver function and possible coma.

Are all cases of cirrhosis associated with alcoholism?
No.

Will moderate drinking cause cirrhosis?
No.

Is cirrhosis usually fatal?
No. Mild or moderate cases do not usually shorten the life span.

What is the treatment for cirrhosis?
1. All toxic influences, such as infection, destruction to the outflow of bile, poisons, alcohol, etc., must be withdrawn.
2. The patient must maintain a good diet and nutritional state, including the intake of adequate amounts of vitamins, minerals, proteins, and carbohydrates.
3. If blood flow through the liver is markedly impaired due to the cirrhosis, it may be necessary to perform a shunting operation. This procedure, a portacaval shunt, allows blood to bypass the obstructed cirrhotic liver.

Can the damage to the liver through cirrhosis be repaired by treatment?
Usually not, although the damage in some cases can be arrested.

Do people with cirrhosis have a tendency to bleed from varicose veins of the esophagus?
Yes.

Can the hemorrhage associated with cirrhosis ever be overcome?
Sometimes by a portacaval shunt operation. This operation connects the portal vein with the vena cava, thus shunting the blood away from the obstructed liver.

Do people with cirrhosis have a tendency to become bloated in the abdomen?
Yes. This is known as ascites, a condition in which fluids

form in the abdominal cavity. It can frequently be controlled by administration of diuretic medications.

TUMORS

Is the liver often invaded by cancer that has spread from some other organ of the body?

Yes, because of the liver's rich blood supply, cancer cells often come to and lodge in liver substance.

Does the liver ever have primary cancer?

Yes, but it is a rather rare disease.

Can tumors of the liver ever be cured through surgery?

Only if they are localized to one or two areas of the liver. Unfortunately, most malignancy of the liver involves too widespread an area to permit surgical removal.

Are there any chemicals that can help to control cancer of the liver?

Some of the anticancer drugs, such as 5 FU, may help to contain the growth of cancer cells in the liver. Unfortunately, permanent cure through these medications cannot be obtained.

Can an entire liver be replaced by a liver graft?

Yes. This has been done in a few dozen cases, but eventually, within a few weeks or months, the rejection phenomenon sets in.

INFECTIONS

Do abscesses ever form in the liver?

Yes. Bacteria can reach the liver through both its arterial and venous blood supply.

What is the treatment for a liver abscess?

Intensive antibiotic therapy, and, in some cases where there is a large, localized abscess, surgical drainage.

HEPATITIS

What is infectious hepatitis?

A viral disease, often occurring in epidemic form.

What is serum hepatitis?
A liver infection caused by the transmission of a virus through blood transfusions.

What is toxic hepatitis?
Liver infection secondary to a drug or harmful substance that an individual has taken.

Is the virus that causes infectious hepatitis the same one that causes serum hepatitis?
No. They are thought to be two distinctly separate viruses.

Is infectious hepatitis contagious?
Yes, but only mildly so.

How long must I wait to be sure I haven't contracted infectious hepatitis?
The incubation period varies from a few days to a few weeks, according to the particular virus that has caused the infection.

What are the symptoms of infectious hepatitis?
1. A feeling of malaise and fatigue.
2. Loss of appetite, nausea, and possibly some vomiting and diarrhea.
3. Mild to moderate fever.
4. Tenderness in the right upper portion of the abdomen.
5. Jaundice, usually coming on five to six days after the initial symptoms.
6. Dark colored urine.
7. Light or clay-colored stools.

Does infectious mononucleosis ever cause hepatitis?
Yes. The virus causing the swelling of the glands, etc., as seen in mononucleosis, also affects the liver.

Does receiving a blood transfusion predispose one to hepatitis?
Yes. To date, there is no way to be positive that blood received through transfusion is free of the virus of hepatitis.

Is one always jaundiced when he has hepatitis?
No.

How reliable are blood, urine, and stool tests in diagnosing hepatitis?

Very reliable. Characteristic findings make the diagnosis obvious in most cases.

What can I do to prevent getting hepatitis, once I have been exposed to a case?

Take injections of gamma globulin.

Should my family get injections of gamma globulin because I have been exposed to someone with hepatitis?

No.

Will gamma globulin prevent hepatitis?

It is thought to be somewhat effective, but its exact role in preventing the disease has not been determined. At best, hepatitis is not very contagious if contact with the patient has been transient. It is most contagious to those who live and sleep with someone who has contracted the infection.

Must I stay in bed with hepatitis?

Yes. Bed rest is essential until the blood chemical examinations return to normal or near-normal.

Do most people recover from hepatitis?

Yes, but it may take several weeks to months until recovery is complete.

Is hepatitis usually associated with permanent liver damage?

No, but it does occur in exceptionally severe cases.

Are there any specific medications to overcome hepatitis?

No.

What is the treatment for hepatitis?

1. Bed rest.
2. Adequate intake of fluids.
3. A high protein, high carbohydrate, low fat diet.
4. Adequate intake of vitamins and minerals.
5. Abstinence from alcohol, or any medications that might be toxic to the liver.

QUESTIONS TO ASK YOUR DOCTOR

Why is my liver functioning improperly?

Is my liver condition contagious?

Is my liver condition curable?

Is my jaundice due primarily to liver disease?

What causes my enlarged liver?

Has my cirrhosis been caused by excessive alcohol?

Can I drink once in a while even though I have cirrhosis?

How severe is my cirrhosis?

Do I need surgery for my cirrhosis?

Do I have ascites?

How soon after contracting hepatitis can I:
   get out of bed?
   shower or shave?
   have visitors?
   eat fatty or fried foods?
   leave the hospital?
   drink alcohol?
   return to work?
   resume all physical activities?
   consider myself wholly recovered?

18. THE KIDNEYS
AND BLADDER

(See also Prostate Gland.)

What is the significance of frequent urination?
   It may be due to a urinary infection, or it may signify
the development of prostate trouble.

Does frequent urination mean that I have a bladder or kidney infection?

It means that these infections must be ruled out as causes.

What is the significance of blood in the urine?

1. It may signify an inflammation of the bladder or urethra.
2. It can be caused by kidney or bladder trouble.
3. It may be due to a tumor in the urinary tract.
4. It can occur if one is taking anticoagulant drugs.

What should one do about the appearance of blood in the urine?

Seek medical attention at once.

Do all kidney stones show up on X-ray?

No. Some are nonopaque and will not show on X-ray examination.

Do all kidney stones cause pain?

Not always. Those that cause the greatest pain are the ones that move from the kidney down the ureter leading to the bladder.

Is there any way to prevent an attack of kidney colic due to stones?

1. Drink large quantities of liquids.
2. Maintain an adequate intake of vitamins.
3. If you have gout, take antigout medications.

These measures may help to prevent an attack, but they are not always preventive.

How will I know when I have passed a stone?

You will feel a sudden pain as you urinate, and you may see a small stone in the toilet bowl. The urine should be strained through gauze to determine whether any small stones have been passed.

How can you tell the difference between kidney stones and gravel?

Gravel often does not appear on X-ray examination; stones frequently do. Also, if you strain your urine, you will see the difference between a stone and gravel.

If I have gotten over an attack of kidney stones, is it likely that I will suffer another attack?

Kidney colic often does recur, as stones tend to be multiple rather than single.

What can I do to prevent attacks of kidney stones?
1. Drink large quantities of fluids in order to keep the urine dilute.
2. If you have a high blood uric acid, you should take medication for it. This will tend to decrease the incidence of uric acid stones.
3. Special diets and vitamins will be recommended by your doctor for other types of stones.

If I take medications against gout and lower my uric acid, will this decrease my chances of getting another kidney stone?
Yes, usually.

Can kidney stones be dissolved?
No, although there have been many experiments and a considerable number of medications given in an attempt to produce dissolution of stones.

Must all kidney stones be removed surgically?
No. About three out of four will pass out spontaneously in the urine within a few days to a few weeks time.

How serious is an operation to remove kidney stones?
It is serious but not dangerous if the general health is adequate.

How can one tell whether he has a kidney tumor?
1. By intravenous pyelographic X-rays.
2. By cystoscopy and retrograde pyelogram X-rays.
3. By renal arteriograms (X-rays showing the blood supply to the kidneys).
4. By surgical exploration of the kidneys.

Are intravenous pyelography X-rays accurate in diagnosing kidney tumors?
In most instances, yes.

Does the kidney always have to be removed for a kidney tumor?
Yes.

Can one lead a normal life after one kidney has been removed?
   Yes, if the other kidney is normal.

Is the removal of a kidney a serious operation?
   Yes, but not dangerous.

Can tuberculosis of the kidney be cured?
   Yes, by intensive treatment with the many effective anti-tuberculosis medications.

How long must the treatment continue for tuberculosis of the kidney?
   Approximately one to two years.

Is it often necessary to remove a kidney because of tuberculosis?
   Not any more, although this was the standard form of treatment a few decades ago.

How do you test kidney function?
   1. Urinalysis.
   2. Blood chemistry, including urea, creatinine, and uric acid determinations.
   3. An intravenous pyelogram X-ray examination.
   4. A cystoscopic examination with X-rays of the entire urinary tract.

If kidney function is impaired, can it be improved by treatment?
   In many instances, it can be helped greatly.

How are most kidney and bladder infections controlled?
   By antibiotics.

How often should I have my urine tested?
   If you have chronic kidney or bladder disease, it should be tested at least once a month. With diabetes, it should be tested daily.

Is urinalysis a good test of my kidney function?
   Yes, but it should be supplemented by other tests, as mentioned above.

Are kidney infections common?
Yes, especially among young women and older men.

What can I do to prevent recurrence of a kidney infection?
Drink plenty of liquids and undergo a thorough, periodic physical examination to rule out a contributing source of kidney infection.

What is pyelitis?
It is an infection in that portion of the kidney in which the urine collects. Symptoms are pain in the loins and lower back, fever, and infected urine.

Are antibiotics successful in combating most cases of pyelitis?
Yes.

Should one give up alcohol because of a chronic kidney condition?
Yes, except for an occasional drink.

Is diabetes a kidney disease?
No. It is a disease of the pancreas.

Can I have normal kidney and bladder functions even though I have diabetes?
Yes.

How can you distinguish between a backache caused by kidney disease and one that is due to back strain?
Muscular back conditions are not associated with abnormal findings on urinalysis, blood chemical examinations, or X-rays of the urinary tract.

Will a kidney transplant control advanced kidney disease?
Yes, in many cases, especially when both kidneys are diseased and uremia is impending or present.

What is meant by an artificial kidney?
It is a machine that takes over the function of the kidney and cleanses the blood of poisonous wastes through a process known as dialysis. In cases of uremia, kidney shutdown, or poisoning affecting kidney function, the use of the artificial kidney may be life-saving.

Is an artificial kidney helpful in controlling chronic kidney disease?

Yes, if it is used on a regular basis, such as two to three times a week.

What is the name of the procedure that is performed when using the artificial kidney?

Hemodialysis or dialysis.

For how long a period of time does dialysis work for someone with chronic kidney disease?

For a year or more, depending on the case. It is an invaluable procedure to tide over a patient who is awaiting a kidney transplant.

Does tobacco damage the kidneys?

No.

Will large amounts of spices aggravate a kidney condition?

Yes. People with chronic kidney disorders should avoid condiments when possible.

Can a focus of infection in the tonsils, sinuses, or prostate gland affect the kidneys?

Yes.

What is uremic poisoning?

It is the accumulation of excess amounts of urea within the bloodstream. If it continues unabated, it may lead to convulsions, coma, and death.

How is uremic poisoning determined?

By blood chemistry examinations.

Is it possible to recover from uremia?

Yes, if the cause is remediable, such as kidney obstruction due to an enlarged prostate or if the uremia is caused by acute poisoning.

Is dialysis helpful in controlling uremia?

Yes, in many cases.

Are birth deformities of the kidneys, ureters, and bladder very common?

Yes, they constitute one of the most frequently encountered defects seen at birth.

Can birth deformities of the urinary tract be corrected?
Yes, but the majority of them require no treatment, as they do not interfere with kidney function.

What are some of the common deformities of the urinary tract that require no treatment?
1. A horseshoe kidney, wherein the two kidneys are fused into one.
2. A double kidney on one side.
3. Double ureters.

What are some of the birth deformities of the urinary tract that might require surgical correction?
1. Exstrophy of the urinary bladder, a deformity in which the bladder is located on the abdominal wall.
2. Constriction of the ureters at the bladder junction.
3. An aberrant (out of place) artery that creates pressure in the kidney outlet.
4. Polycystic kidneys, when kidney function fails. This may necessitate a kidney transplant.

Does bedwetting indicate that a child has a weak bladder?
No. It is a behavioral problem, practically never an indication of an organic disease of the bladder.

How can one tell that he has cystitis?
1. There is frequent urination and pain on urination.
2. There is a sensation, after voiding, of not being completely empty.
3. There may be blood in the urine.
4. The urine may appear cloudy and turbid.

Is it necessary for me to be cystoscoped to make a diagnosis of cystitis?
No. The diagnosis can usually be made by noting the symptoms, by examining the abdomen, and by performing urinalysis.

Is cystitis more common in females?
Yes, because the urethra, the passageway from the bladder

to the outside, is so much shorter in the female. Thus, infections of the bladder can ascend from the outside more easily.

Are bladder infections ever encountered in young girls?
Yes. Such infections are thought to ascend from the outside, or from the rectal area, up the urethra into the bladder.

Is pus and blood in the urine sufficient evidence to make a diagnosis of cystitis?
No. One must also note the symptoms, such as frequent urination and burning on urination, pain in the lower abdomen, fever, etc.

Can most cases of cystitis be cured by the use of antibiotics?
Yes.

Is there a tendency for cystitis to recur?
Yes.

Is cystitis ever present even when urinalysis is negative?
Occasionally. A condition known as interstitial cystitis occurs in older women, often without infection of the urine.

Do women ever get an attack of cystitis shortly after marriage?
Yes. It used to be called "honeymoon cystitis," an infection secondary to intercourse. It is *not* a venereal disease.

Is cystoscopy accurate in diagnosing a tumor of the bladder?
Yes.

How are most bladder tumors removed?
By burning them off with an instrument inserted through a cystoscope.

Do bladder tumors, once removed, ever recur?
Yes, they have a tendency to do that.

Is it necessary to remove the bladder because of a bladder cancer?
Yes. In such cases, the ureters (the collecting tubes from the kidneys) are implanted into the small intestine.

When the bladder has been removed, how does the patient urinate?

The urine is passed into a bag pasted to the abdominal wall.

QUESTIONS TO ASK YOUR DOCTOR

Why is it that I have to urinate so often?

Is the blood in my urine due to a kidney or a bladder tumor, or is it caused by cystitis?

What can I do to avoid another episode of pyelitis?

Will my kidney condition lead to high blood pressure?

Does the swelling of my legs and face mean that I have kidney disease?

Must I limit my fluid intake because of my kidney condition?

Are my backaches caused by kidney disease?

Must I restrict my salt intake because of my kidney disease?

Should I be on a special diet because of my kidney problem?

How soon after an operation for kidney stones can one:
    get out of bed?
    leave the hospital?
    go out of doors?
    bathe or shower?
    drive a car?
    resume marital relations?
    return to work?
    resume all physical activity?

How soon after removal of a kidney can I:
    leave the hospital?
    go out of doors?
    bathe or shower?
    resume marital relations?
    return to work?
    drive a car?
    resume all physical activities?

What can be done to prevent cystitis?

How will I know if I am developing another bladder tumor?

Can my bladder tumor be treated through a cystoscope?

19. THE PROSTATE GLAND

What are the symptoms of an enlarged prostate?
1. Frequency of urination.
2. Difficulty in starting the urinary stream.
3. Inability to empty the bladder completely.

Does prostate trouble affect any particular age group?
Yes, the prostate tends to enlarge as one grows older and is more likely to cause trouble with advancing age.

Why does enlargement of the prostate interfere with urination?
Because the urethra passes directly through the substance of the prostate gland and is surrounded by it.

Is there any relationship between sexual activity and enlargement of the prostate?
No.

What harm does incomplete emptying of the bladder do?
The urine remaining in the bladder becomes infected.

What should I do if I ever have complete inability to void?
Call your doctor immediately. If you cannot reach him, go to the emergency room of the nearest accredited hospital.

How can I tell whether I need surgery because of my enlarged prostate?
By examination of your gland. This is accomplished by rectal digital examination and through cystoscopy.

Is there any satisfactory medical treatment for enlargement of the prostate?
No. Prostatic massage is of very little help.

Will damage to the kidneys result if I allow my enlarged prostate to go untreated?
Yes.

Can anything be done for an enlarged prostate short of surgical intervention?
No.

Is an operation for removal of the prostate dangerous?
No, but it is a serious major operation.

How is it that some people have the prostate removed through a cystoscope while others have an open operation?
It depends on the size of the gland, plus other factors. The larger the gland and the greater the obstruction, the more likely it will be that an open operation will be needed.

Will you be able to tell whether I can have my prostate removed through the cystoscope when you cystoscope me?
Yes.

What anesthesia will I receive if you remove my prostate through the cystoscope?
Either general or spinal anesthesia.

What kind of anesthesia will I receive if I undergo an open operation upon the prostate?
The same, either general or spinal anesthesia.

Is cystoscopy painful without anesthesia?
Yes, moderately, although a local anesthesia is usually administered through the urethra.

How long will I be in the hospital after you remove the prostate through the cystoscope?
Seven to twelve days.

How long will I be hospitalized if I have an open operation for the removal of my prostate?
Two to three weeks.

Will I be able to control dribbling after you remove my prostate?

Yes, but it may take several weeks to overcome this entirely.

Will removal of my prostate relieve my difficulty in voiding?
Yes.

Is it natural to pass blood following prostate removal?
Yes.

Is it natural to have spasms following prostate removal?
Yes.

Will the removal of my prostate interfere with my ability to have sexual intercourse?
Only in 10 to 15 percent of cases.

Does a prostate operation performed through a cystoscope interfere with the subsequent ability to have intercourse?
No.

Does removal of the prostate cause sterility?
Yes, in some cases in which the gland has been removed through an open operation.

Will prostatic removal cause inability to ejaculate?
Only in a minority of instances.

Will you be able to know after surgery whether my condition is benign or cancerous?
Yes. The microscopic examination will tell definitely.

How is a biopsy of the prostate gland taken?
Through a special instrument inserted through the rectum.

Does a prostate ever grow back again once it has been removed?
Very occasionally, and mostly in those cases that have undergone prostatic surgery through a cystoscope.

Are operations upon the prostate ever unsuccessful so that one continues to have difficulty in voiding?
Occasionally, after a transurethral resection has been done through the cystoscope.

If removal of the prostate through the cystoscope does not relieve a difficulty in voiding, is it possible to have an open operation to cure the condition?
Yes.

How long a period of convalescence will there be after a prostate is operated upon?
About six to eight weeks.

Are some people too old to undergo a prostate operation?
If they have complete urinary obstruction, they must be operated upon no matter what their age.

QUESTIONS TO ASK YOUR DOCTOR

Will I receive an anesthetic when you cystoscope me?

Will my operation be done in one stage or more than one stage?

For how long will the catheter be in me after I have had my prostate removed?

Will it be possible for me to ejaculate live sperm after my prostate operation?

What must be done if you discover I have cancer of the prostate?

Is the cancer of my prostate curable?

How soon after my prostate operation can I:
    get out of bed?
    bathe?
    shower?
    go outdoors?
    drive my car?
    return to work?
    resume marital relations?
    resume all physical exercise?

Will an abscessed prostate cause me to become sterile?

Will a gonorrheal infection of my prostate cause me to become sterile?

Will I require special-duty nurses after my operation?

For how many days will I need special nurses?

20. HERNIA

What are the most common types of hernia?
1. Inguinal hernia, in the groin.
2. Femoral hernia, just below the groin in the upper inner thigh.
3. Umbilical, in the navel.
4. Ventral, in the midline of the abdomen.
5. Incisional, though an old operative scar.
6. Epigastric, in the upper midline below the rib margin.
7. Diaphragmatic or hiatus hernia, through the opening in the diaphragm where the esophagus (foodpipe) enters the abdominal cavity.
8. Lumbar, through weakness in the posterior abdominal wall in the flank or loin.

Is a "rupture" the same as a hernia?
Yes.

Do hernias tend to be inherited or to run in families?
No, but the kind of muscles one has may be inherited. A person who has poor muscle development might be more prone to hernia.

Is surgery successful for all types of hernia?
Yes, except that the rate of recurrence is higher for some types, as for hiatus hernia.

What anesthesia will be used for my operation?
Hernia operations can be done under general, spinal, or local anesthesia, depending on the physical condition of the patient and the personal preference of the surgeon and anesthesiologist.

Is spinal anesthesia more dangerous than general?
No.

Can double hernias be operated upon simultaneously?
Yes, but the chances of a recurrence are somewhat greater if both sides are operated on simultaneously.

Do fat people get as good results from hernia operations as thin people?
No. It is wise to lose weight before undergoing an elective hernia operation.

Are children often born with hernias?
Yes, it is one of the most common birth defects.

Should hernias in newborns and young children be operated upon?
Yes, if they are in the groin and the intestine protrudes into the hernia sacs. Small hernias of the navel usually do not require surgery.

Do hernias in infants ever get well by themselves?
Tiny inguinal hernias sometimes do; small umbilical hernias often do. However, most sizable hernias persist as the child grows.

Do inguinal hernias in infants tend to involve both the left and right side of the groin?
Yes, although one of the hernias may not make itself apparent until months or years after the initial hernia has appeared.

When does a hernia of the navel in an infant require surgery?
When it is larger than a nickel and shows no sign of getting smaller during the first year or two of life.

Is it dangerous to operate upon a newborn or a small child for hernia?
No. It is a safe, simple operation. Infants and small children withstand surgery better than adults.

Should hernias in adults be operated upon?
Yes, unless the general condition of the patient prohibits it.

When does a hernia of the navel in an adult require surgery?
When bowel protrudes into it and causes pain or nausea or vomiting.

Is it safe to operate upon a very old person for hernia?
Yes. Such procedures can be done safely under local anesthesia, if necessary.

What are the undesirable effects of wearing a truss?
The tissues tend to be weakened if a truss is worn for a long time. Also, many patients experience considerable discomfort while wearing them.

Which hernias should be treated nonsurgically?
1. Hiatus or diaphragmatic hernias in very stout or old people.
2. Hernias in severe cardiac or pulmonary cases.
3. Hernias in people with marked liver or kidney disease.
4. Hernias that cause no symptoms and contain no intestines in the hernial sacs.
5. Most hernias in markedly overweight patients.

Is the usual hernia operation dangerous?
No.

When is a hernia operation dangerous?
When there is strangulated intestines or large bowel, and the strangulated bowel has become gangrenous.

How will I know if my hernia is beginning to strangulate?
You will have abdominal pain and nausea, and you will be unable to push back the contents of the hernial sac into your abdominal cavity, a condition known as incarcerated hernia.

When is it necessary to operate upon a hernia as an emergency?
When the contents of the hernial sac are incarcerated, that is, cannot be pushed back into the abdominal cavity. Also, when abdominal pain or nausea or vomiting ensues.

Is it ever necessary to remove part of the bowel during the course of surgery for a strangulated hernia?
Yes.

What are the chances of recovering from an operation for strangulated hernia?

Good, if the operation is performed within the first several hours after onset of symptoms; poor, if the strangulation is allowed to go a day or more without operation.

Is it common to have a certain amount of swelling of the testicle after hernia surgery?

Yes.

Is there danger of damage to the testicles during a hernia operation?

No.

Does a hernia operation affect one's sex life?

No.

Will hernia surgery cause me to become sterile?

No.

Can a hernia be produced by lifting something heavy?

Yes, but an underlying weakness of the tissues is usually present. Thus, the predisposition toward hernia is a very important factor in its causation.

Do men get hernias more often than women?

Yes, because they usually do more strenuous work.

Do hernias have a tendency to recur once they have been operated upon?

The recurrence rate is somewhere between 5 and 15 percent, depending upon the type of hernia and the physical condition and activities of the patient.

Will coughing or sneezing after my hernia operation cause it to recur?

No. You may feel as if you have broken some stitches, although this seldom happens.

What are the chances of a hernia recurring?

Approximately 10 percent of inguinal hernias (those in the groin) recur following surgery. Other types may have even higher recurrence rates.

Does one have to wear a belt or support after a hernia operation?
   No, except in rare instances.

If a hernia recurs, can it be operated upon again successfully?
   Yes.

Is it common to have numbness, or pins and needles, or little sticking pains around the region of my hernia wound?
   Yes.

QUESTIONS TO ASK YOUR DOCTOR

How soon should I have an operation for hernia?

What type of operation will you perform on my hernia?

What special preparations are necessary prior to undergoing hernia surgery?

Why shouldn't I treat my hernia with a truss?

Is it necessary to insert a graft to cure my hernia?

What precautions should be taken to prevent a recurrence of my hernia?

How soon after my hernia surgery can I:
   get out of bed?
   leave the hospital?
   walk up and down stairs?
   bathe or shower?
   go outdoors?
   resume marital relations?
   perform household duties?
   drive a car?
   return to work?
   lift heavy objects?
   resume all physical activities?

21. FEMALE DISORDERS

Is it natural for a newlywed woman to have painful intercourse during the first weeks of marriage?

Not necessarily. The maidenhead stretches to permit painless relations in the majority of women. However, it is occasionally necessary to have the maidenhead stretched by a physician to permit intercourse without pain.

What can be done to relieve painful intercourse?

1. Lubricate the vagina.
2. Have your husband lubricate his organ before attempting entrance.
3. The female should relax, spread her legs far apart, and bend her knees high up against the abdomen.

Is it possible that I am too small for my husband?

A normal vagina is large enough to permit entrance of the largest male organ.

Is it normal to have severe pain prior to or during the first day or two of menstruation?

No. Consult your physician to find out the cause of the pain.

Should I go to bed because of my painful menstruation?

Not if you can avoid it. One should attempt to continue all normal activities during menstruation.

What causes severe menstrual cramps?

Contractions of the uterus. In some cases they are caused by endometriosis, an inflammation of the mucous membrane lining the uterus.

Are some women more likely to have menstrual cramps than others?

Yes, women who are emotionally unstable often react more intensely to the pains of menstruation.

What is the treatment for painful menstruation?

It depends upon the cause. Some patients will require hormone therapy while others will respond to pain-relieving medications. A complete pelvic examination must be made before any treatment is started.

Are painful menstruation patterns inherited?

No, but the tendency may be. Also, there are strong environmental factors. If a young girl sees her mother repeatedly suffering with severe menstrual pains, she may develop a similar pattern of behavior when she begins to menstruate.

Is painful menstruation due to an underdeveloped uterus?

No. At one time this was thought to be true, but it is no longer thought to be the cause.

Is it safe to take a shower or to bathe while menstruating?
Yes.

What are the commonest causes other than pregnancy for skipped menstrual periods?

1. Hormone malfunction of the pituitary gland, thyroid gland, adrenal gland, or ovaries.
2. Emotional instability.
3. A debilitating chronic illness.
4. Malnourished, vitamin-deficient states.

Is it natural to have blood clots with a menstrual period?
No, one should not have clots with menstrual periods.

It is natural to have a little swelling of the breasts and face prior to and during the first day of menstruation?
Yes.

Is it natural for me to have an alteration in my menstrual pattern as I approach menopause?
Yes.

What causes scant or abnormally heavy menstruation?
An imbalance in hormone secretions.

Is it harmful to have intercourse during one's menstrual period?

No, but some people find it distasteful.

Is it safe to use a vaginal tampon?
Yes.

Can vaginal tampons be used by young girls?
Yes, virgins can usually use a small-sized tampon.

What is the most common reason for vaginal discharge?
A fungal infection such as trichomonas or monilia. Of course, gonorrhea can cause it too.

Can you tell whether the vaginal discharge is of a contagious or a venereal nature?
Yes, by examining the germ or fungus that has caused the infection.

Is there a detectable odor to normal menstruation?
No.

What is a common cause of odor coming from the vaginal region?
An infection such as trichomonas or monilia.

What can be done to overcome the odor?
1. Periodic douching.
2. Vaginal suppositories for the infection.
3. Medications to overcome any infection.
4. Local treatment of an infected cervix.

What should be used for a douche?
Only mild substances such as boric acid or vinegar diluted in water. Most of the commercially sold douches are satisfactory, if unnecessarily expensive.

Is douching harmful?
Not if properly carried out.

Are strong antiseptics harmful to the vaginal tissues?
Yes.

Can young girls douche even though they are virgins?
Yes, but only on a doctor's advice.

Should one take a douche the day following marital relations?
Yes, but simply as a matter of personal hygiene.

Is douching following intercourse a satisfactory method of contraception?
No. It is very ineffective.

What is the significance of a bloody discharge from the vagina when it is not the time for my period?
There are a great many causes of intermenstrual bleeding, some trivial in that they are due merely to a temporary upset in hormonal activity of the uterus and ovaries, some serious in that they are caused by a tumor of the cervix or uterus. But any unexpected vaginal bleeding should be taken seriously and necessitates a visit to your gynecologist.

What is a cystocele and rectocele?
A relaxation of the ligaments and muscles surrounding the vagina. As a consequence, the bladder and the rectum protrude into the vagina. Retention of urine in the bladder and constipation are common symptoms of these conditions. Either disorder can exist alone, but they generally occur together.

Do cystocele and rectocele always result from improper obstetrical care?
No. They can come from tears in the vagina or vulva at childbirth, but, more often, they are caused by natural weakening of the structures surrounding the vagina due to advancing age.

What is the harm if I allow a cystocele to go untreated?
It may lead to incomplete emptying of the bladder and stagnation of urine. This is frequently followed by urinary infection.

What does one sometimes lose water upon sneezing or coughing?
In the case of cystocele there is often a loss of control of the sphincter at the outlet of the bladder.

What is the treatment for a cystocele?
Surgical repair is the best treatment.

Is the operation for a cystocele and rectocele dangerous?
  No.

Does a cystocele or rectocele tend to get well by itself?
  No.

What are the chances of recurrence of a cystocele or rectocele after operation?
  This seldom occurs.

What type of anesthetic will I have for this operation?
  A general or spinal anesthetic.

Do the stitches have to be removed after an operation for a cystocele or rectocele?
  No. They will absorb by themselves.

Is it possible for me to have another baby after my vagina has been repaired?
  Yes.

What is a Bartholin cyst?
  It is a swelling of the glands at the entrance to the vagina.

What is the treatment for a Bartholin cyst?
  It should be opened and the edges of the cyst stitched to the surrounding mucous membrane. The procedure requires two to three days of hospitalization.

Does a Bartholin cyst tend to recur?
  Not if it has been operated upon.

Is a Bartholin abscess usually the result of a gonorrheal infection?
  No, but it can be secondary to such an infection. Most abcesses of this gland are secondary to infection of a cyst.

What is gonorrhea?
  An infection, transmitted through intercourse, caused by the gonococcus. It results in inflammation of the vagina and outlet of the urethra and, if untreated, may ascend through the uterus to infect the Fallopian tubes and ovaries.

Does gonorrhea affect men and women equally?
  Yes.

Is there immunity to gonorrhea?

No. If one has been exposed to the disease and has used no precautions, he or she will contract it in almost 100 percent of cases.

How is gonorrhea diagnosed?

By examining the secretions from the vagina. The gonococcus germ will be seen on the microscopic slide if gonorrhea is present.

Is gonorrhea in a female curable?

Yes, if treated promptly with antibiotics. During the treatment, the patient must refrain from intercourse.

Can gonorrhea interfere with my having children?

Only if it has infected the Fallopian tubes.

Does gonorrhea during pregnancy affect the child?

Not while it is in the uterus, but on passing through the birth canal the gonorrhea germs may gain access to the infant's eyes. For this reason, every newborn child receives prophylactic treatment within minutes after he is born.

What is vaginitis?

It is any bacterial, fungal, or parasitic infection of the vagina.

What is the treatment for vaginitis?

If caused by bacteria, antibiotic therapy is administered; if it is due to a fungus, antifungal medications are given orally or locally; if it is parasitic in origin, local antiparasitic medications will overcome it.

Do female children get an inflammation of their vaginas with a discharge?

Occasionally one will contract an infection from an adult who is careless about her hygiene.

What causes vaginitis in a child?

It may be gonorrheal in origin, or may be caused by another germ or by a fungus.

What is the treatment for vaginitis in children?

The same as for an adult.

Are birth control pills safe for most women to take?
Yes. Extensive studies have shown that they are harmless unless one has a tendency toward phlebitis (inflammation of the veins) or a tendency toward cysts of the breasts. Such women had best not use birth control pills.

What are the dangers in taking birth control pills?
1. They may be conducive to breast cysts or tumors in certain women who have a predisposition to such disorders.
2. In women who have had phlebitis or large varicose veins, it may be conducive to the development of blood clots.

What are the indications that one should discontinue birth control pills?
1. Severe, repeated headaches and dizziness.
2. Swelling of the ankles and pain in the calves of the legs.
3. Appearance of a lump in the breast.

How medically safe is an intrauterine birth control device?
The majority of women can use these devices without complications.

Is an intrauterine device as effective as birth control pills?
No.

Is an abortion dangerous if performed in a hospital by a qualified gynecologist?
No.

What is meant by a cervical erosion?
It is a form of inflammation of the cervix.

How can it be cured?
In most instances, cauterization of the cervical erosion, a painless procedure, will cure it.

For how long a period of time should one avoid marital relations atfer cauterization of the cervix?
Approximately four to six weeks.

What is a Pap smear?
It is the collection of cells from the cervix and vagina by use of a cotton swab. The cells are smeared onto a slide

which is then examined microscopically for the presence of abnormal cells.

How often should I have a Pap smear taken?
Every year.

Is it painful to take a Pap smear?
Not at all.

At what age should Pap smears be started?
At twenty-one years of age.

Are Pap smears accurate in determining a cancer of the cervix or uterus?
Yes, but they should not be the sole means of arriving at a positive diagnosis.

Can an early cancer of the cervix be cured?
Yes, by means of a hysterectomy.

Are some cancers of the cervix treated by radiation rather than surgery?
Yes.

What is meant by "cancer in situ"?
A cancer which is in such an early stage of its development that it has not invaded the deep tissues of the involved organ.

Do all patients with cancer in situ of the uterus have to undergo a hysterectomy?
Most should, as cancer in situ can be cured through hysterectomy.

Is cancer of the uterus curable?
Yes, if gotten in its early stages.

What is a fibroid tumor of the uterus?
It is benign tumor of the muscle wall of the uterus.

Do fibroids ever turn into malignant tumors of the uterus?
This is thought to occur only rarely.

Must all fibroids be operated upon?
No.

Can women become pregnant even though they have fibroid tumors?

Fibroids may cause sterility in some women; other women can conceive despite fibroids.

When should fibroids be operated upon?

1. When they grow very rapidly.

2. When they are unusually large.

3. When they cause hemorrhage during or in between periods.

4. When they cause bladder symptoms that cannot be relieved.

5. When they cause rectal symptoms that cannot be relieved.

6. When a fibroid undergoes degeneration, or when a fibroid becomes twisted on its own stalk.

What operation is performed for fibroids?

Removal of the entire uterus. In some cases where fibroids are not too numerous and the patient wishes to become pregnant subsequently, only the fibroids—not the uterus—are removed.

Is hysterectomy (removal of the uterus) a dangerous operation?

No, but it requires several weeks of recuperation.

Will I be able to return to normal living after a hysterectomy?

Yes.

Does a hysterectomy always produce a change of life?

Not if the ovaries, or one of the ovaries, have been left in place.

Will I have any menstruation whatever after a hysterectomy?

No, because the entire uterus will be removed.

Why is it that some women have a hysterectomy performed through an abdominal incision while others have the uterus removed through the vagina?

Some wombs are too large to be removed via the vagina.

Will a hysterectomy result in physical changes in my appearance?

No.

Will I tend to grow fat after a hysterectomy?
  No.

Will removal of my uterus affect my sex life?
  No.

What is a "D and C"
  It is a surgical procedure in which the inner lining of the uterus is scraped out. "D" stands for dilatation of the cervix and "C" for curettage, the scraping of the womb.

Will dilatation and curettage indicate the presence of fibroids?
  Yes, in some cases.

Will a dilatation and curettage tell whether I have a cancer of the uterus?
  Yes.

Is a "D and C" a painful procedure?
  No, it is done under anesthesia.

What is a tipped womb?
  A malposition of the uterus which usually causes no symptoms and rarely requires surgical intervention. It causes no difficulty in intercourse or in the ability to conceive.

Does a tipped womb interfere with the ability to carry a baby to term?
  No.

What is an ectopic pregnancy?
  One that takes place within a Fallopian tube. Because it endangers the life of the mother, it must be treated surgically.

If someone has had an ectopic pregnancy, is there a chance of having another such pregnancy?
  Yes, but the chances are greater that a normal pregnancy will take place.

What operation is performed for ectopic pregnancy?
  Removal of the Fallopian tube containing the pregnancy.

What is salpingitis?
  An inflammation of a Fallopian tube.

Is salpingitis always caused by gonorrhea?
   No. In many cases, it is caused by other bacteria.

What is the treatment for salpingitis?
   Bed rest and vigorous antibiotic therapy.

Is it always necessary to operate for salpingitis?
   On the contrary, surgical intervention seldom is necessary
for this condition.

*Does salpingitis frequently result in closed (blocked) Fallopian
tubes?*
   Yes.

*Do I need both ovaries in order to function normally and to
become pregnant?*
   No. As a matter of fact, part of one ovary is usually
sufficient for normal function.

*If one of my ovaries is removed, will I continue to have a
period every month?*
   Yes.

Do cysts of the ovaries ever disappear by themselves?
   Yes, if they are small and are related to menstruation.
Each month one of the ovaries forms a small corpus luteum
cyst which disappears after the egg is discharged.

Do all cysts of the ovaries have to be operated upon?
   No. Large, persistent ones require surgery.

What are the dangers of an ovarian cyst?
   Occasionally, they may rupture or become twisted, or may
become cancerous.

Is an operation for an ovarian cyst dangerous?
   No.

Can I become pregnant even though I have one ovary?
   Yes.

Do tumors of the ovaries ever become cancerous?
   Yes.

Is there a cure for cancer of the ovary?

Yes. Prompt removal of the tumor and the ovary.

CHANGE OF LIFE (MENOPAUSE)

What are the symptoms of change of life?

Some women have no symptoms other than cessation of menstruation. Most women, however, do experience symptoms to a greater or lesser degree. These include irritability, emotional instability, depression, hot flashes and sweats, sleeplessness, etc.

Do all women have serious symptoms from change of life?

No. Some have no symptoms.

If my mother had severe symptoms from menopause, does this mean that I will too?

Not necessarily. However, there is a tendency for daughters to follow their mothers in this regard.

Is it safe for me to take hormones to relieve the symptoms of change of life?

Yes, but only if one is under the care of a competent physician.

Are the hormones likely to cause cancer of the uterus or ovary?

No. This theory has not been accepted by the vast majority of authorities in the field. However, some experts do believe that, in certain cases, giving hormones may cause an existing cancer to grow more rapidly.

Does one often have recurring symptoms of menopause when hormone treatments are discontinued?

Yes.

Will the taking of hormones cause a cancer of my breast?

No. Although female sex hormones have been known to do this in mice, there is no evidence that it causes cancer of the breast in humans.

What other medication is helpful in relieving the symptoms of change of life?

Tranquilizers often give considerable relief.

Is change of life usually associated with a slackening in sexual desire?

On the contrary, many women experience an increase in their desire for sexual relations.

Does change of life encourage the growth of body hair?

No, but there is often a tendency for women to grow hair as they grow older.

Is it natural for the voice to deepen because of change of life?

Many women do have a deeper tone to their voices as they age. It is not due to the menopause, however, but to the natural aging processes.

For how long a period after my menstruation has stopped can I still become pregnant?

Possibly for six to twelve months, but pregnancy during this period is most uncommon.

Is vaginal bleeding after menopause cause for concern?

Yes. It should be investigated by a gynecologist without delay.

Is there a tendency to inherit early menopause or late menopause?

Yes.

Does the early onset of menstruation indicate an early menopause?

No, the earlier the menstruation, the later the menopause is likely to be.

Does an early change of life mean that my life span will be shortened?

No.

QUESTIONS TO ASK YOUR DOCTOR

Why is it that I have painful intercourse?

What is the treatment for my menstrual cramps?

Should I be given hormones to regulate my periods?

What causes the blood clots with my menstrual period?

What causes my irregular menstruation?

What causes my excessive menstruation?

What can I do to prevent a vaginal discharge?

What is the treatment for my vaginal discharge?

How often should I douche?

How soon after an operation for cystocele or rectocele will I
be able to:
  get out of bed?
  leave the hospital?
  go outdoors?
  resume household duties?
  drive my car?
  resume marital relations?
  return to work?
  resume all physical activities?

Is it safe for me to take birth control pills?

Can I take birth control pills indefinitely?

Can I safely use an intrauterine device?

Shall I take douches after cauterization of my cervix?

How long will it take my cervix to heal?

Can I become pregnant despite my fibroids?

Are the fibroids causing my headaches?

How soon after hysterectomy can I:
  get out of bed?
  leave the hospital?
  bathe or shower?
  go outdoors?
  take a douche?
  resume marital relations?

perform household duties?
drive a car?
return to work?
resume all physical activities?

How will you decide whether to remove my ovaries or whether to leave them in place when you do my hysterectomy?

How soon after a "D and C" can I:
get out of bed?
leave the hospital?
walk up and down stairs?
bathe or shower?
take a douche?
go outdoors?
resume marital relations?
perform household duties?
drive a car?
return to work?
resume all physical activities?

Does a tipped womb cause my backaches?

Will an infection of the Fallopian tubes prevent me from becoming pregnant?

Is something wrong that I don't have pain in the abdomen during the time when I should be ovulating?

Is my lack of menstruation caused by disturbed ovarian function?

Does the fact that I bleed so much mean that my ovaries are too active?

Is there any satisfactory hormone treatment for malfunction of the ovaries?

Will ovarian dysfunction interfere with my becoming pregnant?

Will my ovary be removed or just the cyst?

How can you tell whether I have a cyst or a tumor of my ovary?

Is it natural for me to have change of life at my age?

Is it natural for me to continue to menstruate even though I am so old?

How can you tell whether my symptoms are due to change of life?

How long will my change of life last?

Is it safe to continue hormone injections indefinitely?

At what age shall I stop taking female hormones?

Will the taking of hormones help to preserve my youthful appearance?

Will the taking of hormones cause cancer?

How can I tell when it is safe to discontinue birth control?

What can I do to retain my youthful appearance even though I have had change of life?

22. STERILITY
AND FERTILITY

What is sterility?

Sterility, or more properly *infertility*, is the inability to reproduce. The condition may be temporary and reversible or permanent and irreversible. There is no connection between impotence and sterility. In other words, a man may be perfectly capable of having intercourse yet be infertile. The converse is also true.

How often does sterility occur among married couples?

It is estimated that 20 percent of marriages fail to produce a live offspring.

Must the wife have an orgasm in order to conceive?

No. Climax plays no role whatsoever in conception.

How long does it take the average couple to conceive for the first time?

About eight to ten months.

What are some of the common causes of sterility (infertility) in the female?

1. The failure to ovulate. As a result, an egg is not discharged by the ovary.

2. Blocked Fallopian tubes.

3. Glandular disturbance involving the pituitary gland, the thyroid, the adrenal glands, or the ovaries.

4. Failure of the sperm to pass through the cervix.

5. Psychological factors, often difficult to evaluate.

6. Sterility of unknown origin.

What is the most fertile period of the month?

The middle of the menstrual cycle when ovulation takes place.

During how many days of the month is conception possible?

There are only about four to five days of each month when conception is possible.

How does one know that a woman is failing to ovulate?

1. By taking a careful history of menstruation and noting irregularities.

2. By recording basal temperatures over a period of several months. A definite curve will be developed, showing a rise in basal temperature should the patient ovulate. Failure to show this periodic rise in temperature denotes failure to ovulate.

3. By taking an endometrial biopsy of the lining of the uterus just before the expected date of ovulation.

4. By the microscopic examination of vaginal smears.

Can most women who fail to ovulate be treated successfully?

Yes. In many instances, glandular therapy will correct the condition.

What are the common causes of blocked Fallopian tubes?

1. Inflammation, secondary to gonorrhea or some other infection.

2. Previous peritonitis secondary to a ruptured appendix.
3. Spasm of the tubes secondary to emotional factors.
4. Endometriosis.
5. Fibroids that block the entrance from the uterus.

Can blockage of the Fallopian tubes be readily diagnosed?

Yes, either by injecting a gas through the cervix into the uterus (the Rubin test) or by administering a hysterogram (the injection of an opaque dye through the cervix into the uterus, followed by the taking of an X-ray).

Can blocked tubes ever be reopened?

1. In some cases, the performance of the Rubin test itself, by expanding the tubes with gas, will overcome the blockage. It may be necessary to repeat this procedure several times at monthly intervals for it to succeed.

2. In approximately 20 percent of cases, an operation known as a tuboplasty is successful in reopening blocked tubes.

3. Blocked tubes due to emotional factors may clear up when the woman has successfully overcome the problems that caused her stress.

What causes sperm to be unable to penetrate the cervix and gain access to the uterus?

Cervical infection is the most common cause of this condition. When the infection clears up, sperm will again be able to penetrate into the uterus and tubes.

Is sterility ever caused by a cyst on an ovary?

Yes. Upon removing the cyst, conception may again be possible.

Will the prolonged use of contraceptive jellies, birth control pills, or intrauterine devices cause sterility?

No.

Can sterility result from "overindulgence" in sex?

No.

Will taking hormones overcome sterility in the female?

Yes, if there is a proved deficiency of the particular hormone being administered.

What are fertility drugs?

They are hormones given to make a nonovulating female ovulate.

Do the fertility drugs ever result in multiple pregnancy?

Yes, especially a substance known as clomiphene citrate. Twins, triplets, quadruplets, etc., have been known to be produced following its use.

Is the male an important factor in cases of sterility?

Yes. About 30 to 40 percent of all infertile marriages are due to failure of the male, not the female.

What is male sterility?

Inability of a man to produce a sufficient number of live, normal, active sperm.

How can a man know whether he is sterile or infertile?

By undergoing a sperm count. The ejaculation of semen should contain more than 50 to 60 million sperm per cubic centimeter. This count is obtained by microscopic examination of the ejaculate.

What are the common causes of insufficient sperm or total absence of sperm in the semen?

1. Developmental abnormalities which are usually due to chromosomal or genetic defects.

2. Old age.

3. Inflammation of the testicles, such as that following orchitis in severe mumps.

4. Interference with the migration of sperm from the testicle to the ejaculate. An inflammation of the epididymis, the tubes leading from the testicles to the vas deferens, may totally block the passage of sperm.

5. Undescended testicles do not produce live, active sperm.

6. Glandular disorders.

7. A varicocele (this has not yet been proved conclusively).

Can one tell whether the testicles are capable of producing live sperm?

Yes, by a simple surgical procedure known as a testicular biopsy.

Is treatment of male sterility ever successful?

Yes, hormone therapy will help those with glandular deficiencies; eradication of infections involving the testicles, epididymis, or prostate gland may overcome sterility; surgical repair of a blocked vas deferens occasionally will cure sterility; and some urologists think that the surgical correction of a varicocele will successfully relieve male sterility.

What is a varicocele?
Varicose veins of the spermatic cord in and above the scrotum.

What is the vas deferens?
The tube carrying sperm from the testicles to the seminal vesicles where they are stored in preparation for ejaculation.

At what age do most men become sterile?
Usually not until their seventies or eighties. However, they may become impotent at an earlier age.

Is "overindulgence" in sex a cause of premature sterility in the male?
No.

QUESTIONS TO ASK YOUR DOCTOR

What tests must I take to find out if I am fertile?

What is the cause of my sterility?

Will my sterility respond to hormone treatment?

Is it possible that my husband and I both need hormone treatment?

Will my sterility respond to surgical correction?

For how long a period must I take hormones?

How soon after surgery can I expect to regain my fertility?

How expensive is the operation you intend to perform?

When can my husband and I be sure that treatment has failed?

23. PREGNANCY
AND CHILDBIRTH

What are some of the early signs and symptoms of pregnancy?
1. A missed menstrual period.
2. Fullness of the breasts.
3. Increased desire to urinate.
4. Nausea and vomiting, usually in the morning (coming on about six weeks after conception).

How can I tell whether I am pregnant or whether my period is just late?
If you are two weeks late, a pregnancy test performed upon a urine sample will tell whether or not you are pregnant.

Is a missed menstrual period always a sign of pregnancy?
No. There are many reasons other than pregnancy for a missed period.

How reliable are the new pregnancy tests which can be completed within a few minutes?
Very reliable, especially when performed in conjunction with a pelvic examination.

How soon after I become pregnant should I reserve a room at the hospital?
As soon as your doctor has confirmed your pregnancy.

Can I choose my own hospital or must I go to one recommended by my doctor?
You must go to the hospital recommended by your obstetrician.

What precautions must I take during pregnancy?
1. Do not take medicines unless prescribed by your doctor.
2. Avoid people with contagious diseases.

3. Do not undergo X-ray examinations unless necessary.

4. Avoid fatigue.

5. Do not have intercourse during that time of the month when you would ordinarily expect a period.

Is it safe to become pregnant with a heart condition?

Yes, but careful supervision by an internist is necessary.

Is it safe for a diabetic to become pregnant?

Yes, but special care is required throughout the pregnancy.

Can medicines and drugs taken by the mother affect the unborn child?

Some may, others won't. Nothing of this sort should be taken except on the advice of the attending physician.

What is the significance of bleeding during the first few weeks of pregnancy?

It may signify an impending miscarriage, in which case it will eventually develop into heavy bleeding. However, minimal bleeding of a harmless nature is often seen during the first few months of pregnancy as the placenta drops.

What are the main indications for a cesarean section?

1. When the baby's head is too large for the mother's pelvis.

2. Ineffective labor which fails to respond to stimulation.

3. Placenta praevia where the danger of serious hemorrhage is great.

4. Abnormal position of the baby which precludes a natural delivery.

5. Diabetes when an usually large baby is present.

6. Repeated previous stillbirths.

7. An older woman having her first baby.

8. Eclampsia, where convulsions make delivery urgent as a life-saving measure.

9. Abruptio placenta, where the placenta separates from the uterus prior to delivery of the baby.

10. A fibroid tumor of the uterus which obstructs the pelvis.

What kind of anesthesia will be given for a cesarean section?

General, epidural, or spinal anesthesia.

Is it natural to have abdominal cramps during the first few weeks of pregnancy?

They can occur but they are not usually associated with pregnancy.

How soon after pregnancy does morning sickness ensue?

About six to eight weeks after conception.

What can I do to prevent morning sickness?

It cannot be prevented. However, much can be done to relieve its symptoms. Consult your obstetrician.

Can I do anything before I become pregnant to influence the sex of my unborn child?

No. Although a few investigators have claimed that certain factors at conception can influence the sex of the unborn child, most obstetricians do not subscribe to their theories.

What are the chances of my having twins if there is no history of twins in my famliy or my husband's family?

Twins occur once in eighty childbirths.

Can the obstetrician tell whether a woman is having twins?

Yes, in most instances. The obstetrician will hear two or more fetal hearts when listening to the abdomen of women who are having multiple births.

Is heartburn natural during pregnancy?

During the first and last few weeks of pregnancy it is not uncommon.

What is the treatment for heartburn?

Usually a glass of milk will overcome it. No medication should be taken except on the advice of your doctor.

Are dizzy spells or fainting natural during the early part of pregnancy?

They do occur among some patients, but not very often. If they are recurrent, they are abnormal.

Are backaches common during pregnancy?

Yes. They tend to occur during the end of term and are largely due to the unaccustomed weight of the child in the pelvic area.

What can I do about my backaches?
Wear a good back support, sleep on a firm mattress, and avoid unnecessary lifting.

Is swelling of the ankles normal during pregnancy?
Not usually. If it persists, call it to the attention of your obstetrician.

Is it natural to have vaginal discharge during pregnancy?
Yes.

What care is recommended for the breasts during pregnancy?
1. A good supporting brassiere should be worn at all times.
2. Cracked nipples should be treated vigorously.
3. Efforts should be made to avoid excessive manipulation of the pregnant breast.

What special care shall I take to prevent the development of varicose veins?
1. Exercise such as walking, bicycle riding, etc., is an excellent way to encourage venous drainage.
2. Avoid encircling garters or other tight undergarments.
3. Avoid sitting or standing in one position for prolonged periods of time.

Should I wear support stockings for my varicose veins during pregnancy?
Yes, if the veins are large and cause you discomfort.

Can surgery be performed for my varicose veins during the time I am pregnant?
Yes, but it is better to wait until several weeks after delivery.

Do varicose veins ever disappear after delivery?
Yes.

How much weight should I gain during my pregnancy?
As little as possible. Certainly no more than twenty to twenty-five pounds.

Is there anything I can do to regulate my bowels during pregnancy?
1. Eat plenty of fresh fruits and vegetables.

2. Use a lubricant such as mineral oil.

3. Take a bulk-forming substance when necessary.

4. Laxatives, suppositories, and enemas should be used only when advised by your doctor.

How can I prevent hemorrhoids during pregnancy?

By keeping your bowels regular. Even with regularity, some women will develop hemorrhoids as the result of the pressure of the fetus upon veins in the pelvis.

Should my hemorrhoids be removed during pregnancy?

Preferably not.

Will my hemorrhoids go away after pregnancy?

Most do but others will require surgery if they persist after delivery.

Is it natural to have frequent urination during certain periods of pregnancy?

Yes, but the urine should be examined periodically to make sure there is not a urinary infection.

How much sleep should I get during my pregnancy?

Seven to nine hours a night.

Is special care of my teeth necessary during pregnancy?

Yes. See your dentist for specific instructions.

Is it safe for my dentist to give me a general anesthetic when I am pregnant?

No.

Should I take regular douches during pregnancy?

No. Douching should be discontinued during pregnancy.

What physical exercise should I take during my pregnancy?

Take your normal exercise. Walking, swimming, golf, tennis, dancing, and calisthenics are all permitted during normal pregnancy.

Can the doctor tell whether my pelvis is large enough for a normal delivery without X-raying it?

Yes, usually.

What are the symptoms and signs of toxemia of pregnancy?
1. Elevated blood pressure.
2. Albumin in the urine.
3. Abnormal blood chemistry.
4. Abnormal weight gain.
5. Swelling of the ankles and puffiness of the face.

What is done in case of toxemia of pregnancy?
Hospitalization may be required. Termination of pregnancy may be indicated in the most severe cases of toxemia.

At what stage in my pregnancy shall I give up doing housework?
It can be continued until delivery time if you are in good health and are enjoying a normal pregnancy.

How long shall I continue with my regular job?
It can be continued almost until delivery, provided you are in good health and the job is not overly exhausting.

Does physical activity increase the chances of a miscarriage?
No, not if it is the kind and amount of activity that you are accustomed to.

Will going to bed help to prevent a miscarriage?
In most instances, no.

Is there any way, during pregnancy, to tell whether the unborn child is a boy or a girl?
Yes, by performing amniocentesis, a procedure in which some of the fluid around the fetus is withdrawn and examined miscroscopically. To date, this procedure is not recommended merely to find out the sex of the fetus.

Is there any way, during pregnancy, to tell whether the unborn child has any birth defects?
It is possible in some cases through amniocentesis. However, the procedure is recommended only when there is a strong probability that a defect might be present.

Can contagious diseases affect my unborn child?
Yes, especially German measles.

What can people do in the way of prevention of contagious diseases during pregnancy?

Prior to pregnancy, women should be vaccinated against all those contagious diseases that they have never had. After pregnancy, if they have not been so vaccinated, they must avoid contact with people who have or have been exposed to a contagious disease.

Is it harmful to my unborn child if I have the flu or a cold during my pregnancy?

No, but upper respiratory infections may be especially severe during pregnancy, and it is, therefore, necessary to treat them seriously.

Are there any immunizations or vaccinations that I should take now that I know I am pregnant?

No. Do not take them during pregnancy.

Are there any immunizations or vaccinations that I should avoid now that I am pregnant?

Most physicians do not recommend smallpox or German measles vaccination during pregnancy.

Is it safe for me to travel while I am pregnant?

Yes, but long trips by car in excess of 250 miles per day are best avoided.

Is it safe for me to travel to a foreign country?

Yes, unless it is an undeveloped country where modern medical care is unavailable.

What are the chances of the average healthy woman having a healthy, well-formed child?

Of every 100 children, 97 are born without defects. Of the three born with defects, most are minor and correctible.

What can I do to increase my chances of having a normal, healthy baby?

Live a healthy, normal existence during pregnancy. From a genetic point of view, it helps to come from a family with a history of a minimum number of birth defects and to marry a man whose family history also shows a minimum number.

Are mental defects very common if there is no history of such defects on either side of a child's family?

No.

How can I determine when my child will be born?

Subtract three months from the date of onset of your last menstrual period and add ten days. In all probability, your baby will be born within two weeks before or after that date.

What is the effect of an Rh negative blood type in pregnancy?

It will not affect your firstborn. However, unless you are given an injection of a substance known as Rhogam after the birth of your first child, your second child's life may be jeopardized by the development of erythroblastosis (Rh factor disease). Formerly, this caused a great many stillbirths and sick newborns, but today it can be avoided.

Should I take extra vitamins or minerals during my pregnancy?

They are beneficial to many pregnant women, especially if one has diet habits that tend to omit certain types of nutritious foods. Since many women tend to become anemic at this time, iron pills are often recommended.

Is there any special diet that I should follow during pregnancy?

A regular, full diet, high in proteins, fruits, and vegetables, low in fats and carbohydrates.

How much milk should I drink each day?

Three to four glasses.

Can I continue to drink alcoholic beverages during pregnancy?

In moderation—no more than one or two drinks a day.

Is smoking harmful during pregnancy?

Smoking to excess is harmful at all times, including during pregnancy. Moreover, recent studies seem to indicate that it might adversely affect the unborn child.

Is bending, stretching, or raising the arms harmful during pregnancy?

No.

Is it safe to take a shower or bath during pregnancy?

Yes.

If I gain too much weight during pregnancy, does this

necessarily mean that I will have a large baby and a difficult delivery?

No, but it is much better not to be overweight.

Must I limit salt intake during my pregnancy?

Yes.

Can a sudden fright or shock lead to a deformity of my unborn child?

No.

Does the position of the fetus within the uterus ever cause a deformity?

Yes, in very rare instances.

What is the special significance of bleeding during the last two to three months of pregnancy?

It may indicate placenta praevia. Do not fail to notify your obstetrician of any such bleeding.

At what stage of pregnancy will I feel life?

At about four and one-half to five months.

LABOR

How will I know that I am going into labor?

You will feel a hardening of your abdomen with intermittent cramplike pains.

What are false labor pains?

Abdominal cramps not associated with progressive, regular uterine contractions.

How soon after I start having labor pains should I notify my doctor?

Whenever they become regular.

Is it always better to go to the hospital early?

Yes.

What happens to me when I reach the hospital?

You will be admitted to the labor rooms, shaved, given an enema, examined by the resident obstetrician, and placed in bed. The progress of your labor will be noted by the specially trained obstetrical nurses in attendance.

Will the hospital notify my doctor immediately upon my admission?
Yes.

Will medicines be given to relieve my labor pains?
Yes.

Do these drugs adversely affect my unborn child?
No.

Can one tell beforehand whether a labor will be easy or difficult?
One can tell whether the pelvis is adequate but one cannot predict how long or difficult a particular labor will be.

Because I have had a previous difficult labor, does this mean that this one will also be difficult?
No.

DELIVERY

Can I be sure the obstetrician will get to the hospital before I deliver?
Yes. All obstetricians pride themselves on not missing a delivery. It is seldom that they do!

What happens if delivery takes place before the obstetrician reaches the hospital?
If you are to be admitted to a well-staffed, accredited hospital, you can rest assured that a highly trained, competent resident will take charge until your doctor arrives.

Who decides the type of anesthesia that will be used during my delivery?
The obstetrician and the anesthesiologist will consult on this subject prior to your delivery. The ultimate decision will be influenced by what is best for you and safest for your child.

Do stitches have to be removed after I have had my vagina cut in order to facilitate the delivery?

No. They absorb by themselves.

How long does it take for these sutures to absorb?
One to two weeks.

Can you tell what part of the baby is going to come first during delivery?
Yes.

What is a breech delivery?
It is one in which the feet or buttocks come first, rather than the head.

Is a breech delivery dangerous?
No.

What is done when it is discovered beforehand that the baby is in an abnormal position?
At delivery, the obstetrician may put his hand up into the uterus and convert the abnormal position to a normal breech position and deliver it that way.

Can an obstetrician tell beforehand how long a labor will last?
No.

Is a forceps delivery dangerous to the baby?
No.

How is the afterbirth delivered?
By pressure on the uterus from above. It occurs spontaneously within ten to twenty minutes after the child is born.

Are birth injuries very common?
No.

How many cesarean sections can a woman have?
Most women can have three cesareans without danger.

If I once have had a cesarean section, does this mean that I will have one a second or third time?
Usually, but not always. If the cesarean was performed because of an abnormal position of the baby or for some other unusual condition, it is entirely possible that these situations

will not prevail during a second pregnancy. In such an event, a delivery in the normal way may be possible.

How safe is a cesarean section?
  It is a very safe method of delivery. Nevertheless, a delivery through the vagina is preferable, if it is feasible.

How soon after delivery will I see my child?
  Usually within a few hours after birth.

How long after delivery will I be able to get out of bed?
  Probably the day after delivery.

How long will I have to stay in the hospital?
  About four days after a normal delivery.

Can I resume smoking after delivery?
  Yes, but you would be wise to celebrate your baby's birth by giving up cigarettes.

For how long will I have vaginal bleeding after the baby is born?
  For several weeks.

What shall I do if I have any hemorrhage after leaving the hospital?
  Call your obstetrician immediately.

How soon after delivery will I have my first period?
  Within two to three months.

How soon after delivery may I have intercourse?
  When the vaginal bleeding has stopped, anywhere from six to ten weeks.

How soon after delivery is it possible to get pregnant again?
  Within two months.

How soon after delivery can I douche?
  Not until after your first normal menstrual period. This will be several weeks after delivery.

Must I take special precautions against infections following childbirth?

Yes, especially avoid sticking yourself with diaper pins.

Must I be on a special diet after normal delivery?
No, but plenty of milk and foods rich in minerals and vitamins should be part of your daily diet.

Is it normal to feel fatigued after childbirth?
Many women do.

What is postpartum depression?
It is a depressed state of mind coming on soon after delivery and lasting for several months. This kind of mental reaction requires psychiatric care.

QUESTIONS TO ASK YOUR DOCTOR

Am I too old to have a baby?

With my heart condition what special precautions should I take during pregnancy?

As a diabetic, what special precautions are necessary for me to take during pregnancy?

Should I take any special precautions about having intercourse during pregnancy?

What treatment do you recommend for my morning sickness?

What can I do to prevent a miscarriage?

If I have miscarried once, is there a greater chance that I will miscarry again?

Do you recommend natural childbirth?

What are the advantages of natural childbirth?

What are the disadvantages of natural childbirth?

Where can I attend prenatal instruction in natural childbirth?

What should I do if I develop German measles during my pregnancy?

How often shall I come to visit you during pregnancy?

Can I reach you on the telephone whenever I want to during my pregnancy?

How much weight shall I gain during my pregnancy?

What diet shall I follow to lose weight?

Will emotional upset affect the physical development of my unborn child?

Does my unborn child respond to physical and emotional changes in me?

Can you tell now whether I will be able to nurse my child?

Do you believe in inducing the child on a specific date?

What are the advantages and disadvantages of induced labor?

What kind of anesthesia will you give me when my baby is born?

Do you follow the procedure of episiotomy?

Is it necessary to make an incision and cut me prior to the birth of my child?

Can you tell now whether I will be able to deliver normally or require a cesarean section?

Can you tell now whether I will need a forceps delivery?

Will my husband be able to be with me during my labor?

Will my husband be able to watch the delivery?

Will you do the delivery yourself or will you turn it over to one of your assistants?

How will my breasts be treated if I decide not to breast-feed my child?

How soon after delivery can I:
  go out of doors?
  bathe?
  shower?
  drive my car?
  exercise?
  return to work?
  resume marital relations?
  do household chores?
  resume all physical activities?

How soon after delivery is it safe for me to have another baby?

24. THE NEWBORN CHILD

Who will take charge of my baby immediately after he is born?

A pediatrician (child specialist) chosen by you with the help of your obstetrician will examine the baby and from then on will assume its medical care.

Can I tell for sure if my newborn baby is normal?

Yes. Examinations at birth, or before the infant leaves the hospital, can give you complete assurance except in very rare cases.

Is it natural for a newborn baby to have a peculiarly shaped head?

Yes, this is from molding as the head passes through the birth canal.

Is there much danger of the soft spot on a child's head being injured?

No.

What special care must I take of the newborn baby's skin?

It requires very little care except sponging with lukewarm water and periodic oiling.

Is any special care needed for his scalp?
Just sponging with lukewarm water and application of baby oil.

What special care should I give to the baby's eyes, ears, and mouth?
Just washing gently with lukewarm water. The mouth needs no special attention.

What can be done about a baby who is born tongue-tied?
The slight membrane that ties the tongue will be snipped at the time of birth by the obstetrician.

Who examines the baby?
Immediately following birth, the child will be examined by a pediatrician.

Do all babies have jaundice at birth?
No, but occasionally this happens, due to destruction of some of the infant's red blood cells.

Is it natural for my baby's skin to peel during the first few days of life?
Yes.

What special care must I give to the navel?
Keep it clean.

How long does it take before the cord falls off?
One to two weeks.

What special care should be given after my baby's cord has fallen off?
Just washing with lukewarm water.

What is the significance of swelling of the scrotum?
None. It will subside spontaneously.

Should I have my baby circumcised?
Most physicians recommend it for hygienic reasons.

What are the advantages of circumcision?
The penis is easier to keep clean. Also, cancer of the penis is practically never seen in those who are circumcised.

How soon after birth can a circumcision be done?
Anywhere from birth to several weeks after birth.

What special care should be given to the circumcision?
The area should be washed gently with lukewarm water after the bandages fall off.

How long does it take before the circumcision wound heals?
About two weeks.

Can crying cause a hernia in a male baby?
No, but male babies are sometimes born with a hernia.

What is the meaning of a bluish spot at the base of the spine often seen at birth?
This is the so-called mongolian spot. It has no significance, and will most often disappear in time.

Why are eyedrops given to a newborn baby?
To prevent him from getting an eye infection as he passes down the birth canal. Such drops are mandatory in most states to prevent the child from getting gonorrhea of the eyes.

Are the color of my child's eyes at birth indicative of what they will be later on?
No. They will change to their final color within six to eight months.

Is it natural for a newborn's eyes not to work in coordination for the first few days or weeks of birth?
Yes.

How soon after birth does a newborn learn to focus his eyes?
Within several weeks.

How can I tell whether my child is permanently cross-eyed?
You will have to wait until he is a few months of age.

Is it natural for my child to have puffiness around his eyes?
Yes.

Is it natural for the newborn baby to have some discharge from the eyes?
Yes, especially as the result of the drops given at birth.

Will the light of a flashbulb hurt my child's eyes when he is photographed?
   No, but it may frighten him.

Is it natural for the child's breast to be swollen at birth?
   Some infants, both male and female, have this swelling. It is due to the influence of hormones circulating in the mother's blood.

Do some newborn babies have little white spots on their faces?
   Yes. These will disappear spontaneously.

Do some newborn babies' legs appear bowed?
   Yes, almost all newborns look that way. The legs will straighten as the child grows.

How can I know whether any injury has occurred to the limbs of my newborn child?
   Be suspicious if he moves all but one limb. It is natural for him to exercise all four extremities.

How soon after the baby is born can I feed him?
   About ten to twelve hours after birth.

How soon after the baby is born can he have a sponge bath?
   Several days after birth. The vernix with which he is born should be allowed to stay on the skin the first few days.

What temperature should I keep my baby's room?
   About 80° F.

At what temperature should I keep the water in which my baby is bathed?
   It should be just lukewarm to the hands.

How soon after birth can the baby be taken out of doors?
   If the weather is good, about two weeks after birth.

Does the baby have to be taken out of doors every day?
   No. Newborn infants do not require sunlight during the first few weeks of life.

Should I allow my newborn baby to lie in direct sunlight?
   No. It may burn his skin or the conjunctiva of his eyes.

Should I give my newborn a pacifier if he cries a great deal?

There is no objection to the use of a pacifier but make sure all his needs are satisfied before giving it to him. He may be crying because he is thirsty or hungry, or he may be wet or soiled.

Is it wise to allow relatives and friends to pick up and handle a newborn child?

Too much handling by anyone is a poor idea. Newborns require quiet and rest. They will be picked up and fondled sufficiently during feeding time or when their diapers are changed.

Are newborn babies vulnerable to infection?

Yes, from bacteria such as the streptococcus, staphylococcus, pneumococcus, and other germs. However, they are born with an immunity to the contagious diseases of childhood. Such immunity lasts only for the first few months of life.

Is breast-feeding better than bottle-feeding?

Yes, but it is not essential.

Is it necessary to cut my newborn's fingernails?

Yes, because they may scratch his face and eyes if they get too long.

QUESTIONS TO ASK YOUR DOCTOR

Is my baby completely normal?

Should I breast-feed my baby?

How long should I breast-feed my baby?

Should I adhere to a rigid feeding schedule or should I feed my child on demand?

How often shall I weigh my baby?

How can I tell whether or not my child is allergic to certain foods?

How can I distinguish crying due to hunger from crying due to illness or other discomfort?

How often should I bring my child to see you?

25. PLASTIC AND COSMETIC SURGERY UPON THE FACE AND NECK

THE NOSE

Are plastic operations upon the nose expensive?
Usually they are. However, one who is unable to afford a private surgeon can go to the plastic surgery clinic of a large hospital where he may receive care without any charge.

Do most medical and hospital insurance policies cover the cost of nasal plasty.
No. Cosmetic surgery is usually excluded from most health and hospital insurance policies.

What type of anesthesia is used in nasal plasty?
Local anesthesia.

Is it possible to do over a nose that has once been subjected to plastic surgery?
Yes.

Are the results of plastic surgery on the nose permanent?
Yes.

Will I have any difficulty in breathing through my nose after I have undergone plastic surgery?
No.

How long will I have to be in the hospital to undergo a plastic operation on my nose?

Approximately two to four days.

How soon can I get out of bed?
The day after the operation.

How long will it be until all the swelling has gone out of my nose?
Several weeks or months.

Will my eyes be black-and-blue following plastic surgery?
This happens in many cases.

Can I have a bridge built for my nose if it is flat?
Yes.

How is this done?
Through bone grafts taken from your own body.

Can plastic surgery make my nose narrower?
Yes.

Can I have my nostrils made smaller?
Yes.

What special care do I have to take of my nose following plastic surgery?
None, after it has healed fully.

How painful an operation is plastic surgery upon the nose?
There is moderate discomfort but the pain is readily bearable.

Is my nose more subject to injury following plastic operations?
No. .

Can a deviated septum be fixed at the same time as the nose is reshaped?
Yes.

Will plastic operations upon the nose and face frequently help to relieve neuroses?
Yes, in many cases, especially if the patient has focused upon his physical unattractiveness as a cause of his un-

happiness. However, emotionally disturbed people should
receive clearance from a psychiatrist before undergoing
cosmetic surgery.

THE EYES

*Can plastic surgery successfully remove the wrinkles and bags
from my eyelids?*
   Yes. These operations are successful in most cases.

How serious are these operations?
   Not at all serious.

What type of anesthesia is used for eyelid plasty?
   Local anesthesia.

*For how long a period of time will I have to be in the hospital
for such an operation?*
   Approximately two to four days.

*Will I have to wear dark glasses after having my eyelids
plastically repaired?*
   Yes, until the swelling goes down, you may find it more
comfortable to do so.

*How long before I will be able to return to work following a
plastic operation upon my eyelids?*
   Within a week or two.

Can Orientals have the slant in their eyes removed?
   Yes.

How successful is the operation?
   Very successful.

Will the wrinkles and bags around my eyes tend to recur?
   They may, if you are in your sixties or seventies.

If they do recur, can the operation be done over again?
   Yes.

*Can any damage to the eyes result from plastic surgery upon
the lids?*
   No.

Is plastic surgery on the eyes painful?
No, except for slight postoperative discomfort.

THE FACE AND NECK

Can I have my face lifted and the wrinkles removed from my neck all at one operation?
Yes, but many surgeons prefer to do the procedure in two or more stages.

Can markedly neurotic people undergo plastic surgery?
Yes, but only after consultation and clearance by a psychiatrist. Neurotic people tend to be dissatisfied with the results of their surgery.

Is it possible to tell beforehand how much younger I will look following a facial and neck plasty?
No.

What type of anesthesia is used for facial and neck plasty?
Local anesthesia.

How serious an operation is facial and neck plasty?
It is an extensive but not a life-endangering operation.

How long a hospitalization is necessary following plastic operation on the face and neck?
Approximately three to six days.

How successful are the results following facial and neck plasty?
They are usually excellent.

How long will it be before all the swelling goes out of my face and neck?
Several weeks.

What are the dangers of infection following plastic surgery on my face and neck?
Approximately the same as following any operation, that is, about 5 percent.

Do the stitches have to be removed following plastic operations upon my face and neck?

Yes.

What special precautions must I take of my face and neck following plastic operations?
    None.

Can I use the usual makeup and cream following plastic operation upon my face and neck?
    Yes.

Are there any visible scars following facial and neck plasty?
    The scars are so barely visible that they can be hidden with ordinary makeup.

Do wrinkles tend to recur following facial and neck plasty?
    Yes, as one ages.

Can the operation be done over again if wrinkles do recur?
    Yes.

Are there certain plastic surgeons who specialize in facial and neck plasty?
    Yes, but practically all accredited plastic surgeons are equipped to do the procedure.

Can I expose my face to the sun following a facial plasty?
    Yes, but excessive sunburn will tend to damage the skin and cause premature return of wrinkles.

Is it possible to make my lips thinner through plastic surgery?
    Yes.

How successful is the operation?
    Very successful.

Is it possible to build up one's chin by plastic surgery?
    Yes.

THE EARS

How successful are plastic operations for protruding ears?
    Very successful.

Is an operation for protruding ears serious?
    No.

How long a hospital stay is necessary for an operation upon protruding ears?

Two to three days.

At what age should a child have protruding ears operated upon?

Before entering kindergarten or the first grade.

How long must a child be kept out of school following an operation on protruding ears?

A week to ten days.

Is it possible, through plastic surgery, to build up an ear that has been deformed since birth?

Yes.

How successful are operations to restore missing parts to the external ear?

In some cases, very successful; in others, the results are only partially satisfactory.

Will an operation upon a protruding ear alter the hearing in any way?

No.

QUESTIONS TO ASK YOUR DOCTOR

Can I tell beforehand exactly what my nose will look like after it has been fixed?

What can I do if I don't like the end result of the plastic operation upon my nose?

For how long a period of time must I stay out of work following a nasal plasty operation?

Will I have to wear dark glasses for a length of time after undergoing plastic surgery upon my nose?

Is it possible to alter just the tip of my nose without touching the rest of it?

Is it possible to remove a small bump on my nose without altering the rest of its shape?

Will the stitches have to be removed following the operation upon my nose?

Will other people be able to see that I have had a plastic operation done upon my nose?

What is the best time to have a plastic operation done upon my child's nose?

For how long a period will my eyes be swollen following plastic surgery?

What interval will there be between the plastic surgery on my face and on my neck?

How long before I will be able to return to work following facial and neck plasty?

Is there any guarantee as to how long the effects of my plastic surgery will last?

How soon can I use makeup following plastic surgery without fear of infection?

Can you show me before-and-after photos of patients on whom you have performed plastic surgery?

In performing plastic surgery, could you duplicate a sketch or photo of a nose I would like to have?

26. BONES AND JOINTS, MUSCLES AND TENDONS, BURSAE

Should I go to an orthopedic surgeon or a chiropodist when I have a toe infection, an ingrown toenail, or a bothersome corn?

To an orthopedist or general surgeon for an infection or ingrown toenail; to a chiropodist for corns.

When should one be particularly careful about toe or foot infections?
If one is diabetic.

What is the proper way for me to cut my toenails?
Straight across, not down at the sides

Should I treat an ingrown toenail myself?
No.

THE BACK

What is the most common cause of pain in the lower back?
Muscle strain.

Will X-rays reveal the cause for backache?
If it originates from a bone disorder, X-rays will reveal the cause. If the backache is muscular or tendonous in origin, X-rays will probably not show the cause.

If I suffer from chronic backache now, does this mean that I will be subject to recurrent attacks of lower back pain?
Yes.

What can I do to alleviate backache?
1. Sleep on a firm, hard mattress.
2. Take frequent hot tub baths.
3. Take pain-relieving medicines as prescribed by your doctor.
4. Wear a good back support.
5. Indulge regularly in excercises as prescribed by your doctor.
6. Undergo X-ray studies to make sure there is not a slipped disk.

What tests do I need to distinguish between an ordinary back sprain and a slipped disk?
You may require a myelogram X-ray.

If I habitually wear a sacroiliac support, will it cut down on the chances of recurrent back pains?

Yes, if your backache is not due to a slipped disk.

Who is most likely to develop lower back pain?
Those with a curvature of the spine or some other bone deformity.

Will exercises help to straighten out the curvature of my spine?
In all probability, exercise will not correct a major spinal deformity.

Will bad posture habits cause one to develop curvature of the spine?
No, but it may result in chronic backache.

What motions are most likely to cause a recurrence of my back condition?
Sudden twisting motions, or attempts to bend over and lift a heavy object from the floor or ground.

Do infected teeth or tonsils or sinuses play an important part in causing my lower backache?
Usually not; in a small percentage of cases, such infections may be causative factors.

ARTHRITIS AND GOUT

What is the difference between arthritis and rheumatism?
Rheumatism is a lay term rather than a medical one. However, rheumatism is used synonymously with arthritis.

What parts of the body can be involved in arthritis?
Any joint of the body can be involved.

Is arthritis inherited?
No.

Are all age groups affected by arthritis?
Yes, but there is a tendency for arthritis to become more prevalent as one grows older.

What is the most effective medicine for the relief of my arthritis?

Aspirin, or a similar salicylate, is still the most effective medication in relieving pain in most cases of arthritis.

Is there any danger in taking massive doses of aspirin daily?
It is now thought that aspirin is dangerous to those people who already have an ulcer; it is not thought that aspirin causes an ulcer to develop in a normal stomach or duodenum.

For how long a period of time can one safely continue to take aspirin?
Indefinitely, provided no ulcer is present.

Are the patent medicines one reads about effective in relieving the pain of arthritis?
They are no more effective than aspirin, and in most cases they are more expensive.

Do infected teeth, tonsils, or sinuses ever cause a flare-up of arthritis?
Yes, particularly in patients with rheumatoid arthritis.

Will the removal of infected teeth or tonsils help arthritis?
It may if the arthritis is of the rheumatoid type.

How effective are spas in the treatment of arthritis?
They often make one feel better but they do not have curative effects.

Is there any special diet that will help arthritis?
No.

What is the difference between rheumatoid arthritis and osteoarthritis?
Rheumatoid arthritis is usually very painful and when it involves the fingers, it affects mainly the middle joints. Osteoarthritis is often not very painful, is seen mainly among older people, and when it involves the fingers, it affects the joints nearest to the fingertips.

How effective are the treatments for rheumatoid arthritis?
Some people are helped greatly, others are relieved temporarily, and still others do not seem to benefit from any form of treatment.

What is the treatment for osteoarthritis?

There is little that can be done for osteoarthritis, as it is part of the overall aging process. Avoidance of overweight and excess strain upon involved joints is perhaps the best treatment. Pain-relieving medications should be taken when necessary.

Are overweight people more subject to arthritis than those who are underweight?

Yes.

Does arthritis ever lead to loss of one of the limbs?

No, but it can be so crippling as to make a limb almost useless.

Can one drive a car even though he has arthritis?

Yes, if it is not too painful and if the arthritis does not interfere with the driver's ability to control the car.

Is physical exercise, such as golf or tennis, bad for arthritis?

No, provided the pain on exercise is not excessive.

Is swimming helpful for arthritis?

Yes, in many types of cases.

Does untreated arthritis tend to get well by itself?

In some cases of rheumatoid arthritis and gouty arthritis, there may be a spontaneous remission of symptoms. However, recurrent attacks are the general rule.

What is gout?

It is an abnormal metabolic state in which excess amounts of uric acid circulate in the blood. This condition, also called hyperuricemia, may result in severe painful arthritis or in the formation of kidney stones.

How can I tell whether my arthritis is gouty in origin?

By having the blood examined for uric acid. A high uric acid may indicate gout.

Is gout inherited?

Yes.

Can I cut down on my gouty attacks by following a special diet?

Yes, to a certain extent. Alcohol, liver, kidney, meat extracts, sweetbreads, roe, gravies, sardines, anchovies, potato chips, asparagus, mushrooms, peas, spinach, lentils, broths, and bouillons should be eliminated from the diet.

Will the eating of meat bring on attacks of gout?
Only in a minority of cases.

Will the drinking of alcoholic beverages bring on an attack of gout?
It may. People with severe gout should drink very little or not at all.

Can emotional strain bring on an attack of gout?
Yes.

Are there special medications that can relieve my gout?
Yes. Colchicine, Benemid, or a combination of both will relieve acute gout, as may Butazolidin. However, to prevent attacks of gout on a long-term basis, one should be placed on allopurinol therapy.

Are the medications for gout effective?
Yes.

For how long a time can I continue to take allopurinol?
Indefinitely.

FRACTURES

Why are people more susceptible to fractures as they grow older?
Because the bones lose some of the calcium, making them more brittle.

What bones are most likely to be fractured among older people?
The hip and the spine.

Do people with fractures of the hip have to be kept in a cast?
No. The present method is to pin the fractured fragments and to get the patient out of bed within a few days.

How effective is hip-pinning?
　Results are usually good unless the head or neck of the hip bone have been very extensively damaged.

When is an artificial hip used rather than hip-pinning?
　When damage to the hip bone appears to be irreparable.

Do artificial hips usually work well?
　Yes.

How dangerous is an operation for the replacement of a hip?
　It is serious but not dangerous.

Is hip replacement ever carried out for conditions other than a fracture?
　Yes, for advanced arthritis or other diseases of the hip joint.

What is a compound fracture?
　One in which there is a break in the skin through which the broken bone has protruded.

Does the pain of a fracture usually disappear after one has been placed in a cast?
　Yes, within a day or two.

Can one shower or bathe while he is in a cast?
　No, unless he can keep the cast completely out of water.

Does it hurt when a cast is removed?
　No.

Does a bone tend to be weak even after a fracture has healed completely?
　No, it becomes just as strong as before.

Do muscles return to full strength after a fracture has fully healed?
　Yes, in most cases.

OSTEOPOROSIS

What is osteoporosis?
　A depletion of the calcium in the bones. Osteoporosis is

thought to be part and parcel of the aging process. It is especially common in women past the menopause and is thought to be associated with lack of adequate secretions of female hormones. Osteoporosis is also seen following long periods of inactivity, particularly in the limbs.

Does osteoporosis cause symptoms?
   Pain is sometimes associated with the condition, especially when the vertebrae of the spine are affected.

How is it diagnosed?
   By X-rays.

Will the taking of female hormones prevent the onset of osteoporosis?
   Not usually. However, they may slow down the process.

Do men also develop osteoporosis?
   Yes, but not as frequently as women.

Does osteoporosis lead to bone fractures?
   Yes, because the bones are weakened by lack of calcium.

What bones are particularly prone to such fracture in older people?
   The hip and the spinal vertebrae.

What can I do to prevent the possibility of bone fracture from osteoporosis?
   One must take special care not to trip or fall, nor to attempt strenuous physical activity.

If treatment of osteoporosis is successful, will it be seen on repeated X-ray examination?
   Yes, but one should not expect a return to a completely normal picture on X-ray.

Is osteoporosis painful?
   In some cases it is, as in osteoporosis of the vertebral column.

TORN CARTILAGE OF THE KNEE

How can one tell whether there has been a knee sprain or a torn cartilage?

By careful examination of the injured joint.

Will X-rays usually show the presence of a torn cartilage?
Usually not.

Must all torn cartilages of the knee be operated upon?
No, a small number will heal spontaneously.

Are there precautions one can take to prevent a knee from "giving out"?
Yes. One should avoid twisting movements and should refrain from strenuous physical exercise. A knee support is also helpful in safeguarding against excess movements of the knee joint.

Can I perform physical exercise while I have a torn knee cartilage?
Yes, but you will run a great risk of further damaging the joint.

What should one do when a knee locks?
Go to the emergency room of the nearest hospital, unless your doctor is immediately available. Manipulations by an untrained individual may increase the damage to the joint.

What operation is performed for torn cartilage?
The torn portion of the cartilage is removed.

Are the results good from such an operation?
Yes.

Will the scar be very ugly following this type of operation?
There may be an unsightly scar in some cases. Women are especially self-conscious about the scars left following an operation for a torn cartilage.

Does an operation for a torn cartilage ever result in a stiff knee?
Extremely rarely, and then only if the operation is complicated by joint infection.

Is there a tendency for a torn cartilage to recur after it has been removed surgically?
This seldom happens unless there is another severe knee injury.

TENDON LACERATIONS

Must all torn tendons be repaired?

Yes, except for the palmaris longus in the forearm and the plantaris tendon in the leg. A tear of these tendons does not interfere with full function of the arm or leg.

Do tendons ever rupture without a skin laceration?

Yes, a twisting turn or sudden excess strain can cause a tendon to tear. One of the most common such tears is that of the Achilles tendon just above the heel bone.

What are the symptoms of a torn Achilles tendon?

Severe, sudden pain above the heel extending up into the calf of the leg. A complete tear makes it impossible to walk without great pain and, at best, there is a marked limp.

What is the treatment for a torn Achilles tendon?

Through an incision from above the heel up toward the calf, the torn upper portion of the big tendon is stitched to the lower torn part of the tendon, or is implanted into the upper portion of the heel bone.

How successful are operations for repair of a torn Achilles tendon?

They are very successful, but healing may not be complete for several weeks or months, and there may be a residual limp and weakness for several months thereafter.

Can one regain complete use of the leg and foot after a tear of the Achilles tendon?

Yes, but some restriction of movements and some inability to withstand great stress upon the tendon may persist indefinitely.

Should tendons always be repaired at the time of the injury?

Yes, unless the tissues in the area of the injury are badly swollen and obviously infected, or unless tendon grafts will be required to repair the damage.

When are tendon grafts used to repair torn tendons?

When the torn tendon or tendons are located in the palm

of the hand, or when the injury has destroyed so much tendon tissue that the torn fragments cannot be drawn together without tension.

How successful are tendon repairs?
    Results are good in most cases.

BURSITIS

What is bursitis?
    It is an inflammation of a bursa, the pad of fat lying between a joint and its attached muscle and tendons.

What causes bursitis?
    It is most commonly caused by an injury or sudden sprain, or by recurrent strain on a joint. Bacterial infections also have been known to produce this condition.

Is gout a factor in causing bursitis?
    Only in the occasional case.

Is poor diet a cause of bursitis?
    No.

Are infected teeth or tonsils or sinuses ever the cause for bursitis?
    Yes, in rare instances.

Will bursitis always show on X-ray examination?
    Not unless there are calcium deposits in the bursa. Many people, however, will have such deposits.

What are some of the most frequently employed methods of treating bursitis?
    1. The injection of a local anesthetic and a cortisone medication directly into the bursa.
    2. X-ray radiation.
    3. Medications, such as Butazolidin, to relieve symptoms.
    4. Surgical removal of the bursa if it fails to respond to one of the above forms of treatment.

How successful are the injection treatments for acute bursitis?
    They bring about cure in the great majority of cases.

How painful are the injections given to relieve bursitis?
They can be quite painful, and occasionally severe reactions set in for a few hours after the treatment is carried out.

How serious is the surgery for the removal of a bursa?
It is usually not a serious operation.

How long does bursitis last?
Anywhere from a few days in a successfully treated acute case to several months in some cases that fail to respond to ordinary therapy.

Is X-ray therapy dangerous in the treatment of bursitis?
No.

Is the cortisone used in the injection treatment of bursitis likely to cause ulcers or some other condition?
No, the amounts given will have no general effect upon the body.

Does bursitis, once cured, tend to recur?
Yes, if the area is again injured or subjected to undue strain.

MUSCLES

Does one tend to inherit the type of muscles he possesses?
Yes.

Is it natural for the muscles to grow weaker with age?
Not so much that it interferes with average physical activity.

What can I do to prevent loss of muscle tone as I get older?
Exercise regularly.

Will physical exercise strengthen weak muscles?
Yes, if taken regularly.

What is the significance of twitching in muscles?
It is a sign of muscle fatigue.

What is the significance of the thinning out of muscles?

It may be a sign of muscle disease and should be investigated.

Are there accurate ways of measuring muscle disease?
Yes, both by physical examination of reflexes and muscle tone, and by electromyography. Electromyography tests muscle function in much the same way that an electrocardiogram tests the heart.

FLATFEET

Are flatfeet inherited?
No, but there is a tendency to inherit the bone structure of the foot.

Do flatfeet always cause symptoms?
No.

Is there any way to cure flatfeet?
No, but exercises and the wearing of shoes that give proper support will frequently relieve the symptoms caused by flatfeet.

What effect does overweight have on flatfeet?
It aggravates the symptoms.

Can I indulge in all physical activities even though I have marked flatfeet?
Yes.

QUESTIONS TO ASK YOUR DOCTOR

How can you be sure that I do not have a slipped disk?

What specific treatment do I require for my back pain?

How effective are diathermy and whirlpool baths in curing my backache?

How effective will diathermy or whirlpool baths be in preventing recurrence of backaches?

Are there exercises that I should take to strengthen my back?

Will cortisone help to relieve the pain of my arthritis?

How long can I be kept on cortisone?

Is cortisone dangerous for me to take?

How will I know when I must discontinue cortisone?

Are my kidney stones the result of gout?

Will the treatment of my infected sinuses help to clear up my arthritis?

Would a change of climate help my arthritis?

How effective are gold injections in the treatment of arthritis?

Will diathermy or local heat or whirlpool baths help my arthritis?

Are there vaccines that can be given to overcome my type of arthritis?

Will antibiotic drugs help my arthritis?

Is there any type of surgery that will be helpful to relieve the symptoms of my arthritis?

What is the treatment for my rheumatoid arthritis?

What exercises should I take for my arthritis?

Will my arthritis eventually cripple me?

Must I follow a special diet in the treatment of my arthritis?

How long will it take my fracture to heal?

How long will I have to be in a cast?

Will I be able to walk as soon as my cast is removed?

How long will I be on crutches?

How long will I be on a cane?

Will the metal you have used to unite my fracture have to be removed eventually?

What special treatments will I need after my cast is removed?

How soon after my cast is removed will I be able to:
    bear weight and walk?
    go up and down stairs?
    go outdoors?
    drive my car?
    return to work?
    resume all physical activity?

If my knee buckles under me once in a while, does this mean that I have a torn cartilage?

Will torn cartilage require surgery?

How soon after an operation for torn cartilage will I:
    get out of bed?
    walk?
    dispense with crutches?
    dispense with a cane?
    go up and down stairs?
    drive my car?
    return to work?
    resume physical exercise?

Will I have to wear a knee brace following surgery upon my cartilage?

How long will it be necessary for me to wear knee protection?

Is my bursitis due to recurrent strains?

Do I require surgery to cure my bursitis?

Can I work when I have bursitis?

Will bursitis lead to stiffening of my joints?

How many treatments will I need for my bursitis?

Are my flatfeet the cause of pain in my calves and thighs?

Can I relieve the pain in my feet if I purchase special arches?

Should I wear arch supports for my feet even though I have no symptoms?

Will exercise cure my flatfeet?

What exercises shall I do for my flatfeet?

Will my child outgrow his flatfeet?

27. ANESTHESIA

What is the role of the anesthesiologist in an operation?
He not only anesthetizes you but he looks after your general condition while you are being operated upon. He monitors your cardiac action, blood pressure, fluid intake and output, as well as your respiratory function.

Will the anesthesia be given by a nurse or by a doctor?
In most hospitals, physicians give the anesthesia. However, there are many competent nurse anesthetists throughout the country who are excellently trained in this field.

Will I have to pay a separate fee for the anesthesia?
Yes, when it is given by an anesthesiologist with an M.D.

Do medical insurance policies make separate provision for payment of anesthesia fees?
Some do, others don't. Read the provisions carefully before going to the hospital.

Is it important not to eat for several hours before receiving an anesthetic?
Yes. Anesthesia is tolerated best on an empty stomach.

What is the purpose of preoperative medication?
To make the patient drowsy, less aware and anxious, and therefore, more cooperative.

Can I select the type of anesthesia I want?
   No. This is the job of the anesthesiologist. However, you can state your preference and if it is medically advisable, he may grant your preference.

Should I tell the anesthesiologist about a previous bad reaction to an anesthetic?
   Yes.

If I have had trouble with a certain type of anesthesia before, does it necessarily mean that I will be adversely affected again?
   Not at all. Each anesthesia experience with a specific anesthetic is different, and the reaction to the same agent may be entirely different.

Are there certain anesthetics to which certain people are allergic?
   Allergy to anesthesia is extremely rare. In most instances, people wrongly attribute a poor anesthetic experience to an allergy.

Do patients ever give away important secrets while talking as they go under anesthesia?
   No. This is an erroneous idea.

What is the safest anesthesia?
   All types of anesthesia are safe today.

Is one type of anesthesia safer than another?
   No, but one might be safer than another in a particular situation and for a particular patient, such as a heavy smoker, or one with a heart condition.

How long can one safely be kept under anesthesia?
   If given properly, anesthesia can be safely maintained for several hours at a time.

Is it true that people who drink a lot of alcohol are harder to anesthetize than others?
   Yes, they usually require more of the anesthetic agent to put them to sleep.

Is it as safe to anesthetize a child as an adult?
   Yes.

Is the gas that I will inhale unpleasant?

No. Moreover, you will in all probability be put to sleep by an intravenous medication before the gas is administered.

Can the anesthesiologist know accurately that I am fully asleep before the operation begins?

Yes. Surgery is never begun before the patient is fully anesthetized.

Is there a chance of my waking up and feeling the pain during the operation?

No.

Can the anesthesiologist tell whether too much or too little anesthesia is being given?

Yes, he has many accurate methods of determining this.

What is endotracheal anesthesia?

It is anesthesia administered through a tube inserted through the mouth into the trachea. This method affords much greater control over the anesthesia than when the tube is not employed.

What are the aftereffects of endotracheal anesthesia?

Many patients experience a sore throat due to pressure pain from the tube. However, this condition clears up in a day or two.

Are there any bad aftereffects from spinal anesthesia?

No more than from any other type.

Will I get headaches following spinal anesthesia?

About 5 percent of people will.

Is spinal anesthesia more dangerous than other types?

No.

Do patients have to be awake during spinal or local anesthesia?

No. They can be given intravenous medications to permit them to sleep during spinal anesthesia.

What is meant by epidural anesthesia?

It is one in which the anesthetic agent is injected outside the spinal canal where it will anesthetize the nerve roots.

What is caudal anesthesia?
It is one in which the anesthetic agent is injected into the caudal region at the base of the spine. The anesthetic agent does not go into the spinal canal. Caudal anesthesia numbs the rectal and vaginal area.

What is intravenous anesthesia?
It is a sleep-inducing medication. In most instances, it does not obliterate all pain and it is, therefore, supplemented by gas anesthesia.

What is meant by acupuncture anesthesia?
It is a method of anesthesia produced by inserting needles into certain areas of the limbs and body. It is used with alleged success in China but has not gained much popularity in other parts of the world, although at the time of writing, it is being investigated by various medical bodies in the U.S.A. Its method of action is not fully understood.

What is the responsibility of the anesthesiologist to his patient after the operation is over?
He continues to look after him, checking his vital signs until he is at least fully conscious.

Can heart action be monitored during anesthesia?
Yes, a cardioscope is attached to the patient during most major operations. This will show heart action throughout the entire procedure.

Can patients with high blood pressure be given anesthesia safely?
Yes, but they demand special care during the anesthetic period.

QUESTIONS TO ASK YOUR DOCTOR

What kind of anesthesia will I be given for my operation?

Because of a previous bad experience, should I be given this particular type of anesthesia again?

Can a local anesthetic be given instead of a general anesthetic?

Will I be put to sleep before I leave my room?

How soon after the operation is over will I wake up?

Will I feel sick to my stomach when I awaken from the anesthesia?

28. BEFORE AND AFTER SURGERY

How much of an area must be shaved around the operating site?

In order to be certain of a clean operative area, it is customary to shave for several inches or more around the intended incision. Thus, it is usual to shave the entire abdomen for any abdominal procedure and to shave an entire limb if the thigh or leg will be the site of surgery.

Is it necessary to have an enema before going to the operating room?

Since bowel function is sluggish after surgery, most people will receive a cleansing enema the night before going to the operating room. This is not done if there is an inflammatory condition in the intestinal tract.

Is it always necessary to stop eating before surgery?

Yes, one should fast at least eight to ten hours prior to surgery. Anesthetic complications may result if one is operated upon while there is food in the stomach.

Will I be given a sedative before surgery?

Yes. Sedatives are given to obtain a good night's sleep before surgery, and again, in the morning prior to going to the operating room.

Why is it necessary to get all undressed just to have a simple minor operative procedure performed?

Street clothes may be contaminated and in order to safeguard the sterility of the operating room area, people are made to undress and put on hospital gear.

Why is it necessary to go to the operating room on a stretcher when one is perfectly able to walk?

1. Shoes should not be worn to an operating room because they transmit germs, as do clothing.

2. Some people become ill or feel faint even when contemplating the most minor type of operation. They should, therefore, be lying down. In this position, such symptoms are less likely to occur.

How soon after you get to the operating room floor are you operated upon?

It may take anywhere from a few minutes to an hour or more before surgery is begun, depending upon whether the operating room is free and whether the surgeon has been able to keep to his operating schedule.

What is done with valuables while a patient is in the operating room?

They should be given to the floor nurse for safekeeping, along with any dentures that might be worn.

How soon after surgery is the patient brought back to his room?

If he has had general or spinal anesthesia, he first goes to the recovery room. He will not go back to his own room until he has fully recovered consciousness after the operation. This may take anywhere from a half hour to ten or twelve hours.

When shall I tell my family to come to the hospital after I am operated upon?

If you are having general or spinal anesthesia, it is best that they not come to see you for at least several hours after surgery. In all probability, you will spend a few hours in the recovery room where no visitors are permitted.

Will there be someone in the operating room to monitor my heart action during the operation?

In most instances, the heart function as well as the respiratory function is monitored by the doctor-anesthesiologist who is in attendance. In the case of a seriously ill person, the job is done by an internist.

What will be done to relieve the pain in my wound?

There are many excellent drugs that will relieve a great deal of the pain postoperatively.

Will the scar be permanent?

All scars are permanent, but many are not significantly disfiguring.

How can I prevent an excessive scar from developing in my incision?

There is no way to prevent an overgrown scar. Fortunately, most people do not form keloids (overgrown scars).

How long will it take for the scar to flatten out?

Most scars take several months to flatten out and turn white.

How soon after surgery can most patients get out of bed?

Usually the day following the operation. There are, of course, many exceptions in which the patient is kept in bed for several days after surgery.

How do most patients feel when they first get out of bed?

It is natural for most to feel dizzy and weak.

Is it painful to have stitches removed?

No. There is just a slight pulling sensation.

Can one go home from the hospital before his stitches are removed?

Yes, in a great many instances.

What is the significance of a pink discharge from the wound?

It may mean there is serum in it, or it may mean that the wound is healing poorly and is separating.

What is serum?

It is a pinkish red fluid that sometimes develops beneath a surgical wound.

Is it natural for wounds to develop serum?

Some do, others don't. Wounds in fat people or in fatty areas of the body are more likely to develop serum.

Is it common for some wounds to develop an infection?

Yes, if the operation involves handling tissues that contain bacteria, such as the appendix or intestines.

Are wounds very painful for a long period after surgery?

There may be some painful sensations for days or weeks after surgery but the pain is usually not severe and is tolerable.

Is it natural to have numbness around an incision?

Yes.

Why does one feel "pins and needles" in a wound?

It is most likely due to regrowth of tiny severed nerve filaments.

Will full sensation in the wound area return?

Yes, except for the scar itself, and a small area surrounding the scar.

Is it natural for a healing wound to itch?

Yes.

How can I prevent getting a rupture of my wound?

Avoid strenuous physical effort for several months.

Will bending or stretching hurt a surgical wound?

No.

How soon after surgery can one have a shampoo?

Within a week.

Is it necessary to take vitamins or tonics for prolonged periods of time after an operation?

Usually not, except in chronic conditions where there has been marked debility.

Is it natural to feel tired and depressed following surgery?

Many people do, but in most instances these feelings will pass within a few weeks' time.

QUESTIONS TO ASK YOUR DOCTOR

At what time will I be operated upon?

Will they have to pass a stomach tube into me before I go to the operating room?

Will a catheter be inserted into my bladder before surgery?

Will I have to be fed intravenously after surgery, and if so, for how long?

Will you do the operation yourself or will one of your assistants do the operation?

Can my internist be present at the operation if I want him?

How long will the operation take to perform?

Will I need blood transfusions?

Will I go to the recovery room before being brought back to my regular room?

How long do you think I will be in the recovery room?

Will I go to the intensive care unit before coming back to my room?

Will you tell me the truth about your findings during the operation, even if it means that I must know the worst?

Will I require special nurses? For how long? Around the clock?

How long a period of time am I likely to spend in the recovery room following surgery?

How big an incision will I have?

Will the scar from my wound be unsightly?

Will I have to receive transfusions during the surgery?

For how long a period will I be in pain after my surgery?

Will I have to have a tube in my nose going down into my stomach following surgery? If so, for how long?

Will I have to have a catheter in my bladder following surgery, and if so, for how long?

Will I have to have any drains in my incision?

Is it painful when these are removed?

How soon after surgery will I be able to eat?

Must I follow a special diet after surgery?

How long will it take before my bowel function returns to normal?

When, after surgery, will I be able to have visitors?

How soon after my operation can I:
   walk?
   take a bath or shower?
   go outdoors?
   go up and down stairs?
   take a ride in a car?
   drive my car?
   resume physical activities?
   do housework?
   resume marital relations?
   go back to work?

When will my stitches be removed?

Is it common for a wound of my type to develop serum in it?

What are the chances of my wound becoming infected?

Will I have bleeding from my wound?

How often will it be necessary to change my wound dressing after the operation?

How long must I wear a dressing on my wound?

How soon after my operation will I be able to leave the hospital?

Once I am discharged from the hospital will I have to come to your office for dressing changes?

How long does it take a wound of my type to heal?

When will the swelling go down around my incision?

Will it harm my wound to get it wet?

Should I wear a special support over my wound?

Is it safe to wear a girdle?

What are the chances of my developing a rupture within my wound?

29. CONVALESCENCE

QUESTIONS TO ASK YOUR DOCTOR

How long will it take for me to convalesce from this illness?

Should I go to a convalescent home to recuperate from my illness?

For how long should I stay in a convalescent home?

Can I do my own housework during my convalescent period?

Should I have someone come in to do my chores during my convalescence?

How long will it be before I am able to take care of myself completely?

Will special diet and the taking of vitamins and tonics speed my convalescence?

How much physical activity can I embark upon during my convalescence?

Are there special exercises that will speed my convalescence?

Can I do office work at home during my convalescence?

Is it necessary that I avoid emotional strain during my convalescence?

Must I take special precautions in intercourse after surgery and will it affect my ability to enjoy sex?

Will the operation in any way affect my ability to have children?

Will I have to wear a special support following surgery?

Will the operation force me to change my mode of living?

Will the operation affect my span of life?

What are the chances of my getting the condition back again?

What precautions can be taken to prevent recurrence of my condition?

What can be done if a recurrence does take place?

How often should I come in for a periodic check-up?

How much sleep should I get during my convalescence?

Is it safe for me to take an airplane trip during my convalescent period?

How soon after my operation will I be able to go away for a vacation?

Is there an advantage in going to a warm climate to speed my convalescence?

Must I avoid high altitude while convalescing from my illness?

30. MEDICATIONS
AND PRESCRIPTIONS

Is it safe to medicate oneself without a doctor's advice?

It is absurd to assume that every indisposition requires calling a doctor. Of course, one can take a laxative once in a while for constipation, or an aspirin tablet because of an occasional headache. However, a physician should be consulted before taking medicine for what is obviously an unusual symptom or serious illness.

If a doctor has once prescribed a medicine, is it safe to take it again at a later date when symptoms recur?

Yes, if you can be sure it is the same condition. If you are in doubt, telephone your doctor.

How can one tell if a medication is still effective?

Many prescriptions have labels that give an expiration date. Any change in color or consistency of a preparation should lead one to believe that it should no longer be used. When in doubt, telephone your physician.

Is it safe to give a relative or friend a medicine that has been prescribed for oneself?

No. This may result in a serious mistake, as a layman is seldom in a position to make an accurate diagnosis of another's illness.

Why is it certain drugs can be bought without a doctor's prescription and others require it?

The sale of drugs is under the control of federal, state, and local health authorities. The decision as to whether a medication requires a prescription is generally based upon the possible toxic action as well as its addictive potentialities.

Are the various advertisements one reads in the papers, hears on radio, or sees on television usually reliable?

Naturally, most drug manufacturers are overenthusiastic

concerning the value of their products, but the federal government prohibits actual falsification of drug actions. However, one should be medicated by a doctor, not by a commercial advertisement.

Should one ever reach for a medicine in the dark?

No. This is a dangerous practice. Turn on the lights and be thoroughly awake so that you can read the label clearly before taking a medicine.

How can one safeguard against taking the wrong medicine?

It is a good practice to write the name of the drug on the label of the bottle. Ask your doctor its name when he hands you the prescription.

What medicines are dangerous to have around the house?

All medications and drugs are potentially dangerous if a small child gets hold of them. Aspirin, bicarbonate of soda, laxatives, and other seemingly innocuous medicines can cause severe toxic reactions if taken in large doses by a child. *All* medicines should be kept well out of the reach of children, especially strong antiseptics, insecticides, cleaning fluids, lye, alcohol, etc.

What makes a drug habit-forming?

* The inherent character of the drug.
* The character and personality of the individual who takes the drug.
* Any drug that relieves discomfort, produces sleep, or creates a pleasant state of mind or body is potentially habit-forming.

Is there a difference between a habit-forming drug and one to which an individual has become addicted?

Yes. Drug addiction causes a physical and mental dependency upon the substance. Withdrawal of such a drug results in intense physical, physiological, and emotional disturbance. Withdrawal of a habit-forming drug may cause some psychological and emotional distress, but rarely produces physical symptoms.

Why do some medications lose their effectiveness if taken repeatedly over a prolonged period of time?

The exact cause of this phenomenon is not clearly understood. It is known that certain bacteria will develop resistance to antibiotic drugs. Also, increased tolerance to the effect of certain pain-relieving drugs, narcotics, sleeping pills, and laxatives sometimes occurs in people. On the other hand, most medications continue indefinitely to exercise their therapeutic properties.

Is it true that the less medication one takes, the better?

Yes. There is a tendency today, probably because of the constant pressure of advertising, for people to take too many medications.

Are there satisfactory measures to combat overdoses of drugs?

Yes. There are precise methods of treating overdosages of almost every medication. The most important point to remember is not to delay one moment in getting medical help. Also, vomiting should be induced as soon as possible.

Why do physicians sometimes insist upon a return visit before renewing a prescription?

* To check on the progress of the patient and the effect of the medication.
* To reaffirm or to change a questionable diagnosis.
* To alter dosage or to change the medication to another one.
* To note whether maximum benefit has been obtained from use of the medication.

Should pregnant women be especially careful about taking medicines or drugs?

Yes, especially during the first twelve weeks of pregnancy when the drug might have its most powerful effect upon the rapidly growing embryo. Certain drugs that are beneficial to the mother might have serious, harmful effects upon the embryo.

Is it bad practice to take a medication over a period of months or years without consulting your doctor?

Yes. Certain medications, while effective and harmless for short periods of time, may cause toxic symptoms if taken for too long.

QUESTIONS TO ASK YOUR DOCTOR

Can I get this medicine at any drugstore?

Do I need a prescription for this medicine or can I buy it over the counter?

Is this medicine very expensive?

Where can I get it the most cheaply?

Are you prescribing a brand name or a generic name?

Shall I have this prescription renewed when it runs out?

Can I have it renewed by the druggist without coming back to see you?

Will you renew this prescription if I call you on the telephone?

How long do I have to take this medicine?

How long will it keep?

Does it tend to lose its effect when taken over a long period of time?

Does this medicine have any side effects I should know about?

Is this medicine dangerous to keep within reach of children?

How will I know if the medicine is affecting me badly?

Is there any penicillin in this medicine?

Is this medicine safe to take even though I have a stomach ulcer?

Is this medication bad for people who have allergies?

Is this medicine habit-forming?

Will I have to get up at night to take the medicine?

Is it best to take this medicine before, during, or after meals?

Is an overdose of this medicine dangerous?

How soon after I take this medicine will it begin to benefit me?

Can I safely take this medicine again if my condition should recur several months later?

What is the name of this medication so I can write it down on the bottle?

Is this medication safe to take should I become pregnant?

Are there foods I should avoid when I take this medication?

Is this medication safe to take even though I have diabetes?

Does one ever develop an allergy to this medication after taking it over a long period of time?

Will this medication alter my bowel function?

Is this medication a hormone?

Is it possible that this medication might stimulate the growth of a tumor in my body?

Does this medication contain cortisone?

Will this medication keep me awake at night?

Will this medication tend to make me feel drowsy?

Will this medication in any way affect my vision?

Is it safe to drive my car while I am taking this medication?

31. ADDICTION TO DRUGS

What is the nature of a drug that makes it potentially addictive?

It is the chemical composition of the drug that determines addiction.

Is there a difference between a habit-forming drug and one to which there is true addiction?

Yes. One may become accustomed to taking a drug without having a true physical addiction to it. As examples, one may become dependent upon a tranquilizer without becoming addicted to it and when one stops taking it, withdrawal symptoms do not develop. Heroin and morphine, on the other hand, can produce real addiction with severe withdrawal symptoms when one stops taking them.

As I become more dependent upon a drug, do I need larger doses to produce satisfactory effects?

Usually, yes.

How can I tell whether I am likely to become addicted to a drug?

All people can become addicted to drugs such as morphine or heroin if they take enough of them for a sufficiently prolonged time.

Are some people more susceptible to addiction than others?

Yes. Neurotic, insecure people are the most likely victims.

Can true drug addiction ever be cured?

Yes, although the longer one has been addicted, the more difficult it is to cure the habit.

Does a non-habit-forming drug ever become habit-forming?

Yes, if taken over a long enough period of time. This applies especially to sedatives, stimulating drugs, and laxatives.

Is there a tendency for drug addictions to be inherited?

No.

Are there any pain-relieving drugs I can take which are not habit-forming?

Yes. There are several excellent ones that have no addictive potential. They can be prescribed by your doctor.

Are there any sleep-producing drugs that I can take that are not habit-forming?

Yes, but one does have a tendency to rely upon these medications if taken over a period of months or years, and for this reason they should not be taken routinely.

Are there any stimulating drugs that I can take that are not habit-forming?

Most of these medications contain amphetamines which do induce habit formation. Therefore, they should be taken only on your doctor's prescription.

Does one become truly addicted only to a narcotic such as morphine or heroin?

No. There are other addictive chemicals, the most prevalent of which is alcohol.

Is there such a thing as a true addiction to the barbiturates or to the stimulating (amphetamine) drugs?

No, but the dependency upon them has about the same effect as a true addiction.

Does one ever become addicted to laxatives?

No, but marked dependence upon them in order to have the bowels function is frequent.

Are massive doses of aspirin harmful?

Yes, if one has an ulcer, aspirin may induce bleeding.

Can one become addicted to aspirin?

No.

Can one become addicted to hormones?

No.

Is methadone a good method of treating morphine or heroin addiction?

It seems to be the best method available at this time. It

substitutes a less harmful addiction for a very dangerous one.

How will I know that a prescription that is given me is or is not habit-forming?

Your doctor will tell you when he prescribes it.

How can I tell whether a drug bought across the counter has habit-forming tendencies?

It will be clearly marked as such.

32. ALCOHOL

Is alcoholism a true addiction?

Yes, in every sense of the term.

How can I tell whether I am a true alcoholic or merely a heavy drinker?

When you crave a drink and have symptoms of withdrawal when you refrain from drinking, you are an alcoholic.

If I can stop drinking whenever I want to, am I a true alcoholic?

Many alcoholics think they can stop whenever they want to, but in actuality they do not do so.

If I drink steadily but moderately over a period of years, are the chances greater that I will become a real addict?

Yes.

Is alcoholism inherited?

Not in the sense that it is passed on through the genes. But statistics show that the children of alcoholics have an increased tendency to drink in excess.

Is there a chemical basis for alcoholism?

Some investigators in the field believe that one must be chemically prone to becoming an alcoholic. If one is not so constituted, he will never become a true alcoholic even if he drinks heavily.

What causes a "hangover"?

It is thought that edema (swelling) of the brain with excess fluid around the brain causes the symptoms of a hangover.

Is there any medical cure for a hangover?

Aspirin to relieve the headache is perhaps the best treatment.

What organs are most severly damaged by the excessive use of alcohol?

The liver, brain, heart, blood vessels, the pancreas, and the kidneys.

Can I drink even though I have had a coronary?

Yes, but only in moderation.

Can I drink even though I have diabetes?

Drinking large quantities of alcohol makes it difficult to regulate a diabetic's diet.

Can I drink even though I have had hepatitis?

One should not drink for approximately six months after an attack of hepatitis.

Can I drink even though my kidneys are not in good condition?

People with kidney impairment should refrain from all but an occasional drink of alcohol.

Where can I go to get treatment to cure my habit of excess drinking?

1. See your family doctor.
2. Obtain psychiatric advice.
3. Join Alcoholics Anonymous.

Is it safe to take the medicine known as Antabuse?

Yes. This often prevents drinking because the patient knows he will be violently sick if he drinks after taking Antabuse.

What are the chances of getting cured of chronic alcoholism?

Excellent, if one truly has the desire to overcome the addiction.

Is hypnosis a helpful method of treatment for alcoholism?

It has helped a considerable number of people. After all, hypnosis is a form of psychotherapy.

How helpful is Alcoholics Anonymous?

It has helped tens of thousands of people to overcome alcoholism.

If I am cured of drinking, is it possible for me to have a relapse?

Unfortunately, yes.

Will heavy drinking shorten my span of life?

Yes.

Is it safe to take sleeping pills after one has been drinking a lot?

No. Excessive drinking causes depressed heart and lung action. Sedatives do the same. A combination of both may cause heart failure or suffocation during sleep.

Should an expectant mother cut down on drinking?

Yes. Heavy drinking can damage the unborn child, as alcohol passes through the placenta into the bloodstream of the fetus. A drink a day will do no harm.

Should one take any precautions about drinking before undergoing surgery?

Yes. It is wisest to stop drinking several days before surgery as this will lead to smoother anesthesia.

Will psychotherapy help a drinking problem?

Yes, in many cases it helps a great deal.

What effect does drinking have on a stomach ulcer?

Alcohol irritates the raw surface of the ulcer and should be avoided.

Is it safe for me to drink even though I have colitis?

No. Alcohol may cause increased intestinal activity, thus aggravating the colitis.

What is a safe amount for anyone to drink each day?

No more than two ounces of a hard liquor, more than two cans of beer or two glasses of wine.

Is it safe for me to take an occasional drink even though I am a chronic alcoholic?

No. It is well known that alcoholics who take even one drink may lose control and revert to heavy drinking.

QUESTIONS TO ASK YOUR DOCTOR

Since I tend to drink heavily, how can I prevent myself from becoming a true alcoholic?

Should I be hospitalized to overcome my drinking problem?

Are there any tests to determine whether or not I have a physical tendency to become addicted to alcohol?

How can I tell whether my drinking has already damaged my liver, kidneys, or brain?

Does drinking affect the eyesight?

How much is it safe for me to drink a day?

33. VITAMINS

Are vitamins essential to life?

Yes.

How can one tell whether he needs supplemental vitamins?

If he eats a normal diet and feels in good health, the chances are that vitamin intake is adequate.

Will the taking of large doses of vitamin C prevent me from catching colds?

Some people think so, but it has not been proved by medical investigation.

Can lack of vitamins be the cause of visual disturbances?
Yes, but only if there is a profound and prolonged deficiency in vitamin intake.

Is a lack of vitamins ever the cause for skin conditions?
Yes.

Can lack of vitamin A ever cause eye trouble?
Yes. A condition known as xerophthalmia may result.

Can lack of vitamins be the cause for cavities in teeth?
Usually not. That is more likely to be caused by mineral rather than vitamin deficiency.

Which foods are particularly rich in the various vitamins?
See Table of Vitamins in the back of this book (page 338).

Are the commercially advertised multivitamin pills satisfactory to restore vitamin deficiency?
Yes, in most cases. In some instances, a doctor will want to prescribe massive doses of a specific vitamin.

When is it necessary to take vitamins by injection?
When there is an acute vitamin deficiency that must be overcome quickly. Also, when a gastrointestinal disorder interferes with the absorption of ingested vitamins.

Is it possible to take an overdose of vitamins?
Yes.

What are some of the harmful effects of taking an overdose of vitamins?
1. Hypervitaminosis D in children is a definite disease entity.
2. The taking of excessive vitamin C may lead to stomach upset and diarrhea.

Should all people routinely take vitamin pills to maintain good health?

Not if they are in good health and eat a normal diet.

Do normally growing small children require extra vitamin intake?

Usually they do, because their rate of growth is so rapid.

Do elderly people require extra vitamins?

Usually they do because their vitamin intake by mouth is often inadequate.

Should supplementary vitamins be given to a pregnant woman?

Yes.

Will the taking of vitamins cause a gain in weight?

Only if one is underweight due to a vitamin deficiency. People of normal weight will not gain from taking vitamins as they contain no calories.

Will the taking of extra vitamins add calories to my food?

No. Vitamins contain no calories.

Are vitamins helpful in quieting the nerves?

Not if one is on a normal diet.

Will vitamins help to overcome anemia?

Yes, but only if the anemia is associated with a vitamin deficiency, as in pernicious anemia.

If one takes extra vitamins, will he have increased physical energy?

Only if there is an existing vitamin deficiency.

If one takes mineral oil regularly, will it interfere with the absorption of vitamins?

Not if the mineral oil is taken before going to bed at night, a few hours after the evening meal.

Does it make much difference which brand of vitamins is purchased?

No. All companies that sell vitamins must have their

products conform to the high standards set by the Federal Food and Drug Administration.

Is there any difference in the effect of synthetic vitamins and natural vitamins ingested in one's food?
No.

Do I have a vitamin deficiency?

Are there tests to diagnose which specific vitamin I lack?

Is my failing potency due to a vitamin lack?

Will I increase my potency by taking vitamin E?

Can I improve my vision by taking vitamin K?

Is my skin condition due to a vitamin deficiency?

Can I take supplementary vitamins for an indefinite period of time?

Is my fatigue due to a lack of vitamins?

Are my frequent colds due to vitamin deficiencies?

34. DIABETES

Is diabetes inherited?
Yes.

What are my chances of inheriting diabetes?
This will depend upon whether diabetes is present on both sides of your family. If only one parent or uncle or aunt has diabetes, your chances are good not to inherit the disease. If

it exists on both sides of the family, your chances are considerably poorer.

If one parent is diabetic, one out of four children will probably be diabetic. If both parents have diabetes, most of their children will develop the condition.

Is it wise for a diabetic to marry?

Yes, but he should receive counseling before embarking upon a family.

Is it wise for a diabetic to have children?

Yes, but it should be understood beforehand that the pregnancy might be complicated and the chances of a stillbirth are greater.

How can you diagnose diabetes?

By examining the blood, utilizing a test known as the glucose tolerance test. The finding of an elevated blood sugar does not always mean diabetes, as blood sugar levels can be high in a nondiabetic person if the test is taken shortly after eating a big meal containing large quantities of carbohydrates. Similarly, sugar in the urine is not always a sign of diabetes, though it may be.

How common is diabetes?

About 2 percent of the population are diabetic.

Does infection cause diabetes?

No, but it will intensify a preexisting diabetes. Many people who never knew they were diabetic first evidence symptoms and signs of the disease during or after an infection.

Will eating large amounts of sweets and carbohydrates cause diabetes?

No, but it will aggravate the condition and may cause an unknown, hidden diabetes to become symptomatic and apparent.

What are the symptoms of diabetes?
1. There may be no symptoms in mild cases.
2. Excessive thirst.
3. Excessive urination.

  4. Excessive appetite.
  5. Loss of weight.
  6. Loss of energy.
  7. Itching of skin.
  8. Coma, in extreme cases.

How is diabetes diagnosed positively?
  1. By finding an elevated blood sugar.
  2. By finding sugar in the urine.
  3. By finding a characteristic curve on performance of a glucose tolerance blood test.

Does sugar in the urine always indicate diabetes?
  No. There are a few uncommon conditions that can give a positive test for sugar in the urine.

How can one avoid diabetes?
  Since it is an inherent condition, one cannot avoid it. However, one can avoid active symptoms in some cases by eating a balanced diet low in carbohydrates and by keeping one's weight at a normal level.

Is it bad for a diabetic to be overweight?
  Yes.

Can I drink alcohol even though I have diabetes?
  Only in small quantities.

Should a diabetic test his urine daily before giving himself an injection of insulin?
  Yes.

What are the symptoms of insulin shock?
  Tremors, spots before the eyes, sweating, weakness, dizziness, confusion, a hollow feeling in the pit of the stomach, a desire to eat, fainting, convulsions.

What can I do if I feel shock coming on?
  Drink a glass of a sweet fruit juice, eat some candy or sugar, lie down.

Should a diabetic test himself to make sure he doesn't have acidosis?

Yes. This is done by a simple urine test.

Is it safe for a diabetic to become pregnant?

Yes, if the diabetes is under good control. Permission from an internist should be obtained first.

Is the pregnancy likely to be complicated?

Not necessarily. But there is an increased incidence of complicated pregnancies among diabetic women.

Are diabetics especially prone to infection?

Yes, if their diabetes is not under good continuous control. No, if it is well controlled.

What special care should diabetics take to avoid infection?

1. They should not walk barefoot.
2. They should not cut toenails down in the corners.
3. They should consult a doctor early in the onset of any potential illness or infection.

Which diabetics are most liable to infection, and where?

The older diabetic, who should take special care of his toenails and feet because the circulation to his feet is probably not as good as it once was.

Does the diabetic live as long as the nondiabetic?

As a matter of fact, the span of life of a diabetic is as long as that of a nondiabetic. This is because the diabetic learns to take good medical care of himself at all times.

What foods should the diabetic avoid?

He can eat everything as long as it conforms to his pre-determined, medically prescribed diet. Diabetics who take insulin or oral medications are frequently instructed by their physicians to eat everything.

Can diabetics safely undergo surgery?

Yes, but a medical specialist should regulate his status prior to and after surgery.

Can diabetics engage in strenuous physical exercise?

Yes, but such exercise burns extra sugar. It may, therefore, be necessary to alter the dosage of insulin or oral medications.

Can diabetes ever improve by itself?
One does not outgrow diabetes but as one learns to regulate the disease, its symptoms may disappear.

Are self-administered insulin injections painful?
Only slightly. Most diabetics get used to the pain very easily.

Can diabetic children be treated successfully with pills rather than insulin?
Not usually.

QUESTIONS TO ASK YOUR DOCTOR

What kind of diet must I follow?

What do I do about my insulin if I go off my diet?

What do I do about my antidiabetes pills if I go off my diet?

How can I regulate myself when I take a few drinks of alcohol?

How long should it take me to learn how to give myself insulin?

Must I take insulin indefinitely?

Why can't I be treated with the antidiabetes pills?

Can I look forward to a time when I can switch from insulin injections to antidiabetes pills?

At what age can my child be taught to give himself insulin?

35. OVERWEIGHT

Is a tendency to overweight inherited?
This question has not been clarified but it is a fact that obesity seems to occur in some families among most of its members. This may be due to their particular eating habits or to a constitutional inborn tendency to overweight.

Why are most people overweight?
Because they eat more each day than their body requires.

Is glandular malfunction a common cause of overweight?
No. It is a rare cause.

How can I tell if my glands are the cause of my overweight?
By having a thorough physical examination, including an evaluation of thyroid and pituitary gland function.

Will someone lose weight by taking thyroid pills?
Usually not. Most overweight is caused by overeating, not by a thyroid deficiency.

Should one medicate himself with thyroid?
No.

Will weight-reducing pills cause weight loss?
Only if they are accompanied by lessening of food intake. The pills may reduce appetite, thereby resulting in less caloric intake.

Are there any harmful effects from taking weight-reducing pills?
Yes. Many of them contain amphetamines and these drugs may cause a rise in blood pressure, sleeplessness, and nervousness.

Are there medicines that will cause loss of appetite by sickening the stomach?

Yes, but they should be taken on your doctor's advice.

How effective is physical exercise in producing weight loss?

Only mildly effective, although the number of calories consumed by moderate exercise is measurable. Restriction of food intake is a much quicker and more efficient way to lose weight.

Why is it that some people I know eat a lot of food and remain thin?

Because they eat nonfattening foods.

Will all overweight people lose weight if they diet properly?

Yes.

Will I live longer if I lose weight?

Vital statistics tell us that thin people have longer life spans than fat people.

Of what value are the so-called miracle diets?

They may help one to lose weight for a time, but their value is limited because they cannot be continued indefinitely and because they do not lead to a more sensible pattern of eating. Once off them, there is a tendency to put on weight quickly.

Are my chances of getting a coronary attack, high blood pressure, arthritis, or diabetes greater because I am overweight?

Yes.

What foods should I avoid to lose weight?

See diets in the back of this book (pages 331-336).

Are various types of baths helpful in weight loss?

To a limited extent, largely because they make one aware of the need to care for the body properly. The weight lost in the transpiration of water from the body is only temporary and is usually quickly regained. Food restriction is a much more important factor in weight loss.

Is spot-reducing possible?

Massages, slenderizing machines, rollers, and such devices merely delude the public. There is no such thing as spot-reducing.

Do vitamins tend to increase one's appetite?

No.

Is there a tendency to gain weight when someone stops smoking?

Yes, because then the tendency is to reach for food instead of a cigarette.

Will I become nervous if I diet strenuously?

Not if your diet is a sensible one and you avoid weight-reducing pills.

What are the side effects of a weight-reducing diet?

A tendency to become constipated, bad breath, and hunger pains.

How can I ease the hunger pangs which I always feel when I am on a diet?

By eating low calorie foods such as celery, lettuce, carrots, etc.

Is fasting a safe way to lose weight?

Only under the strict supervision of a doctor.

Must one drink a large amount of liquids while on a strenuous diet?

Yes, in order to avoid acidosis and to keep kidney function normal.

Should one restrict his salt intake while on a diet?

Yes, as salt results in retention of body fluids.

Is there a tendency to develop an attack of gout while on a strict diet?

Only if one has a constitutional tendency toward gout and has a high blood uric acid.

What can one do to avoid an attack of gout while dieting?
He can take antigout medications.

Will the taking of saccharin or other sweetening agents be harmful to one's general health?
No.

Are commercially packaged, low calorie foods helpful in weight loss?
Yes.

Do older people have more weight problems than younger people?
There is a tendency to put on weight as one passes into the fifties or sixties, but only if the body is neglected.

How is it that some people eat very little but still gain weight?
This is not true!

How many calories should a good reducing diet contain?
See diets in the back of this book (page 331).

How can I tell if I am overweight?
See the Weight Charts in the back of this book (page 336).

Is psychotherapy helpful in weight loss?
Many physicians think so, on the assumption that overeating is a neurotic manifestation. Psychotherapy may thereby overcome such a neurotic tendency.

Is hypnosis helpful in getting one to diet?
In people who can be hypnotized, it may be temporarily helpful.

See special diets in the back of this book (pages 331-336).

QUESTIONS TO ASK YOUR DOCTOR

Should I take weight-reducing pills?

How often should I come and see you if I am on weight-reducing pills?

How much weight must I lose?

Is heredity the cause of my overweight?

If I am overweight, what are the chances that my children will also be overweight?

How effective would injections be in helping me to lose weight?

Have I put on weight because I am at the menopause?

Should I take vitamin pills while I am on a strict diet?

36. CANCER AND ALLIED TUMORS

Is cancer contagious?

No. It must be stated, though, that the influence of viruses in the metamorphosis of a normal cell to a cancerous one has not yet been fully evaluated.

Am I likely to develop cancer if other members of my family have had the disease?

Not necessarily. Cancer is not inherited, although there may be an inherent tendency toward the development of certain types of tumors.

Is it safe for me to marry someone if several members of his family have cancer?

Yes. However, before you have children, it is a good idea to receive genetic counseling.

If I have a familial tendency toward cancer is there any way that I can prevent myself from developing this disease?

Yes, by thorough physical examinations—including cancer detection techniques—carried out twice a year by your physician.

Can I take any immunizing injections against cancer?

None are presently available. This may be possible at sometime in the future.

If I have a benign tumor, is there a chance it may become malignant?

Yes, although most malignant tumors start out as malignancies.

How can one tell whether a benign tumor is turning into a cancer?

This is extremely difficult to determine in most internal tumors. For this reason, surgical removal of all tumors is advocated early in the course of their growth.

Is there such a thing as an exceptionally malignant cancer or an exceptionally benign cancer?

Yes, certain cancers grow very rapidly while others are slow-growing and show little tendency to spread.

Do I have immunity to cancer because I am young?

No, but young people are less likely to develop certain kinds of cancer than older people.

Does obesity have anything to do with the development of cancer or other tumors?

For some unknown reason, the incidence of cancer is higher among overweight individuals.

Am I likely to develop cancer because I smoke?

Yes! Not only is cancer of the lip, tongue, cheeks, larynx, and lungs more prevalent among smokers but other types of cancer occur more often among this group.

Will the increased tendency toward cancer development diminish if I stop smoking?

Yes.

Is there a greater tendency to develop cancer when one lives in an area with marked air pollution?

In all probability, yes. However, the air pollution alone will not increase the tendency. It must be present along with other unfavorable factors.

Am I more likely to develop cancer because I drink heavily?

The incidence of cancer is slightly higher among those who drink heavily over many years time.

Is there any way to prevent spread of cancer from one part of the body to another?

Yes, by early surgical removal and by postoperative treatments with chemicals, or X-ray, or both.

How can I tell if I have a hidden cancer?

By submitting yourself to periodic health check-ups, including a complete history of any symptoms that have recently developed.

What are the danger signals of early cancer?

See Danger Signals, page 298.

How accurate is the Pap test in telling whether or not I have a cancer of the cervix or uterus?

It is accurate but it is not the sole method of arriving at a diagnosis. A pelvic examination, a biopsy of the cervix, and a scraping of the uterus should also be carried out if cancer in this area is suspected.

Is there any satisfactory blood test to determine whether I have cancer or a predisposition to cancer?

No, but encouraging progress has recently been reported on research along these lines.

Will cancer always show on X-ray examination?

No. Certain cancers of lymph glands, blood, and soft tissues do not show up on X-rays.

Can a surgeon always tell whether a tumor is cancerous when he removes it?

Not always. For this reason, all tissues removed are subjected to microscopic examination.

How long does it usually take to get a microscopic report after removal of a tumor?

If a frozen section examination is done, the answer will be forthcoming in a few minutes; if paraffin sections are made, it may take a few days before a final diagnosis can be rendered.

Is there a possibility that cancer will disappear by itself without treatment?

This, unfortunately, happens only in extremely rare cases.

Does cancer usually end fatally if it is untreated?

Yes, although there are some types, such as skin cancer, which do not always result in fatalities.

Does loss of weight indicate the presence of cancer?

Weight loss is not always an early sign of malignancy but often develops as a cancer advances.

Do people with cancer usually show anemia early in the course of their disease?

Some do; most don't show it until late in the disease.

Is loss of appetite a sign of early cancer?

Yes, if the cancer is in the upper gastrointestinal tract. It may be a late or nonexistent symptom in malignancies located elsewhere in the body.

Does the size of a cancer usually have much to do with its degree of malignancy?

Yes, in many cases, because the larger cancers have been present for a longer period of time.

Danger Signals of Possible Cancer

The presence of one or more of the signs listed below does NOT necessarily mean that one has cancer. However, their presence should be an indication for medical consultation and examination.

1. The appearance of a lump or thickening in or beneath the skin, in the breast, or anywhere else on the body.

2. The increase in size of any lump that one knows has been in existence for a long time.

3. A change in color, and increase in size, or bleeding from any mole, wart, or ulceration on the skin.

4. The coughing of blood, especially when unaccompanied by a respiratory infection.

5. The vomiting of blood.

6. Blood in the stool.

7. Blood in the urine.

8. Hoarseness that lasts for more than two weeks.

9. Difficulty in swallowing.

10. Any chronic cough, whether associated with smoking or not.

11. Repeated headaches, especially when associated with blurred vision, loss of balance, or muscle weaknesses.

12. A persistent, unexplained loss of appetite.

13. A change in bowel habit.

14. Vaginal bleeding not associated with menstruation.

15. A sore that does not heal.

QUESTIONS TO ASK YOUR DOCTOR

Will you tell me the truth if I have cancer?

Must my cancer be treated by surgery, or can it be treated by X-rays or chemicals?

How will I know if my cancer has spread to other organs?

How will I know if I have been completely cured after treatment for a cancer?

Will there be a tendency for my tumor to recur after it has been removed surgically?

How can you minimize the chances of recurrence of my cancer?

Can I return to normal life after my cancer has been removed?

Will the removal of the cancer affect my sex life?

Will I be able to resume my physical activities after the cancer has been removed?

Will I be able to become pregnant after my cancer is removed?

Will pregnancy in any way affect the recurrence of my cancer?

After the treatment of my tumor, how often should I return for follow-up examination?

What tests will be made to establish a positive diagnosis of cancer in my case?

Can a positive diagnosis of cancer be made while I am under anesthesia?

Should I tell my family that I have cancer?

Will I be able to return to a normal existence after my tumor has been treated?

What are the chances of full recovery from my cancer after it has been removed?

How long do you think it will take me to recover fully?

37. X-RAYS

Is there any danger in being X-rayed?

Not if it is done for diagnostic purposes and you are in the hands of a trained technician. The amount of exposure to X-rays is so slight that harm cannot result. Restraint is used, however, in X-raying women who are pregnant.

Is it safe to X-ray my child?

Yes, if the X-rays are carried out by a qualified radiologist.

Are birth deformities more likely to develop in my offspring if I have undergone X-ray treatment?

No.

Is there any danger of getting a shock from an X-ray machine?

No. They are all shockproofed.

Do all the tissues of the body show up on X-ray?

No. Most soft tissues will not show up unless contrast media, such as barium or iodine solution, are given beforehand.

Can X-rays confirm diagnoses in all cases?

No.

Does a negative X-ray necessarily mean that there is no disease?

No. X-rays are only an aid in diagnosis, not the definitive means of reaching one.

Are X-ray films the property of the doctor or do I own them?

They are part of your permanent medical record and thus the property of your doctor or hospital. You pay him for the *interpretation* of the X-rays, not for the films.

Will X-ray doctors give me the X-rays if I want them?
They may release them to you if you agree to return them.

What is fluoroscopy?
X-raying part of the body and recording the rays on a fluorescent screen. This is done to view various organs in motion.

Is it safe to be fluoroscoped?
Yes, provided such examination is conducted by a qualified radiologist.

Do X-rays taken for diagnostic purposes result in overexposure?
No. Radiologists are always careful not to permit overexposure.

Does one usually get an overdose of X-rays from the usual methods of examination?
No.

Will an overdose of X-rays hurt my reproductive organs?
Only if an extraordinary number of X-rays are taken within a short period of time. It is extremely rare that such exposure will occur.

Will all breast tumors show up on X-rays of the breast?
No, the majority will not.

Will an X-ray show definitely whether a fractured bone is present?
Yes.

Will X-rays show the presence of a muscle sprain or a tear in a ligament or a torn cartilage?
No.

Will X-rays show whether or not I have a slipped disk?
In some cases they will, in others they will not.

What is a myelogram?
An X-ray of the spinal cord carried out after the injection of a dye which will show on the film.

Are myelograms dangerous?
No.

Will a myelogram usually show whether or not I have a slipped disk?
Yes.

What is X-ray therapy?
The use of X-rays in the treatment of a disease such as cancer.

Are X-ray treatments only given for maligant conditions?
No. There are a considerable number of nontumorous diseases in which X-ray treatments are helpful.

Does radioactive cobalt emit X-rays?
Yes.

Is X-ray therapy safe?
Yes. There is no danger from the controlled doses of radiation given by a trained X-ray therapist.

Is there any pain or discomfort from undergoing X-ray therapy?
There is no pain, but in a certain number of patients there may be nausea, loss of appetite, and a general feeling of weakness. This may have its onset during the last two or three weeks of X-ray therapy and it may persist for a few weeks after the therapy had been completed.

Will my skin get red or brown after repeated X-ray treatments?
Yes, in most cases.

Will X-ray treatments cause the permanent loss of hair in an area being treated?
In many instances this will happen.

Will X-ray therapy destroy the normal cells around the diseased cells?
Usually not.

Does radium have the same effect as X-rays?
Yes.

Do radioactive isotopes have the same effect as X-rays?
   Yes.

Will radioactive iodine cure my goiter?
   In some cases. However, in other patients surgical removal of the goiter is necessary to effect a cure.

Are there radioactive isotopes other than iodine that are helpful in treating disease?
   Yes, there are many, including radioactive gold, phosphorus, cesium, strontium, iron, and cobalt.

QUESTIONS TO ASK YOUR DOCTOR

May I eat before I undergo my X-ray examination?

Why must I have so many X-ray treatments for my condition?

Will X-ray therapy produce a cure in my condition?

Will X-ray therapy prevent my tumor from spreading to other parts of my body?

Can my condition be treated by X-rays rather than surgery?

PART III

1. FIRST AID

ARTIFICIAL RESPIRATION

Mouth-to-mouth breathing is the most efficient method of artificial respiration. To perform it:

1. Place the stricken person flat on his back.

2. Loosen the collar or any clothing that is constricting the neck or chest.

3. Lift up the chin so that the head is extended. This will produce the best airway from the mouth to the lungs.

4. With your fingers, pinch the stricken person's nostrils so that they are closed.

5. Take a deep breath, place your mouth directly over the stricken person's mouth, and blow out as hard as you can.

6. Take away your mouth so that the air you have blown into the other person's lungs can be expelled.

7. Repeat this maneuver every five to six seconds (ten to twelve times a minute).

8. Do not stop mouth-to-mouth resuscitation as long as the stricken person has a pulse or heartbeat.

9. As soon as you tire, have someone else continue the artificial respiration.

10. Wipe out the stricken person's mouth if mucus collects and interferes with free passage of air.

11. Do not stop artificial respiration until you are positive the pulse and heartbeat have stopped. This may necessitate mouth-to-mouth resuscitation for anywhere from a few minutes to more than an hour.

12. Do not stop mouth-to-mouth breathing immediately after the stricken person takes a breath or two on his own. Continue the maneuver until regular breathing is resumed.

13. After resumption of breathing, keep the stricken person quiet and warm, and do not let him move until a doctor or an ambulance arrives.

14. Do not fear that you will catch a disease from the stricken person. Remember, you may be saving a life!

FIRST AID IN HEART ATTACKS

1. Place the victim in a semi-sitting position.

2. Do not permit the victim to walk or move about.

3. Discover whether the patient has any special heart medication in his clothing. If so, administer the medication according to the patient's instructions.

4. Encourage deep breathing.

5. If breathing stops, give mouth-to-mouth artificial respiration.

6. If heart stops, give CARDIAC MASSAGE.
    * Place the patient flat on his back on a firm surface. (If he is on a soft bed, gently place him on the floor.)
    * Kneel and straddle the patient.
    * Place the base of your palm of the right hand flat upon the patient's breastbone.
    * Place the palm of your left hand over the right hand and press down so that the breastbone is depressed between one and two inches.
    * Release the pressure.
    * Repeat the pressure every one to two seconds until the heartbeat returns. You can determine this by leaning down and placing your ear to the chest.
    * If no heartbeat is heard, continue the cardiac massage for at least ten to fifteen minutes.

* Do not stop the cardiac massage when only an occasional beat is heard. Continue until a regular rhythm returns.
* If the patient is resuscitated, do not permit him to move. Send for an ambulance and medical aid.

FIRST AID FOR BLEEDING

1. Apply pressure directly over the bleeding wound, using a sterile gauze pad (if available), a clean handkerchief, or a napkin.

2. Pressure on the wound should be firm and continued for five to fifteen minutes. Use the fingers or the palm of the hand to create the pressure. Bandage the area with firm compression.

3. If the wound continues to bleed despite pressure, and if the wound is in the arm or leg, a tourniquet should be applied two to four inches above the site of the hemorrhage. The tourniquet should never be left in place for more than ten to fifteen minutes.

4. A handkerchief, tie, scarf, shirt, or belt can be fashioned into a temporary tourniquet.

5. A tourniquet should *never* be applied until all attempts have been made to control bleeding by direct pressure on the wound. Tourniquets, if kept in place too long, may do permanent damage to the limb's blood supply.

6. The wound should be cleansed thoroughly with plain soap and water. Do NOT use iodine or other strong antiseptics to clean a wound.

7. When applying a bandage, be sure not to apply it so tightly that it obstructs circulation.

8. Never apply a tourniquet to the neck, chest, or abdomen.

9. Internal bleeding can often be diagnosed by the passage of blood in the stool, by passing jet-black stools, or by the coughing up or vomiting of blood. In this case the victim should lie perfectly quiet and flat, and immediate medical aid should be summoned. Do *not* give the patient anything to drink, nor any medication.

FIRST AID FOR CHOKING

1. If the patient is a child, turn him upside down and slap him on the back.

2. Encourage the victim to cough.

3. If the obstructing substance is not coughed up, put your index finger in the victim's mouth and sweep it around the back of the throat. This will often dislodge the foreign body, as many of them are stuck, within reach, just below the back of the tongue.

4. If choking continues, *but patient is able to breathe,* transport him as soon as possible to the nearest hospital.

5. If the patient turns blue and is completely unable to breathe, and if medical help is not available—*and when it is obvious that the victim is choking to death*—perform an emergency TRACHEOTOMY:
    * Take a knife in one hand.
    * Steady the windpipe in the other hand.
    * Stab a hole in the windpipe in the midline below the Adam's apple.
    * Twist the knife blade while keeping it in place in the windpipe. This will keep the hole open and allow the patient to keep breathing.
    * Transport the patient to the nearest hospital.

FIRST AID IN FRACTURES OR DISLOCATIONS

1. Do NOT move the patient if medical aid is available. In such instances, do not touch the injured part.

2. Do NOT permit a patient to stand on an injured leg.

3. Do NOT try to straighten a broken arm or leg, if an ambulance or doctor is available.

4. Do NOT try to push back a protruding bone if there is a break in the skin.

5. Do NOT apply a tourniquet unless the bleeding is profuse and you have been unable to stop it by direct pressure.

6. Place a sterile gauze pad or a clean handkerchief over any break in the skin.

7. If patient must be moved, splint the broken limb before moving:

   * An umbrella, cane, or straight piece of wood can be used as a splint. Use handkerchiefs, ties, scarfs, or a torn shirt to keep the splint from moving.

   * Place a handkerchief or some article of clothing between the splint and the body when tying the splint in place. This will prevent damage from too much pressure.

   * A broken shoulder, collarbone, or arm should be splinted by wrapping the arm securely to the body. Use a shirt, scarf, or bandage to accomplish this.

   * If the broken arm is in a hanging position, splint it in that position to the side of the body.

   * If the broken arm is bent at the elbow, splint it in that position to the body.

   * A broken leg should be splinted by tying it snugly to the other leg.

   * Give the same first aid to a dislocation as to a fracture. Do not try to replace the dislocated bone if medical help is available. If no medical aid is available, pull steadily and firmly on the dislocated arm or leg and splint to the body.

   * Move the patient in a lying-down position.

   * If the injury is to the neck or back, keep the patient's body straight. *Do not bend the neck or lift the head.* Place the patient face down on his stomach. If the patient must be moved, transport him in this position.

FIRST AID FOR BURNS

1. Burned areas should be placed under cold running water for ten to fifteen minutes.

2. If the burned area is dirty, mild soap should be applied gently while the area is under running water.

3. A clean gauze dressing should be applied to the burn.

4. Blisters should be left alone. Do NOT open them.

5. Do NOT put butter or ointments on burned areas (your doctor will apply such medication, if indicated).

6. If the burned area is extensive, the patient should drink large quantities of water.

7. If the patient shows signs of shock (rapid, weak pulse, shortness of breath, profuse sweating, ashen gray appearance, anxiety), he should be covered with warm blankets and kept still.

8. All burns, except mild, minor ones, should be treated by a doctor. Take the patient to a doctor or to the nearest hospital.

9. Burns from *chemicals* should be flushed immediately with cold running water. This applies especially to burns of the eye.

FIRST AID IN CONVULSIONS OR FAINTING

1. Make sure there has been no head injury. Look for lacerations and large bumps.

2. Allow the patient to lie down and give him plenty of room so that he can thrash about freely.

3. Loosen tight collars, belts, and other clothing.

4. Place a folded handkerchief between the patient's teeth if he is convulsing. BEWARE OF BEING BITTEN ACCIDENTALLY. Keep your fingers out of a convulsing patient's mouth.

5. Do NOT try to restrain the convulsing movements.

6. Do NOT throw cold water in the patient's face.

7. If the patient is still but unconscious, permit him to lie flat but elevate his feet and legs about twelve inches above body level.

8. If the person is unknown to you, search his clothing. He may have a card informing the first-aider that he is subject to convulsions and bearing instructions on what to do and who to call.

9. Do not leave a patient alone after he has recovered from a faint or convulsion. It may require anywhere from one

half hour to one hour for him to regain full knowledge of his situation.

10. Do NOT pick up a convulsing child during the convulsion. Rarely does a convulsion or faint last more than a few minutes. It is better to keep the child in bed and to summon an ambulance or doctor.

11. Do NOT place a convulsing child in water.

12. Anyone who has had a fainting spell or convulsion should be seen by a doctor shortly thereafter.

FIRST AID IN POISONING

Whenever a poison has been taken, the stomach should be emptied as soon as possible. The quickest way to do this is to cause vomiting by placing your fingers down the back of the throat, or by giving the victim warm salt water to drink (a teaspoon of salt to a large glass of water). The next move is to administer the specific antidote to the poison that has been ingested.

The Poison	*The Antidote*
Acids	Milk, raw eggs, gelatin, bicarbonate of soda gargle
Alcohol	Black coffee
Alkalines	Milk, wine, lemon or apple juice
Ammonia	Inhale vinegar solution
Arsenic	Milk
Barbiturates	Black coffee, a strong laxative
Belladonna	Black coffee, charcoal tablets
Benzene	Milk
Botulism	Castor oil, charcoal tablets, a soap-suds enema
Carbon dioxide	Fresh air, mouth-to-mouth resuscitation, oxygen

Chlorine gas	Inhale warm steam
Cocaine	Any barbiturate
Cyanide	Artificial respiration, oxygen
Iodine	Milk, raw eggs, bicarbonate of soda, laxatives
Lead	Milk, whites of eggs, Epsom salts
Lysol	Milk, raw eggs, gelatin
Mercury	Milk, raw eggs, bicarbonate of soda
Morphine or heroin	Black coffee, strong tea, charcoal tablets
Mushrooms	Flour paste, strong tea, charcoal tablets
Snake bite	Make a criss-cross incision in the area of the bite, suck out the wound, place the tourniquet above the site of the bite, keep the patient still until medical aid arrives.
Strychnine	Any barbiturate, small amount of alcohol, artificial respiration, if necessary
Wood alcohol	Black coffee

* When victim begins to vomit, place him face down with his head to the side. This will prevent aspiration of vomit into the lungs.

* Save the poison container to show the doctor. This will help in determining specific treatment to be undertaken in the hospital.

* Breathing is often difficult after ingesting or inhaling poison. Therefore, loosen all tight clothing and, if necessary, assist breathing with artificial respiration.

FIRST AID IN SUFFOCATION FROM GASES

1. Open all windows and doors wide to let in fresh air.

2. Begin artificial respiration by mouth-to-mouth breathing if the patient is not breathing on his own.

3. Continue artificial respiration as long as there is a heartbeat.

4. If patient is conscious, encourage deep breathing.

5. Call the police and ask for a pulmotor if breathing has ceased or is irregular.

6. Keep the patient warm.

7. Do not allow patient to get up even after he has recovered.

FIRST AID IN ELECTRIC SHOCK

1. DO NOT TOUCH ANYONE WHO IS STILL IN CONTACT WITH ELECTRICITY. You may be shocked too!

2. Disconnect the electric current immediately, if at all possible.

3. Detach the victim from the electric contact immediately. Do this with a *dry stick* or other piece of wood, rolled-up newspapers, or dry rubber gloves, shoving the wire away.

4. If possible, use an axe or other tool that has a *wooden handle* to break the wire bearing the current.

5. If victim is not breathing, give mouth-to-mouth artificial respiration (see page 308). Continue as long as there is a heartbeat.

6. Give first aid to any burned area (see section on Burns).

7. Keep patient warm and in a half-sitting position if he is breathing.

8. Send for an ambulance or doctor.

2. IMMUNIZATIONS
AND VACCINATIONS

* Most pediatricians believe that it is better to protect a child against childhood diseases than to let him get natural immunity through catching the disease. Even the most minor of the childhood diseases can sometimes lead to serious complications.

* Allergic children must be vaccinated carefully when the vacine is derived from chick embryos. A determination of allergy to eggs must first be made, and, if found to be positive, consultation with an allergist is advisable.

* Childhood contagious diseases tend to be more severe when contracted by adults, especially measles, mumps, whooping cough, and chicken pox.

* Recent studies would seem to indicate that the incidence of smallpox in the United States is lower than the incidence of complications following smallpox vaccination. Nonetheless, one should be guided by his pediatrician's or family physician's advice regarding the advisability of vaccination.

* The United States Public Health Office will advise what immunizations and vaccinations are necessary when traveling to a foreign land. Contact the local office of the U.S. Public Health Service or your local department of health office.

Immunization and Vaccination

Disease	Material used	When given	Number of injections	Spacing of injections	Reactions	Duration of immunity	Recall or booster injections	Remarks
Diphtheria	Diphtheria toxoid	Infancy and childhood, or on exposure	3	1 month	None to slight	Varies	1st booster— after 1 year 2d and 3d— 2-year intervals 4th and 5th— 3-year intervals and on exposure to disease	All three (diphtheria, tetanus and whooping cough) may be combined in a single injection (in young children only)
Whooping cough	Pertussis vaccine	Infancy and childhood, or on exposure	3	1 month	Slight to moderate	Varies		
Tetanus	Tetanus toxoid	Infancy and childhood, or after injury	3	1 month	None to slight	Varies		
Smallpox	Cowpox virus	Infancy, childhood, and adulthood	1	....	Moderate	Several years	5-7 years and for foreign travel	....
Poliomyelitis	Salk polio vaccine	Infancy to 40 years or older	3–4	First two 1 month apart, third 7 months later	None	Unknown (probably long)	4th injection one year after 3d injection	Now used only occasionally
	Sabin polio vaccine	3, 4, 5 months of age	No injections; 3 oral doses	1 month	None	Probably permanent	Not necessary	
Typhoid fever	Typhoid, para-typhoid vaccine	When traveling to suspicious area	3	1-4 weeks	Moderate	1-3 years	Every 1-3 years	....
Mumps	Mumps vaccine	During adolescence or adulthood	2	1 week	Bad if sensitive to eggs	Unknown	None	Not given to those sensitive to eggs
Infectious hepatitis	Gamma globulin	On exposure to case of infectious hepatitis	1	....	None	4-6 weeks	None	....
Scarlet fever	Penicillin	On exposure to case of scarlet fever	3	Daily	None	4-6 weeks	Same procedure if reexposed	May give penicillin only in adequate dosage
Rabies	Rabies vaccine	Following suspicious animal bite	14	Daily	Slight	3-6 months	if bitten again after 3 months	May not need full series if animal is found not infected
Cholera	Cholera vaccine	When traveling to suspicious area	2	7-10 days	Slight	Short	Every 6-12 months	....

Immunization and Vaccination (cont'd)

Disease	Material used	When given	Number of injections	Spacing of injections	Reactions	Duration of immunity	Recall or booster injections	Remarks
Typhus fever	Typhus vaccine	When traveling to suspicious area	2–3	1 week	Slight	Short	Every 12 months	....
Yellow fever	Yellow fever vaccine	When traveling to suspicious area	1	....	May be moderate	Long	Every 6 years	Must be careful of reactions in those sensitive to eggs
Plague	Plague vaccine	When traveling to suspicious area	2–3	1 week	Slight	Short	Every 6-12 months	....
Influenza	Influenza vaccine	During epidemics	2	1 week	Slight	Short	....	....
Rocky Mountain spotted fever	Rocky Mountain spotted fever vaccine	When exposed to ticks in suspicious areas	3	1 week	Moderate	Short	Annually	Must be careful of reactions in those sensitive to eggs
Measles	Measles vaccine	9 to 12 months of age	3	1 month	Moderate	Long	None	....
German measles	German measles virus	Childhood; adulthood for females of childbearing age	1	....	None	Unknown (probably long)	None	Woman should not be pregnant, nor become pregnant for 2 months
Chicken pox	None							

318

3. VITAL SIGNS

Normal temperature: Adult 98.6° Fahrenheit
                                Child 99.0° Fahrenheit

Normal pulse rates: Adult 72 per minute
                                Child 80 per minute

Normal respiratory rate: 16-18 per minute

Normal blood pressure: 110/70 to 130/85

* Some healthy people habitually run a lower than normal temperature, such as 98°F; other equally healthy people habitually run a higher than normal temperature, such as 99° F.

* A rise in temperature above one degree usually denotes the presence of an infection.

* Extremely low temperatures may be caused by a debilitated state, or by prolonged exposure to cold.

* The pulse rate usually rises 10 to 40 or more beats per minute when performing strenuous physical exercise, or when in a frightened or disturbed emotional state.

* Some healthy people habitually run a low pulse rate of 60 to 70 beats per minute; other healthy people habitually run a high pulse rate of 80 to 90 per minute.

* With each one-degree rise of temperature above normal, there is usually an increase in pulse rate of 10 beats per minute.

* A persistent low pulse rate (below 50 per minute) may indicate the presence of a heart block.

* A persistent high pulse rate (above 100 per minute) may indicate the presence of an overactive thyroid gland, or may be evidence of a heart disorder.

* Pulse rates are invariable slower during sleep and rest than during waking hours and physical activity.

* Respiratory rates above normal may be associated with:
  1. Strenuous physical exercise.
  2. Emotional states.
  3. Respiratory infections.
  4. High altitudes.
  5. Cardiac disorders.
  6. Blockage of the respiratory passageway.

* The blood pressure figure *above* the "/" line is called the *systolic* pressure, that is, the force of blood populsion through the arteries during heart contraction. The blood pressure figure *below* the "/" line is called the *diastolic* pressure, that is, the force of blood propulsion through the arteries during relaxation of the heart.

* In healthy people, blood pressure readings may be as low as 100/70 during sleep or rest, and as high as 140/90 during strenuous physical exercise or periods of excitement.

* It is *not* true that normal systolic blood pressure should be 100 plus one's age. In elderly healthy people, pressure ranges are considered to be normal up to 140/90.

* Persistent low blood pressure is not usually serious, unless it is habitually below 90/60. Such low pressures may indicate marked debility, or may be associated with serious anemia, chronic disease, or malfunction of the adrenal glands.

* Persistent high blood pressure is abnormal, and may be caused by hardening of the arteries, kidney disease, heart disease, or other serious illness. Emotional instability may cause transient high blood pressure, but this is not an indication of organic disease.

4. BLOOD, URINE, AND STOOL TESTS

Blood Counts

	Normal	Above normal may indicate:	Below normal may indicate:
Red blood cells	Male: 4,700,000 to 5,500,000	Polycythemia; dehydration	Anemia; blood loss
	Female: 4,400,000 to 5,200,000	Polycythemia; dehydration	Anemia; blood loss
White blood cells	Male: 8,000 to 10,000	Infection; blood disease	Viral infection; blood disorders
	Female: 8,000 to 10,000	Infection; blood disease	Viral infection; blood disorders
Hemoglobin	Male: 14–15 Gm.	Polycythemia; dehydration	Anemia; blood loss
	Female: 13.5–14.5 Gm.	Polycythemia; dehydration	Anemia; blood loss
Hematocrit	Male: 42–52%	Dehydration	Anemia; blood loss
	Female: 38–48%	Dehydration	Anemia; blood loss
Blood platelets	Male: 250,000–350,000 cu. mm.		Bleeding tendency
	Female: 250,000–350,000 cu. mm.		Bleeding tendency

Differential Count

	Normal	Above normal may indicate:	Below normal may indicate:
Polys	50–65%	Systemic infection	Lowered body resistance
Band forms	1–5%	Acute infection	
Lymphocytes	20–40%	Subacute or chronic infections; mononucleosis	
Monocytes	1–5%	Subacute or chronic infections; mononucleosis	
Eosinophiles	1–4%	Allergic response	
Basophiles	0–1%	Blood disorder	
Bleeding time	Less than 5 minutes	Bleeding tendency	

Differential Count (cont'd)

	Normal	Above normal may indicate:	Below normal may indicate:
Coagulation time	Less than 12 minutes	Bleeding tendency; hemophilia	
Prothrombin time	14–16 seconds	Bleeding tendency; liver disease	
Sickle cell prep	Negative	Positive prep indicates tendency toward sickle cell anemia	

Blood Chemistries

	Normal	Above normal may indicate:	Below normal may indicate:
Calcium	8.5–10.5 mg.%	Tumor or over-activity of parathyroid glands	Weakness or disease
Phosphorus	2.5–4.5 mg.%	Disorder of parathyroid glands	Disorder of parathyroid glands
Glucose (sugar)	65–110 mg.%	Diabetes mellitus	Hyperinsulinism or pancreatic tumor
Urea nitrogen	10–20 mg.%	Kidney disease	
Uric acid	2.5–8 mg.%	Gout	
Cholesterol	150–300 mg.%	Premature hardening of arteries; thyroid disorder	
Total protein	6–8 Gm.%		Debilitated state; starvation; chronic illness
Albumin	3.5–5 Gm.%		Upset in protein metabolism
Total bilirubin	0.2–1.0 mg.%	Jaundice; liver disease; gallbladder disease	
Alkaline phosphatase	30–85 mu./ml.	Obstruction of flow of bile	
Lactic dehydrogenese	90–200 mu./ml.	Tissue damage	
SGOT (enzyme)	10–50 mu./ml.	Tissue damage, as in coronary thrombosis or liver disease	
Amylase	60–160 mg.%	Inflammation of pancreas	
Lipose	0.2–1.5 units	Inflammation of pancreas	

Blood Chemistries (cont'd)

	Normal	Above normal may indicate:	Below normal may indicate:
Thymol turbidity	0.4 units	Liver disease	
Creatinine	1–2.5 mg.%	Urinary obstruction; kidney disease	
Sodium	135–145 mEq.	Water retention; upset in adrenal function	Upset in chemical balance
Potassium	4–5.7 mEq.	Impending heart malfunction	Upset in chemical balance
Chlorides	97–106 mEq.	Water retention; upset in adrenal function	Upset in chemical balance
Total lipids	600–800 mg.%	Upset in fat metabolism	
Phospholipids	250–350 mg.%	Upset in fat metabolism	
Fibrinogen	0.2–0.6 Gm.%		Bleeding tendency
T3	25–35%	Overactive thyroid gland	Underactive thyroid gland
T4	3–6 mEq.	Overactive thyroid gland	Underactive thyroid gland
PBI	3.5–8 mEq.	Overactive thyroid gland	Underactive thyroid gland
pCO_2	35–45 mm.Hg.	Acidosis	Alkalosis
pH	7.35–7.45	Alkalosis	Acidosis
pO_2 (arterial)	95–104 mm.HG.	Alkalosis	Acidosis

* Chemical findings may vary according to whether blood has been taken after eating, or after several hours of fasting. When abnormal results have been obtained, the test should be repeated.

* Blood chemical determinations should be made once yearly on all adults as part of their general health check-up.

* Anemia will not result from drawing several vials of blood for testing. Adults have between five and six quarts of circulating blood in their bodies. Rarely are more than two ounces ever taken for blood tests.

* Blood chemistries and blood counts are taken routinely on every patient admitted to a hospital.

* It is essential to test the bleeding time and coagulation time on every infant and young child before he undergoes even the most minor operative procedure.

* Blood grouping (typing) is performed each time a patient undergoes major surgery in which a transfusion may become necessary. The patient's blood is always crossmatched for compatability with the donor's blood.

* Rh compatability between patient and donor is determined in all cases prior to giving a blood transfusion.

* Many diseases, including several forms of anemia and leukemia, can be diagnosed by a simple blood count. However, other blood and lymph diseases cannot be diagnosed by a blood count and may require sampling of the bone marrow or the surgical removal of a lymph gland.

* Many diseases, including nephritis, uremia, diabetes, hepatitis, pancreatitis, etc., can be diagnosed through chemical analysis of the blood. However, clinical evaluation of the patient is essential to confirm the blood chemical findings.

Urine Analysis

	Normal	Abnormal
Amount in 24 hours	1200–1500 cc. (between 1 and 1½ quarts)	Markedly decreased amounts, or failure to excrete urine, indicates: (a) kidney disease, (b) obstruction to outflow of urine from bladder, etc.
Color	Water color to amber	(a) Very dark urine may indicate marked concentration due to excessive perspiration or inadequate drinking of fluids. (b) Dark brownish urine may accompany jaundice. (c) Reddish urine may indicate bleeding from kidney, ureter, bladder, prostate, or urethra.
Specific gravity	1.017–1.020	Very low specific gravities (on repeated examinations) may indicate inadequate kidney function. Very high specific gravity indicates a concentrated urine.
Acidity	Slightly acid (pH 5.3)	Markedly acid or alkaline urine is often caused by the diet one follows or medications one takes. Acidity and alkalinity can be altered by changing diet or giving appropriate medication.
Albumin	None	Presence of albumin may indicate nephritis, nephrosis, or other kidney disorders.
Sugar	None	Presence usually indicates diabetes.

Urine Analysis (cont'd)

	Normal	Abnormal
Urea	30 Gm. in 24-hour specimen	
Uric acid	0.4 to 1.0 Gm. in 24-hour specimen	Marked alterations may indicate kidney or liver disease.
Ammonia	0.5 to 1.0 Gm. in 24-hour specimen	
Red blood cells	Very occasionally, cell is seen on microscopic examination	A large number of red cells indicates bleeding from some point in the genitourinary tract.
White blood cells	Very occasionally, cell is seen on microscopic examination	A large number of white blood cells indicates an infection originating somewhere in the genitourinary tract.
Pus cells	None	A large number of pus cells indicates an infection in the genitourinary tract.

* Urinalysis should be a routine procedure, carried out during every complete physical examination. It should be performed at least once yearly.

* Blood in the urine may be serious. Anyone who has even the smallest amount of blood in the urine should consult his physician.

* Untreated diabetes usually is associated with sugar in the urine. However, one can have diabetes, with a high blood sugar level, and still have urine that is free of sugar.

* Burning on urination may be due to inadequate intake of fluids with too great a concentration of urine, or it may be a sign of a urinary infection.

* Very dark urine may be due to inadequate fluid intake, or may be caused by jaundice.

* Frequency of urination in a middle-aged or elderly male may be due to an enlarged prostate gland, or to a urinary infection.

* Frequency of urination in a female may be due to a urinary infection, or to a weakened muscle structure of the bladder or urethra.

* Albumin in the urine, if persistent, may indicate kidney disease.

* People normally void more often than usual in cold

weather, when under emotional stress, and when they eat
or drink a great deal.

STOOL EXAMINATION

* Blood in the stool, or blood mixed with the stool, whether
bright red or dark in color, is abnormal and warrants a
visit to your physician.

* Blood may indicate hemorrhoids, a polyp in the colon, a
bowel tumor, or may be due merely to passage of a large,
impacted bolus of stool.

* Persistent diarrhea may indicate a dysentery infection, a
parasitic infection, or the presence of colitis.

* Stool examination for parasites is essential when diarrhea
is persistent, especially after returning from a trip to a
foreign land.

* Jet-black stools usually indicate that bleeding has occurred
in the upper gastrointestinal tract. The taking of iron pills
may also color the stool black, or a greenish black color.

* Inabilty to move one's bowels may be due merely to constipation, or may be an indication of a bowel tumor. Any
persistent change in bowel habit and in the character of
the stool should be reported to your physician.

* Mucus in the stool usually has little medical significance.

* Some healthy people normally move their bowels once or
twice daily; other healthy people normally move their
bowels only every other day.

* Laxatives should not be given for constipation if the
constipation is associated with abdominal pain.

5. MEDICINES AND MEDICAL SUPPLIES TO BE KEPT IN THE HOME

MEDICINES

Bottle of 5-grain aspirin tablets
Bottle of antiacid tablets
Box of powdered bicarbonate of soda
Box of powdered Epsom salts
Bottle of mild laxative tablets
Bottle of mineral oil
Bottle of milk of magnesia
1 ounce of paregoric
1 bottle of eyewash
Bottle of 5-grain salt tablets
Bottle of rubbing alcohol (70%)
Bottle of mild mouthwash
Bottle of oil of cloves
Bottle of witch hazel
Bottle of antibiotic capsules (to be taken only after consulting your doctor)
Bottle of hydrogen peroxide

SUPPLIES

Rolls of 2- and 3-inch Ace (elastic) bandages
Rolls of 1- and 2-inch adhesive tape
Rolls of 1- and 2-inch gauze bandage
Box of assorted Band-Aids
Roll of absorbent cotton
Box of 2 x 2-inch, and 4 x 4-inch gauze pads
Box of cotton-tipped applicators
Tube of Vaseline

*All containers should be child-proof and kept out of the reach of children.

Eye cup
Bedpan
Electric pad
Flashlight
Oral and rectal thermometer
Douche bag and attachments
Enema bag and attachments
Enamel basin
Plastic drinking tube
Ice bag
Hot water bag
Rubber pad
Steam inhalator and attachments
Tweezers
Scissors
Urinal
Rubber tubing for tourniquet

* There is no such thing as completely "harmless" medicine. If someone is sensitive, even a seemingly innocuous medication may cause a severe reaction. For this reason, *all* medicines should be treated with respect.

* People should always turn on the bathroom light before reaching into the cabinet to take a medicine. The selection of the wrong drug may have dire consequences.

* A medication that has only a mild effect upon an adult may be extremely toxic to a child. It is, therefore, important to keep all drugs out of a child's reach as well as all household cleaning materials which often contain harmful substances.

* Drugs should be clearly labeled. If there is any doubt about a drug's identity, it is a good policy to discard it.

* Before taking a drug, it is a wise practice to read the label twice.

* When in doubt about the freshness of a medicine, call your doctor. If he cannot be reached, throw away the medicine.

* Powerful drugs, such as sleeping pills, narcotics, strong antiseptics, tranquilizers, etc., should not be kept in the family medicine cabinet where they might fall into the hands of children. Such medications are best placed under lock and key.

* Strong antiseptics such as iodine are purposely omitted from the home medicine cabinet. Ordinary soap and water are much more effective in cleansing a wound than strong antiseptics.

6. DELIVERY CALCULATIONS (OBSTETRICAL)

* Normal pregnancy lasts about 280 days, plus or minus 10 days.

* A premature baby is one born more than three weeks prior to the calculated date. This happens frequently.

* A postmature baby is one born more than three weeks after the calculated date. This happens infrequently.

* To roughly calculate the expected birth date, *count back three months* from the date of the onset of the last menstrual period and then *add five to ten days*. Thus, if your last menstrual period began on January 1st, your baby will most likely be born between October 6th and October 11th.

* Women with irregular menstrual periods may find it more difficult to calculate expected dates of delivery than those who have a regular menstrual cycle.

7. SPECIAL DIETS

Low Caloric*
Diet for Overweight People

Breakfast	Lunch	Dinner
Orange juice or ½ grapefruit (no sugar)	Vegetable, meat, fish or fruit salad with juice of lemon and/or vinegar, or 1 portion of lean meat	1 portion of boiled or broiled lean meat, fish or fowl
1 boiled egg		
1 slice of toast	Dessert: 1 portion of fresh fruit or low-sugar canned fruit	2 vegetables such as: spinach, lettuce, tomato, celery, cucumber, cabbage, onion, peppers, asparagus, string beans, etc.
1 cup of tea or coffee with saccharin and milk		
	Tea, coffee, with saccharin and skimmed milk	Dessert: Jell-O, fresh or stewed fruit
		Tea, coffee or skimmed milk

Avoid

Bread, rolls, crackers, butter, cream, cheese, beans, potato, noodles, spaghetti, cereals, sugar, nuts, cake, pie, pastry, ice cream, candy, gravies, sauces, fried foods, meat fats, etc.

*Courtesy of *The New Illustrated Medical Encyclopedia for Home Use.* Abradale Press, N. Y.

High Caloric*
Diet for Underweight or Undernourished People

Breakfast	Lunch	Dinner
Fruit juice with sugar or grapefruit with sugar	1 (or 2) meat or egg sandwich, or 1 large portion of meat or fowl	1 plate of cream soup
1 cup of cereal with cream and sugar		1 large portion of meat, fish, or fowl
	2 vegetables with butter	
2 scrambled or fried eggs	1 potato, or portion of spaghetti or noodles	1 potato, or portion of spaghetti or noodles
		2 vegetables with butter
2–3 slices of bread or toast with butter and jam	2–3 slices of bread and butter	2–3 slices of bread and butter
	Dessert: Fruit, cake, pie, ice cream, etc.	Green salad with Russian or Roquefort dressing
Tea or coffee with cream and sugar		
	Milk with cream	Dessert: Same as for lunch
	Midday Snack	**Bedtime Snack**
	Malted milk, ice cream soda, eggnog, with cake or crackers	Sandwich or meats and milk, tea or coffee with cream and sugar

*Courtesy of *The New Illustrated Medical Encyclopedia for Home Use.* Abradale Press, N. Y.

Gout Diet*
(Low Purine)

Foods	Include	Avoid
Breads	All	None
Cereals	All	None
Soups	Milk soups made with vegetables	Bouillon, broth, consommé
Meat, fish, eggs or cheese	Fish, fowl, shellfish, meats (except those listed), eggs, cheese	Kidney, liver, meat extracts, sweetbreads, roe, sardines, anchovies
Potato or substitute	White potato, sweet potato, hominy, macaroni, rice	Fried potato, potato chips
Fats	Butter	None
Vegetables	All (except those listed)	Asparagus, beans, lentils, mushrooms, peas, spinach
Desserts	Simple cakes, cookies, custard, gelatin, pudding, etc.	Mince pie
Sweets	All	None
Beverages	Carbonated beverages, coffee, milk, tea	None
Miscellaneous	Spices, cream sauces, nuts, salt, condiments	Alcohol, gravy, yeast

Elimination Diet (for allergic persons)*

Foods	Include	Avoid
Breads	Quick bread, yeast bread, crackers—if made without eggs	Bread or rolls containing eggs or nuts
Cereals	All, except ⟶	Chocolate-flavored cereals
Soups	All	None
Meat, fish, eggs or cheese	Any meat or fowl except fresh pork; cottage cheese	Fresh pork, fish, seafood, eggs, all cheeses except cottage cheese
Vegetables	All, except ⟶	Corn, tomatoes
Potato or substitute	Potato, hominy, rice, macaroni	Noodles containing eggs
Fats	Butter, cream, French dressing without pepper, lard, margarine, oil	Salad dressings containing eggs or pepper
Fruits	All fruits, except ⟶	Fresh strawberries, raspberries, huckleberries, blackberries, melon
Desserts	Cakes, cookies, gelatin, puddings, ice cream—if prepared without eggs, chocolate, cocoa or nuts	Baked custard, desserts containing eggs, chocolate, cocoa or nuts
Sweets	Candy, jelly, sugar, honey, syrup	Chocolate, nuts, candy containing eggs
Beverages	Carbonated beverages, decaffeinated coffee, milk	Cocoa, chocolate, coffee, tea

*Courtesy of *The New Illustrated Medical Encyclopedia for Home Use*. Abradale Press, N. Y.

Low Fat, Low Cholesterol, High Protein Diet*

Foods	Include	Avoid
Meat and other protein foods	Lean meats (trim off fat): veal, beef, ham, chicken, turkey, lamb Non-oily fish: haddock, cod, halibut, freshwater fish, flounder, bluefish, bass White of egg only	Fried meats, fat meats, fresh pork, egg yolk, fish canned in oil, mackerel, herring, salmon, shad, brains, tuna, liver,† sweetbreads,† shellfish,† bacon,† kidney†
Fats	Margarine, corn oil, peanut oil, vegetable shortening used sparingly	Butter, lard, suet and other animal fats
Cereals	Any cereals (preferably whole grain), bread, wheat cakes made without eggs, macaroni, spaghetti, noodles made without eggs	Noodles made with eggs, breads and hot breads made with eggs
Dairy products	Skim milk, buttermilk, cheese made from skim milk (dry cottage cheese)	Whole milk, cream, most cheeses, ice cream
Fruits	Any fruit or juice	Avocado
Vegetables	Potatoes, baked without butter, or mashed with water or skim milk, any vegetable prepared without oil or fat	None
Desserts and sweets	Gelatin desserts, ices and sherbets, tapioca and rice puddings made with fruit and juices Plain cookies, angel food and other cakes made without egg yolks and butter Jams, jellies, honey, candy made without butter or cream	Rich desserts made with fat, cream, egg yolks Rich candy made with butter Ice cream, pastry, chocolate
Beverages	Tea, coffee, cereal drinks, buttermilk, skim milk, soft drinks	Whole milk, alcohol
Soups, etc.	Clear broth, vegetable soup made without whole milk or fat,	Cream soups, gravies, cream sauce
Miscellaneous	Salt, spices, vinegar, popcorn without butter, relishes, pickles, catsup, low fat yeast extracts	Olives, mayonnaise, oily dressing, fried foods, potato chips, brewer's yeast

*Courtesy of U.S. Vitamin and Pharmaceutical Corp.
†Note: The following foods are of high nutritive value, but are omitted from the diet because of their moderate cholesterol content. Any one (but not more than one) of these foods may be eaten once a day in an amount not to exceed that suggested:

Liver — 3 ounces
Kidney — 3 ounces
Sweetbreads — 3 ounces
Lobster — 3 ounces
Canadian bacon — 3 ounces
Peanut butter — 1 tablespoon
Whole milk — 1 glass (6 ounces)

Low Carbohydrate (Sugar) Diet

Breakfast	Lunch	Dinner
1 portion of fruit, canned or stewed without sugar	Meat, fish, seafood, vegetable or fresh fruit salad	Clear soup
2 soft- or hard-boiled eggs	2 salt crackers	1 portion of any meat, fish, seafood, or fowl
1 slice of bread or toast	Gelatin sweetened with saccharin	Any 2 of the following vegetables: asparagus, string beans, watercress, celery, cucumber, cabbage, tomato, lettuce, eggplant, beets, carrot, endive
Coffee or tea with saccharin, or milk	Tea, milk, or coffee	Unsweetened canned fruit, or fresh fruit or gelatin
		Tea, milk or coffee with saccharin

Avoid

More than 1 slice of bread, potato, noodles, spaghetti, macaroni, lima beans, baked beans, corn, rice, gravies, sugar, cake, pie, pastry, ice cream, carbonated beverages, sweetened canned fruits, nuts, cream sauces, beer

Low Salt (Low Sodium) Diet*

Foods	Include	Avoid
Meat and meat substitutes	Lamb, beef, pork, veal, rabbit, liver, chicken, turkey, duck, goose, fresh cod, halibut, fresh salmon, freshwater fish, one egg daily	Salted, canned, smoked meats, frankfurters, bacon, ham, sausage, liverwurst and other spiced meats, brain, kidney, tongue, salt or canned fish, haddock, shellfish (oysters, clams, lobster, shrimp), salt pork
Vegetables	Fresh, frozen or specially canned without salt: asparagus, string beans, broccoli, brussels sprouts, cabbage, cauliflower, corn, cucumber, eggplant, endive, lettuce, mushrooms, okra, onions, parsnips, peas, peppers, potato, rutabaga, soy beans, squash, sweet potato, tomato, lima beans	All canned vegetables and relishes, beets, beet greens, chard, kale, celery, spinach, sauerkraut, rhubarb, potato chips, pickles
Fruits	Any raw, cooked, canned fruit or juice, apricots, avocado, banana, blackberries, blueberries, cranberries, dates, grapes, grapefruit, lemons, oranges, peaches, pears, pineapple, plums, raspberries, strawberries . . . and other fresh and frozen fruits	Dried fruits containing benzoate of soda, raisins, prunes
Cereals and bread	Salt-free cereal: barley, farina, oatmeal, pettijohn's, ralston, rice, wheatena, puffed wheat or rice, shredded wheat, macaroni, spaghetti, noodles, yeast bread prepared without salt	Most commercially prepared cereals, bread, crackers, pretzels, hot bread, etc., made with salt, baking powder or soda

Low Salt (Low Sodium) Diet (cont'd)

Foods	Include	Avoid
Desserts	Ice cream or puddings made with milk allowance, unsalted fruit pies, gelatin desserts, custards	Those prepared with salt, baking powder or soda, or egg white
Soups	Unsalted soups and broths, cream soups out of milk allowance	Canned soups, and those made with bouillon cubes
Dairy products	Whole milk 1 pt. per day (dialyzed milk may be used more freely, if available), unsalted cottage cheese—1 oz. per day, unsalted butter, homemade ice cream, cream—⅛ cup per day	All hard cheeses, all salted cheeses, salt butter, oleomargarine, buttermilk, commercial ice cream
Beverages	Coffee, tea, cocoa, wine, fruit juices; beer and soft drinks—8 oz. per day	
Fats	Lard, oil, vegetable fat	Salted shortening, bacon fat, salad dressing
Seasonings, condiments	Pepper, garlic, paprika, vinegar, herbs, dry mustard, onion, vanilla, lemon, cinnamon	Catsup, chili sauce, prepared horseradish, pickles, relishes, steak sauce, salad dressings
Miscellaneous	Sugar, syrup, candy, jam or jelly made without benzoate of soda, unsalted nuts, popcorn	Olives, salted nuts and peanut butter

*Courtesy of U.S. Vitamin and Pharmaceutical Corp.

Diet for People with Ulcer of Stomach or Duodenum

	Foods Permitted
Breads	White toast, crackers, rolls
Cereals	Farina, cream of wheat, rice
Soups	Cream soups, such as asparagus, tomato, beets, pea
Meats, fish, eggs or cheese	Scraped beef, minced white meat of chicken, lamb chops, broiled liver, sweetbreads, fresh fish, salmon, eggs, cottage or cream cheese
Vegetables	Cooked beets, asparagus, carrots, peas, beets, squash, string beans
Potato, etc.	Baked or mashed potato, corn purée, lima bean purée, macaroni, noodles, rice
Butter	Butter, margarine, cream
Fruits	Avocado, banana, canned or stewed apples, apricots, cherries, peaches, pears; dilute orange juice, prune juice, prune whip
Desserts	Sponge cake, crackers, cookies, custard, Jell-O, rice or bread pudding, ice cream, sherbet
Sweets	Jellies, plain candies, sugar, honey
Beverages	*Milk,* milk drinks, tea, decaffeinated coffee

General Instructions

1. Eat, or drink milk every 2 to 3 hours.
2. Drink milk and eat lightly before retiring at night and if you wake up during the night.
3. Eat slowly and chew food thoroughly.
4. Adhere strictly to diet and AVOID the following: SMOKING; ALCOHOL; COFFEE; and mustard, chili sauce, horseradish, other spices and condiments. Also avoid gravies, hot sauces, nuts, pickles, etc.

Low Roughage, Low Residue Diet*

Foods	Include	Avoid
Breads	White, enriched or fine rye bread, crackers, toast	Whole wheat, graham, dark rye bread
Cereals	Refined cereals, corn, rice, wheat, dry cereals prepared from cooked oatmeal	Whole grain cereals
Soups	Bouillon, broth	Cream soups, vegetable soup
Meat, fish, eggs or cheese	Bacon, tender meat, fish, fowl, canned fish, eggs, cheese	Tough meat
Vegetables	None	All
Potato or substitute	Potato, macaroni, noodles, refined rice	Hominy, unrefined rice
Fats	Butter, cream, margarine	None
Fruits	None	All
Desserts	Plain cakes, cookies, custard, gelatin, ice cream, pie, pudding, all without fruits or nuts	Desserts containing fruits or nuts
Sweets	Hard candy, jelly, syrup, honey	Candy containing fruits, jams or nuts
Miscellaneous	Cream sauce, gravy, peanut butter, vinegar	Nuts, olives, pickles, popcorn, relish

*Courtesy of *The New Illustrated Medical Encyclopedia for Home Use.* Abradale Press, N. Y.

8. NORMAL WEIGHT CHARTS

Men—25 Years Old or Older*

(Weight in pounds, with clothes)

Height		Small Frame	Medium Frame	Large Frame
(With shoes, 1 inch heels)				
Feet	*Inches*			
5	2	112–120	118–129	126–141
5	3	115–123	121–133	129–141
5	4	118–126	124–136	132–148

Men—25 Years Old or Older (cont'd)

Height		Small Frame	Medium Frame	Large Frame
5	5	121–129	127–139	135–152
5	6	124–133	130–143	138–156
5	7	128–137	134–147	142–161
5	8	132–141	138–152	147–166
5	9	136–145	142–156	151–170
5	10	140–150	146–160	155–174
5	11	144–154	150–165	159–179
6	0	148–158	154–170	164–184
6	1	152–162	158–175	168–189
6	2	156–167	162–180	173–194
6	3	160–171	167–185	178–199
6	4	164–175	172–190	182–204

Women—25 Years Old or Older*
(Weight in pounds, with clothes)

Height		Small Frame	Medium Frame	Large Frame
(With shoes, 2 inch heels)				
Feet	Inches			
4	10	92– 98	96–107	104–119
4	11	94–101	98–110	106–122
5	0	96–104	101–113	109–125
5	1	99–107	104–116	112–128
5	2	102–110	107–119	115–131
5	3	105–113	110–122	118–134
5	4	108–116	113–126	121–138
5	5	111–119	116–130	125–142
5	6	114–123	120–135	129–146
5	7	118–127	124–139	133–150
5	8	122–131	128–143	137–154
5	9	126–135	132–147	141–158
5	10	130–140	136–151	145–163
5	11	134–144	140–155	149–168
6	0	138–148	144–159	153–173

For girls between 18 and 25, subtract 1 pound for each year under 25.

*Courtesy of the Metropolitan Life Insurance Company.

* Anyone more than 10 percent above his normal weight, as shown in the accompanying chart, is sufficiently overweight to require a reducing diet.

* Anyone more than 10 percent below his normal weight, as shown in the accompanying chart, is sufficiently underweight as to require a high calorie diet.

* Dieting, recommended by your physician, is the best way to take off weight.

* Exercise does *not* by itself cause much permanent weight loss.

* Overeating is the sole cause of weight gain in almost all people.

* Disturbed metabolism causes weight gain in only a tiny percentage of all overweight people.

* Any healthy person who eats less than his daily caloric needs will lose weight. Conversely, any healthy person who eats more than his daily caloric needs will gain weight.

* People who say, "I don't know why I am gaining weight; I eat very little," are not telling the truth!

* Weight-reducing pills should never be taken unless prescribed by your doctor.

9. VITAMINS AND VITAMIN-DEFICIENCY DISEASES

Vitamin	Found in:	Deficiency may result in:
Vitamin A	Milk, butter, cheese, eggs, liver, green vegetables	Xerophthalmia (an eye disease), night blindness, skin disease
Vitamin B₁ (thiamine)	Meat, grains, eggs, yeast, potato, most vegetables	Beriberi, neuritis, heart malfunction
Vitamin B₂ (riboflavin)	Eggs, milk, cheese, butter, meats, liver	Keratoses (a skin disease), cheiloses (cracking of the skin at the corners of the mouth); glossitis (inflammation of the tongue), photophobia (inability to withstand strong light)
Vitamin B₆	Cereals, yeast, fish, most vegetables	Neuritis, skin disorders
Vitamin B₁₂	Meat, liver, eggs, milk	Pernicious anemia, nerve inflammations
Niacin (nicotinic acid)	Grains, yeast, meats	Pellagra (a skin disease), nerve disorders, glossitis (inflammation of the tongue)
Vitamin C (ascorbic acid)	Oranges, grapefruit, lemons, limes, tomatoes, potatoes	Scurvy, hemorrhage from the gums and beneath the skin
Vitamin D	Cod liver oil, fish livers, eggs, butter, milk, sunlight	Rickets, bone deformities such as bowlegs, pigeon breast, tetany (convulsions, occurring mostly in infants)

Vitamin	Found in:	Deficiency may result in:
Folic acid	Green vegetables, yeast, liver	Anemia, often pernicious in type
Vitamin K	Most vegetables, liver, fish; found in sufficient quantities in most normal diets	Bleeding tendency, bleeding in the newborn
Vitamin E	Wheat-germ oil, cereals	May be associated with habitual abortion, sterility, muscle weakness

* Most healthy children and adults obtain sufficient vitamins in their daily diets so that supplementary vitamins are unnecessary.

* Nursing infants and those on bottle formulas require additional vitamins, especially A, C, and D.

* Elderly people often eat inadequate diets and may require a multivitamin tablet each day.

* People whose diet must be deficient in certain foods because of an ulcer, colitis, or some other gastrointestinal disorder usually require supplementary vitamins.

* The taking of vitamins will *not* cause a healthy person to gain weight. Naturally, those with vitamin-deficiency disorders may gain weight as they recover from their deficiency state.

* Alcoholics usually develop a vitamin deficiency as a result of inadequate food intake.

* Mineral oil as a bowel lubricant will not interfere with vitamin absorption if taken in moderate quantities just before retiring at night.

* Harm can result from excessive intake of vitamins, especially vitamin D, and to a lesser degree, vitamin C.

* It has not been proved that intake of large quantities of vitamin C will protect against upper respiratory infections.

* It has not been proved that intake of large quantities of vitamin E will increase virility or influence fertility.

* Iron, in combination with vitamins, is indicated only when the patient is anemic, or during pregnancy.

* Ask your doctor which vitamin product to take. Do not depend upon commercial advertisements.

* Bottles containing vitamins should be kept out of a small child's reach. Overdoses can cause serious disturbance.

10. LIFE EXPECTANCY TABLES

	Females			Males	
At age:	May expect to live to	Age:	At age:	May expect to live to	Age:
Newborn		75.0	Newborn		67.6
1 year		76.4	1 year		69.3
2 years		76.5	2 years		69.4
3 years		76.5	3 years		69.4
4 years		76.6	4 years		69.5
5 years		76.6	5 years		69.5
6 years		76.6	6 years		69.6
7 years		76.7	7 years		69.6
8 years		76.7	8 years		69.6
9 years		76.7	9 years		69.7
10 years		76.7	10 years		69.7
15 years		76.8	15 years		69.8
20 years		77.0	20 years		70.2
25 years		77.2	25 years		70.7
30 years		77.4	30 years		71.2
35 years		77.7	35 years		71.6
40 years		78.0	40 years		72.1
45 years		78.5	45 years		72.8
50 years		79.2	50 years		73.8
55 years		80.0	55 years		75.0
60 years		81.0	60 years		76.7
61 years		81.3	61 years		77.1
62 years		81.5	62 years		77.5
63 years		81.7	63 years		77.9
64 years		82.0	64 years		78.3
65 years		82.3	65 years		78.8
66 years		82.6	66 years		79.2
67 years		82.9	67 years		79.7
68 years		83.2	68 years		80.2
69 years		83.5	69 years		80.7
70 years		83.9	70 years		81.2
71 years		84.2	71 years		81.8
72 years		84.6	72 years		82.4
73 years		85.0	73 years		83.0
74 years		85.4	74 years		83.6
75 years		85.9	75 years		84.2
76 years		86.3	76 years		84.8
77 years		86.7	77 years		85.4
78 years		87.2	78 years		86.1
79 years		87.7	79 years		86.7
80 years		88.2	80 years		87.3
81 years		88.7	81 years		88.0
82 years		89.2	82 years		88.7
83 years		89.8	83 years		89.3
84 years		90.3	84 years		90.0
85 years		90.9	85 years		90.7

INDEX

Electric shock, first aid in, 315
Electrocardiogram, 135
Electroencephalogram, 91-92
Electrolysis, 58
Electroshock therapy, 85
Emotional strain, heart condition and, 134, 136, 138
Emphysema, 142, 149-50, 154
Encephalitis, 96-97
Endocarditis, 132
Endotracheal anesthesia, 262
Entropion, 112
Epigastric hernia, 196
Epilepsy, 92, 95-96, 100
Erythroblastosis, 227
Exercises
    for arm swelling following breast removal, 160
    arthritis and, 249
    breathing, 144
    diabetes and, 288-89
    for flatfeet, 260
    heart condition and, 133, 137, 138
    muscle, 256
    for sagging breast, 156
    shortness of breath and, 143
    with torn knee cartilage, 253
    for weight loss, 291
Eyes
    allergy-caused inflammation of, 65
    check-up on, 17
    facts on, 106-21
    of newborn, 236-37
    plastic and cosmetic surgery around, 241-45
    tumor of, 118-19, 121-22
    vitamins and, 283

Face
    infections of, 70
    plastic and cosmetic surgery on, 239-45
Facial paralysis, 94

Fainting
    facts on, 90-91
    first aid in, 312-13
    during pregnancy, 222
Fallopian tubes, blockage of, 216-17
False labor, 228
Family doctors, choosing, 3-4
Farsightedness, 108-9
Fatty liver, 178
Fees, medical, 12-13
Feet, flat, 257
Female disorders, 200-16
Femoral hernia, 196
Fertility, 216-19
Fertility drugs, 218
Fibrillation, 131
Fibroid tumors
    cesarean section and uterine, 221
    facts on, 208-9
    surgery on, 209
First aid
    facts on, 307-15
    for foreign body in ear, 122
    kit, for travel, 79
Flatfeet, 257, 260
Fluoroscopy, 301
Food, see Diet
Food allergies, 64-65
    diarrhea and, 169
Forceps delivery, 230
Foreign bodies in eyes, 110-11
Fractures
    facts on, 250-51, 258
    first aid in, 310-11
    of skull, 97-98, 101
Frigidity, 104-106

Gallbladder
    cancer of, 174
    facts on, 173-77
    surgery on, 174-75
Gallstones, 173
Gastrectomy, 166
Gastroscopy, 165

More SIGNET Books of Special Interest